Praise for THE CASE FOR (

"John Washington makes a strong, eloquent, and even inspiring case for the relaxation and ultimately the abolition of border controls."
—J. M. Coetzee, Nobel Prize–winning novelist and essayist

"With precise and convincing examples, John Washington obliterates any argument against a world without borders. I am forever changed by reading this book. *The Case for Open Borders* is the text I needed in order to continue to dream of a world where the right to move is no longer a radical act but, instead, a right we need to protect in the twenty-first century and beyond.
—Javier Zamora, author of *Solito*

"*The Case for Open Borders* reveals the extent to which today's global borders have become, at their very core, irredeemably inhumane. Through riveting reporting and wide-ranging citations and case studies, John Washington deconstructs a host of broken metaphors, facile analogies, and fallacious arguments—deconstructing modern notions of scarcity, enforcement, and 'order.' This is essential reading, a powerhouse manual for reimagining a world without walls."
—Francisco Cantú, author of *The Line Becomes a River*

"Perhaps the most profound book you'll read this year. Washington cleaves through all the cruel obfuscations and militaristic cant that derange our border and immigration politics and offers a better, human alternative. Borders will not save us or our rapidly broiling planet, but Washington's reportorial courage and ethical clarity just might."
—Junot Díaz, author of *This Is How You Lose Her*

"John Washington's *The Case for Open Borders* is a compelling, empathetic argument, a far-reaching look into the origins of borders. Washington is one of our most thoughtful, creative, and humane journalists, and this new work will make people think differently, in new, surprising ways, about what they think they already know about what divides and unites the world. Highly recommended."
—Greg Grandin, author of *The End of the Myth*

THE CASE
FOR OPEN
BORDERS

John Washington

Haymarket Books
Chicago, IL

Published in 2023 by
Haymarket Books
P.O. Box 180165
Chicago, IL 60618
773-583-7884
www.haymarketbooks.org
info@haymarketbooks.org

ISBN: 979-8-88890-072-7

Distributed to the trade in the US through Consortium Book Sales and Distribution (www.cbsd.com) and internationally through Ingram Publisher Services International (www.ingramcontent.com).

This book was published with the generous support of Lannan Foundation, Wallace Action Fund, and the Marguerite Casey Foundation.

Special discounts are available for bulk purchases by organizations and institutions. Please email info@haymarketbooks.org for more information.

Cover design by Rachel Cohen.
Cover art: *Haka (and Riot)* © Julie Mehretu, Los Angeles County Museum of Art. Photo by Tom Powel Imaging.

Printed in Canada by union labor.

Library of Congress Cataloging-in-Publication data is available.

10 9 8 7 6 5 4 3 2 1

For Daniela

Contents

But 'tis a single Hair —
A filament — a law —
A Cobweb — wove in Adamant —
A Battlement — of Straw —

A limit like the Veil
Unto the Lady's face —
But every Mesh — a Citadel —
And Dragons — in the Crease —

—EMILY DICKINSON

We are unlearning certain things, and that is good, provided
that while unlearning one thing we are learning another. No
vacuum in the human heart! Certain forms are torn down, and
so they should be, but on condition that they are followed by
reconstructions.

—VICTOR HUGO, *Les Misérables*

PREFACE

I like borders. Borders are places of connection, clash, and blend. They define cultures—languages, arts, cuisines, habits—by exhibiting, testing, mingling, and breaking their distinctiveness and insularity. Borders are where humans trade in goods, ideas, and beliefs. They are places of ingenuity, *mezcla*, neologism, and entrepôt. Borders mark difference and possibility: as sites of beauty and definition, alloy and creation, they spark vibrant and unexpected harmony. "Something only is what it is," as the philosopher G. W. F. Hegel put it, "in its limit and through its limit."

Infamously, however, regimes of crushing violence and dispiriting exploitation sully the creative and polyphonic potential of borders. As we deny, cast out, and crack down, we have turned our thresholds into barricades.

Given the proliferation of such walling off of human beings, of human decency, and of human potential, how do we respond?

* * *

A lot of people living in the world's borderlands experience what scholars refer to as a *human rights encounter*. In such an encounter, when you meet someone who has crossed the border despite being legally barred from doing so, you're presented with a choice: you can help the person with water, shelter, or a ride—but if you do so, you risk being arrested, prosecuted, and even imprisoned. Where I live, in Arizona within an hour of the US–Mexico border, offering such help may constitute a class 1 misdemeanor (or a felony) carrying a fine of up to $1,000 and possibly months in prison. Or: you can obey the law, do nothing, and take no risk. You decide. Not deciding isn't an option.

Instead of *encounters*, it makes more sense to call these moments *confrontations*: humanity confronting law.

My first such confrontation (I've since had plenty of others) took place in the mid-2000s when I met with a young border crosser in distress in Southern California. A friend and I were driving down an empty road in the Anza-Borrego desert, about eighty miles east of San Diego and fifteen miles north of the border. The valley we were cutting through lies between the peninsular mountain range to the west, from which on clear days you could catch distant flashes of the Pacific, and the flat expanse of the Imperial Valley to the east. The desert is slowly undulating scrubland with shocks of gullied badlands and occasional palm oases. Our plan was to cook over a fire, drink some whiskey, sleep under the open sky. We were only a few miles from where we'd intended to camp—a primitive site close to a series of winding canyons—when we saw a figure standing by the road.

This was before I spoke Spanish, before I knew much about the border or migration, apart from my mother's stories of her flight from Romania. I pulled to a stop. The figure—a kid, seemingly in his late teens—stepped into the road.

He was wearing a thin, black hooded jacket, heavily dusted jeans, and a broken-billed hat. There were pimples on his cheeks. He carried an empty gallon bottle. His eyes looked recently sparked back to life.

Across the language divide—Agua, he said, and, instead of miming drinking, gripped his neck, as if something there had gone wrong—he let us know he was pained and thirsty, that he'd walked a long time, and that he wanted a ride to the next town. My friend and I looked at each other, then back at the kid. We handed him some water, still not sure what to do. I tried to tell him that the next town was far, that there were Border Patrol agents around. We gave him a half bag of oranges and topped him off on water. I mumbled through an apology, wished him luck, and then we drove on.

Twenty minutes later, as we were hefting supplies out of the car, I stopped. What the hell had we been thinking? How could we have left him on the side of the road? We jumped in the car and sped back toward where we had seen him. He wasn't there. We drove back and forth, walked the shoulder, called out. There was no sign of him, no trace. We weren't even sure exactly where—in the stretches of bush and cactus, wash and hummock—we had first seen him.

That night we drank our whiskey, crawled into sleeping bags, and slept rough. As I woke up the next morning to dawn's brilliance, and a slight headache, I took a long pull from my water bottle before starting on the coffee. Where had that young man, that boy, slept? How much water did he have left? Had he finished the oranges? Had he walked all night through the thornbushes, hiding in arroyos, risking his life and freedom walking the unlit road?

I committed a violent act that day—a violent act of omission. The Germans once used the term *Mauerkrankheit*, or "wall sickness." It is a violence, a sickness—the wall creeping into the head—that is one of the most dangerous developments in the world today, imperiling millions of people who are forced from their homes by war, economic despoilment, or climate crises, and then barred (both by law and by the everyday practice of people like me who refuse to act with decency and humanity) from finding homes elsewhere.

My actions that day in the Anza-Borrego were my fault. But to take responsibility for a wrong doesn't mean that you can't also point a finger at others, that you can't call out the system that trains and expects you to favor and protect those on the inside of the wall and to disfavor and neglect those outside of it.

Looking back at that experience in the Southern California desert, what strikes me is how ignorant I was. Not only was I ignorant of the border crosser's legal situation (and mine), how likely either of us were to be caught if I had given him a ride, or what the exact charges or penalties would have been. And not only was I ignorant of his situation—where he had come from (most likely Southern Mexico or Central America), the history of his homeland and the current reality and struggles there, or of my country's stance toward and history with his country: despoiling and destabilizing it, invading and exploiting its people. But I was also ignorant of his most elemental situation as a human. I was ignorant of, and empty of, empathy.

I didn't see his most basic and obvious plight: tired, hungry, thirsty, in danger. Instead of seeing that and having compassion, I was scared. Scared for myself despite all my surrounding comforts: the food, water, and whiskey packed in my trunk, my apartment waiting for me back in the city, and my ready ability to forget his struggle. I was ignorant of his most basic state even while I looked right at it. And that is a profound and deeply rooted ignorance.

But I know something now, in a way that feels like the deepest sense of knowing there is: I should have helped that kid.

That the force of the border could have blinded me to that glaringly obvious and simple truth reveals, in turn, something else: its tentacles had me so tightly gripped that I couldn't see its power. "Walls cut deep into us," writes political philosopher Wendy Brown, "into our psyche, our souls." And I know, too, that I don't want something so deep inside me that so profoundly alters—that so poisons—who I am and how I am toward other people.

In the ensuing decade and a half, I've started trying to fill in some of my gaps of ignorance (plenty of them persist), to cure myself of the wall sickness. After these years of listening and reporting on migration and borders (including crossing them frequently, for both research and leisure), this is what I have come to: people should be able to move and migrate where they need or want to.

It is the abandonment of people on the side of the road that we should prosecute (in whatever constructive way we can). We should fear not the act of crossing a line but the society that compels anyone to deny a desperate person basic aid, to leave them stranded on the side of a desert road.

But not everyone lives in the borderlands. Not everybody is forced into a human rights encounter, to choose between helping or not helping someone desperately thirsty, hungry, and tired. And yet, we are all confronted.

As members of society on "this" side of the wall (even as many who physically live on "this" side are relegated to "that" side by paper walls, or by state marginalization and oppression), as taxpayers contributing to border agencies whose officers hunt down, whip, shackle, detain, and deport people trying to cross those walls, we are all, somehow and in some way, daily confronted. Each one of us decides.

Introduction: What Confronts Us

There are more closed borders today than ever before in human history. In the last fifty years, sixty-three border walls have been built between countries, and watchdogs count at least 2,250 immigration detention centers across the globe, sites of human warehousing and squalid misery. Meanwhile, in 2023, the number of displaced people around the world neared 110 million.

More than zones of trade and cultural communication, of liminal possibility and convergent creativity, borders are increasingly sites of violence and refusal. They are black flags of rightlessness, marginalization, and exploitation—where human life and democracy are sacrificed to the dragons in the crease. In 2022, the remains of nearly nine hundred migrants were found along the US–Mexico border, the deadliest year on record. The same year, while crossing the Mediterranean, at least 2,062 migrants died.[1]

Closed borders are a tool and manifestation of power concentration, providing cover and excuse for lurking domination and deep-seated marginalization and exploitation. Borders are not some essential skin without which the organism of the state is overexposed and dies. Nor are they—remotely—designators of juridical rule or sovereignty, as power and the rule of law both wax

---

1 All of these numbers are significant lowballs. Many migrants, the world over, are lost and never found—never tallied among the dead. By the time you are reading this, more walls will likely have gone up. And the official number of detention centers, while disturbing, doesn't count the jails and prisons where migrants are temporarily held before being transported to immigration authorities, nor does it factor in the safe houses where kidnappers and smugglers, often working directly with or with the acquiescence of authorities, trap migrants for extended periods.

and wane inside and outside the legal demarcations of the state. So, what are borders?

Borders are all of the above and all of the below. Both mirror and window, they reflect and expose both sides of the line. They are a springboard and a trapdoor, sites of unity and discord, sparking wars and ending them. As fetishistic monuments and inoperative manifestations of nationalist desperation, they are a relatively recent political invention[2] and remain both poorly controlled and poorly understood, even as they metastasize, extend, and function far beyond and before the lines they objectify. Opening borders will help, but it isn't nearly enough.

"Contemporary life is bordered from all around and in every direction," writes philosopher Thomas Nail in *Theory of the Border*. "From the biometric data that divides the smallest aspects of our bodies to the aerial drones that patrol the immense expanse of our domestic and international airspace, we are defined by borders." So much more than barriers erected along international boundaries, borders are complex interconnected technologies of policing and surveillance. While militarized lines are increasingly used as nationalist bugle calls and moral blinders, facial recognition and data shackles make physical fortifications increasingly redundant: belt and suspenders, moat and portcullis, Border Patrol and ICE. Borders today are simultaneously creeping outward and boring intimately inward, increasingly infiltrating everyday life. The twenty-first century is a century of borders.

And yet—still—we are mobile. Migration is not peripheral or anomalous to what humans are, but a defining anthropological feature. As journalist Suketu Mehta puts it in *This Land Is Our Land*: "People are not plants." What is at stake is whether we respond to human mobility, further fostered by climate change and

---

2   While Andorra, the nugget of a country smashed between Spain/Catalonia and France, has the oldest remaining border in the world (established in 1278), clearly delineated and strictly controlled borders did not globally proliferate until the twentieth century.

ever-ripening political crises, by criminalizing, hounding, harass-
ing, and murdering people, or by offering them welcome and reprieve. Closed borders do not solve who we are. Rather, they bedev-
il—and redevil—other looming injustices.

This book asks one of the important questions of our time: Who
belongs?

* * *

I focus much of the book on the United States, not only because I
live here as a citizen of the country and because I know and have
crossed its borders far more than those of other countries, but also
because the United States has a unique immigration history.

For one hundred years, from around 1800 to around 1900,
three-quarters of all global immigration was to the United States.
In the twentieth and the twenty-first centuries, the United States
remained, by far, the country with the highest levels of immigration. Over one hundred million people have migrated to the United States since the late eighteenth century, and the United States
currently has, by far, the largest population of immigrants in the
world.[3] All through that history, the United States has wrestled with
its border: how, where, and why to place it; how, when, and why to
guard it. The United States has also deported far more people than
any other nation: around sixty million have been forcibly removed
from the country in the last 140 years. The US–Mexico border, the
most transited and among the most contested borders in the world,
is some 1,950 miles long (its exact length depends on who you ask
and how you measure along the alternatively rocky, riverine, desert
landscape) and has had over $400 billion of "security" poured into

---

3   Despite the high overall numbers, the United States takes in fewer migrants
    and refugees per capita than many other countries. The United States ranks
    nineteenth in the world in per capita immigration and fifty-fourth in the
    world in per capita refugee settlement—below Sudan, Ethiopia, Uganda,
    Lebanon, Turkey, and Jordan.

it in just the last twenty years. While, on average, two hundred million legal border crossings are clocked across the US–Mexico border every year, only a small percentage of those border crossers suffer the brunt of a violent and impune enforcement regime, are locked up and then thrown back to where they came.

Despite the constantly and expensively reinforced schism, the US–Mexico borderlands remain a unique zone of cultural and linguistic blend. Cities such as Juárez in Chihuahua and El Paso in Texas, or Nogales in Arizona and Nogales in Sonora, were once relatively seamless conurbations in which people lived, visited, shopped, and traveled back and forth with minimal friction—until, that is, the cities were hewn in two by a militarized border wall, economic chicanery exploiting tax loopholes and cheap labor, and bogeyman scare tactics used to shore up nationalistic voting blocks. The oft-cited and oft-exaggerated distinction between El Paso as one of the safest cities in America and Juárez as suffering from uncontrollable violence does not arise because the border wall protects El Paso from the violence or poverty of Juárez. On the contrary, the wage gap and security disparity are border-born—created and widened by the wall. Transnational corporations draw massive numbers of workers to Juárez, where those same corporations then exploit, at near-starvation wages, the dearth of labor protections and the precarity of a workforce that is at once uprooted and immobilized. And with US illicit drug demand constant over the years, a hardened border makes trafficking and smuggling more lucrative for the paramilitary cartels and the corrupt state agents (on both sides of the line) with whom they work, further tightening their stranglehold on the population. More than marking the difference between people, borders make the difference—imaginary lines fissuring families, cultures, economies, and ecosystems.

* * *

Historians, critics, and everyday observers have pointed out that the United States did not live up to any semblance of a true democracy until after 1965, when Black people (with a population of around eleven million at the time) were given the vote. But what about immigrants? What about the tens of millions of people—migrants both documented and not—who live in this country, some of whom have been here for decades, and who aren't able to participate in at least one key aspect of democracy: voting? Why are they overlooked? Why are they disenfranchised, marginalized, arrested, detained, and deported?

Because they are a horde, an invasion, an army. Because they are contagious and thieving ne'er-do-wells. Because they are mooching layabouts and rapists. Such vitriolic and racist hyperbole extends to the unhitched-from-reality descriptions of current border policy, with anti-immigrant cavilers claiming that the border is "open," that migrants are taking jobs, resources, the teacher's attention, or "our" place in line. Such ignorance—often malicious, sometimes misinformed—spilleth over, but it's worth giving a few examples of the current anti-immigrant hallucination proliferating in the United States.

Ohio Representative Jim Jordan, while visiting Yuma, Arizona in 2023, referred to "this border that's no longer a border, this open border chaos on our southern border." In a House Judiciary Committee hearing, Jordan put it even more bluntly: "Under President Biden, *there is no border*, and Americans are paying the price." Wisconsin senator Ron Johnson similarly commented, "The Biden administration's policies are as close to a completely open border as anyone could possibly imagine." Texas Representative Chip Roy discussed "the impact of open borders," which he called "hardly a lie, hardly a figment of our imagination." And Florida's governor, Ron DeSantis, announced legislation meant to "protect Floridians from federal open border policies."

According to research from the nonprofit Media Matters, the Fox News network mentioned the term "open borders" 3,282 times between November 1, 2020, and March 16, 2023. An ad-tracking project from the immigration reform advocacy organization America's Voice counted over six hundred different paid ads from Republican campaigns during the '22 midterms that claimed that the US–Mexico border was "open."

Such fantasy is not relegated to politicians' or pundits' rhetorical excesses. As a reporter in Arizona, I spend a fair amount of time sitting in county board of supervisors and city council meetings. During the call-to-audience sessions, a few community members inevitably rail against—to county supervisors or city council members, who have no authority on border or immigration policy—the country's "open borders." Plenty of these folks seem on the verge of popping blood vessels as they flick spit into the microphone and exercise their anxieties. I don't want to mock or minimize their ire, as regular folk have plenty to contend with these days. But, as regards the border, what are they and those aforementioned politicians and pundits talking about?

The term "open borders"—that shopworn shibboleth—has been drained of all basic meaning. In fact, total annual migration to the United States has been decreasing from a peak that crested just before 2000. As of the spring of 2023, the current administration has, in just over two years, deported over four million people from the country. Successive administrations, Republican and Democrat alike, fund, arm, train, and staff the agencies tasked with blocking migrants' entry and with kicking others out of the country. Even those migrants allowed in are forced to wade through a years- and sometimes decades-long bureaucratic and antagonistic gauntlet in order to "regularize"—the term of art in immigration-speak for achieving legal status. Undocumented migrants, many left without any hope of such "regularization," face the ever-looming snare of roving immigration agents, road checkpoints, high-tech surveillance, and the precarity of living without papers. At any given point, tens of thousands of migrants are packed into squalid detention centers for no other reason than having crossed the border. The

US Supreme Court has given police a green light to racially profile migrants. And hundreds of migrants, in search of safety and dignity, die every year trying to get into the United States because they are forced to evade triple walls, manned and unmanned aircraft, ground sensors and surveillance towers, and the country's largest law enforcement agency, the US Border Patrol. Open borders we have not.

As of 2023, more than forty-five million immigrants live in the US—just under 14 percent of the total population. That percentage has fluctuated for the past 170 years between 10 and 15 percent, with a record high approaching 15 percent in 1890. Despite consistent howling to the contrary, the country is not being overrun.

By 2065, according to Pew Research, there could be as many as seventy-eight million foreign-born residents in the United States. (With dropping birth rates, the foreign-born percentage of the population is expected to break 15 percent, but even anti-immigrant doomsayers don't put it close to 20 percent.) Many of those seventy-eight million may be citizens or on the path to citizenship, but depending on how politics shake out in coming decades, many, perhaps most, will not be full members of society, unable to vote and potentially subject to deportation for even trying. Many of them, again depending on how politics play, will face laws that specifically target them, barring their access to many basic rights: to work, to drive, to equal access to education and health services, or to vote.[4]

In Southern Arizona, humanitarian organizations have extensively documented emergency services' consistently disparate responses between presumed citizens and noncitizens who make

---

4 I don't contend anyone who moves anywhere should immediately be able to vote in that new community. A wait time and establishing residency makes sense before offering access to the ballot. But what makes less sense is having a large and permanent and yet precarious class of residents who pay taxes but have no say in how those taxes are spent and who are unable to fully participate in civic life.

9-1-1 calls when they are lost in the borderland wilderness. When those calling are presumed to be citizens, rescue teams across multiple agencies are summoned, mobilized, and deployed, with a nearly 100 percent rescue success rate. With just a couple vague landmarks to guide their search, helicopters, quads, and the cavalry will come out to search for distressed citizens. When presumed noncitizens call, they get transferred from the sheriff's office to the Border Patrol, who might patch them to the next county over, which then patches them back to the sheriff in a potentially deadly cycle of telephonic handwashing. No summoning, no mobilization, no deployment. No rescue.[5]

In Arizona, it is illegal to drive a distressed border crosser to the hospital. A recently proposed bill in Florida would make driving an undocumented migrant anywhere punishable by up to five years in prison.

These are just a few examples of how migrants are marginalized into the corners of rightlessness and lawlessness: fewer rights, no vote, little safety, no home. Borders in full effect.

A political system that implements different laws for different groups of people is, by definition, a system of apartheid.

* * *

Liberals don't do much better: often they are in line with the anti-immigrant right when it comes to policy proposals, if not rhetoric. In a *New York Times* essay called "The Open Borders Trap," Jason DeParle writes of the "moral dilemma" posed by immigration:

---

5   I spoke with one group of volunteers dedicated to looking for distressed migrants who recounted a three-day search for a 23-year-old man stranded on top of a freezing desert mountain ridge. The man was savvy, had called 9-1-1 and, after futilely waiting another night to be rescued, then called the group's emergency hotline with his exact geographic coordinates. No officials were willing to send out a rescue team until a volunteer called in and said they were themselves in distress. That's when the Border Patrol finally showed up.

"There are more potential migrants than the country can accept. To the extent that they're fleeing poverty and violence, it's unfair to keep them out. But with nearly two billion people living on less than $3.20 a day, it's impossible to let them all in. Hence the need to set limits and enforce them humanely." It's myopic, however, to think that "limits"—in whatever form DeParle is envisioning them—*could* be enforced: more and worse catastrophes are coming, and those fleeing them will not be held back by immigration laws or walls. The straw man of "letting them all in" obscures other urgent solutions and approaches. Indeed, it is both morally stunted and dangerously unimaginative to think that closing borders is any sort of solution to the financial rapacity maintaining the wage gaps between those with hardly enough to get by and those with too much to manage.

Another issue to which DeParle makes only passing reference is that the status quo of closed borders is premised on a pernicious and paradoxical concoction of both limitlessness and strict limits: the idea that extractive and exploitative capitalism has no bounds and can, forevermore and without catastrophic consequence, keep overfeeding and overfueling rich Western countries at the expense of poorer countries, on whose populations are imposed strict limits of mobility and other basic rights.

The call for open borders is the call to reset these limits: to acknowledge that closed borders cannot reconcile the grotesque levels of wealth predicated on human immiseration or the voracious extraction precipitating the cascading climate crisis. It is such gross exploitation and malapert consumption that we should limit, not the freedom of movement.

In 2021, Cecilia Muñoz, formerly Barack Obama's top immigration advisor and a member of Joe Biden's presidential transition staff, said that she understands some of the advocates' frustration with Biden's continuation of hard-line immigration tactics advanced during the Trump presidency, but that the Biden administration has "terrible options." "Some advocates have not grappled with the

difference, if any, between their position and an open-borders position. And an open-borders position is anathema in the country,"
said Muñoz. "It's like pushing the administration right off a cliff."[6]

In 2020, one unnamed government official called the fact that
migrants sometimes miss court dates "a grave threat to America's
sovereignty. And a threat to, really, the foundations of American
society itself." (Despite persistent and erroneous claims, migrants
rarely miss court, and when they do it's usually because the government makes a paperwork mistake.)

A threat to American sovereignty and the foundations of society?
Did the almost total absence of federal immigration enforcement
for the first 150 years of the United States' existence undermine the
rise of the global superpower? Or did it, rather, for good or for ill,
help it rise?

The call for open borders is not a pie-in-the-sky dream but an
urgent response to the reality that closed-borders advocates deny:
people move and will not stop moving. To expect them to, or try
to stop them, is to incite misery, enormous and futile expenditure,

---

6   In the spring of 2022, along with a co-reporter from the *Intercept*, José
    Olivares, I interviewed a female Venezuelan migrant who claimed to have
    been sexually abused by a member of the medical staff while in Stewart, a
    notoriously abusive ICE detention center in Georgia. We got sidetracked in
    the conversation when she mentioned how she had first arrived to Stewart.
    As she and about fifty other women were being "processed" in a Border
    Patrol facility in Texas, she said, they were crammed into a small room,
    where they were forced to wait for hours with no food and little water.
    Increasingly desperate and claustrophobic, they heard what sounded like
    the jangling of chains approaching, and then a few Border Patrol agents
    opened the door with large metal boxes filled with shackles. The agents
    began calling out the women's names, one by one, bringing them to the
    doorway where they were shackled at the wrists, ankles, and waist. "I was in
    shock," the woman said. "I couldn't believe this was happening." She said
    that at least four women fainted from fear. Each of the fifty or so women
    was eventually chained up, marched out the door, and loaded onto buses
    that headed for a nearby airport, where they were shipped to detention
    camps spread throughout the country. What "cliff," I would ask Muñoz,
    has the administration already hurtled over?

and war. To try to stop humans from moving is to try to stop humans from being human.

* * *

This book isn't a strategic guide to action (though I address possible paths forward in chapter 7). It is a call for action, an attempt to chip away at a disgraceful and pervasive ethical code. It shines a spotlight on the noxious and generational harms of closed borders and makes an urgent call to open them.

The reasons for the urgency are multiform: borders can't stay closed if we are to achieve climate justice, nor can they stay closed if we are to achieve racial justice. Indeed, borders not only fragment societies, derail solidarity, and stymie responses to the many self-catalyzing global crises; they also perpetuate the crises by allowing carbon emitters to operate unregulated and by serving as a crutch and excuse for institutional/individual racism, as they both deepen and exacerbate a regime of global inequality that relies on an immobilized and racialized underclass. Both the gratuitous, environmentally toxic luxuries some of us enjoy and the basic freedoms some of us are denied depend on the sprawling and tentacular system of borders. The following pages probe and, I hope, bolster this argument.

Today, where one is born—on what side of what political line—disproportionately determines one's income, wealth, and longevity. There is more than twenty-five years' difference in life expectancy between a woman in Somalia and one in Switzerland. There is a decade's difference between a woman living in Honduras and a woman living in New York. There is a 1,000 percent wage gap between workers with practically identical jobs in Haiti and the United States. Who wouldn't want a few extra years, an extra decade or two to live, or decent wages for their hard work? Instead of offering that chance, wealthier states build walls and relegate billions of people to premature death and destitution. Those who have won the so-called birthright lottery and enjoy the immense privileges of wealth, liberty, nutrition, education, and longevity, and who believe they have the right to bar people from those unearned entitlements, should imagine themselves in the position of those who have "lost" the birthright lottery.

Anti-immigrant advocates frequently and falsely portray border crossings in apocalyptic terms, skewing the perception of a basic human act to appear as a contest between the weight of a nation and the weight of an individual. But immigration—an exercise of an elemental human freedom—is a boon to communities. Studies have consistently shown that migrants engage in less criminal activity and are healthier than native populations. Even mass migration adds to the prosperity of migrants and natives alike (see chapter 4). Therefore, while not a threat itself, opening borders would amend past and correct current wrongs (see appendix, point 15), pulling us closer to modern conceptions of equality, justice, and freedom.

Open borders is not a call for cultural homogenization. It is not an appeal to empty ideals of equality. Migration is a fomenter and catalyst of culture, not its killer. Migration is not a leveler of human will or capacity but an opportunity, a platform, a runway.

"Borders don't have to be tools of exclusion," Nick Estes, an organizer, historian, and cofounder of advocacy group The Red Nation, told me. They can allow a human—and humane—flow. But first: we must open the gates.

* * *

Migrants aren't passive victims of global crises, nor are they swept—or drowned—by political tides. On the contrary, migrants are active and dynamic agents who affect and determine their life paths, choosing—albeit often under strained or precarious circumstances—to seek safety and opportunity, subverting, as they do so, systems of apartheid and inequality. They actively resist global regimes meant to exploit, deny, and immobilize them. They should be welcomed, dignified as they are, and respected. Opening borders doesn't give migrants a chance at life (since migrants find and make life where they are) but ends the active and inhumane campaigns waged against them.

To get there, there's much work to do. Pundits, politicians, academics, journalists, and laypeople still balk and belch at the term. "Open borders" is at once verboten, anathema, and a catchall, memeified and mischaracterizing smear utilized by left, right, and center. Part of the problem is that few understand what the idea of open borders means. "I am not calling for open borders," Suketu Mehta writes, "I am calling for open hearts." But emotional willingness is not enough. Without real, revolutionary material transformation, you can put your hope in a slogan, on a poster, or into the White House—and then watch it fizzle.

Open gates may sound scary, idealistic, naive, impossible, or self-destructive. Change can be unsettling, especially in a world increasingly destabilized by an economic system that alternately spikes, then crashes, and an accelerating global climate crisis. "The other faces me," as philosopher Emmanuel Levinas writes, "and puts me in question and obliges me." Careful consideration of the grievous harms that closed borders currently wage against hundreds of millions of people, and understanding and analyzing the evidence of what open borders would indeed herald, will not only allay widespread fears but win over new advocates and activists. To look beyond the self, to welcome the other, to be *obliged*, puts the self on edge, in question, on the line. It is also what makes us human.

* * *

But how do we break out of apartheid when many don't recognize it for what it is?

Reflecting on our capacity to foster and implement profound societal change, climate activist and human ecologist Andreas Malm writes:

> The roster of historical analogies begins with slavery. If the abolitionists could turn the tables on that nefarious institution, so long taken for granted as a natural part of modern economies, through boycotts, mass meetings and thundering denunciations of iniquity, then we will do the same; just like us, they were first disparaged as crackpots and unreasonably impatient radicals, until righteousness gained the upper hand. Morals and strategy blend here. Abolition is conceived as a reprogramming of ethical codes—slavery went from foundation to abomination and fossil fuels will go the same way.

Malm's call for climate justice is similar to the call for open borders: what may today seem crackpot (open borders) could tomorrow be a moral given.

If you're looking for quick summations of this book's arguments, see the appendix. You can use the more succinct explanations there for quick reference, as well as glean numbers, facts, and overviews of complex arguments. The rest of the book is more discursive, winding, descriptive, historical, and sometimes personal. I don't purport to have clear or ready answers—except one—but I do have some observations about why borders are lunkheaded and shortsighted, why they make the world worse, as well as how we might do things better. And yet, I admit: it's complicated.

This book also answers the question posed earlier: Who belongs?

1

Abu Yassin and the
Friendship Dam

"I dream of being warm," said Ahmad Yassin Leila, reacting to the whirlwind of destruction that met him and his young family as they sought shelter in Idlib, Syria, in early 2020. Abu Yassin, as he is known, his wife, and their four children had arrived to this northwestern province near the Turkish border after the Syrian regime's heavy artillery siege of their Damascus neighborhood of East Ghouta had forced them from their home three years earlier. Since then, they had been on the run from the pervasive violence—shock wave, caved ceiling, scurrying shrapnel—that seemed to follow wherever they fled. The Syrian government had been bombarding Idlib for months with tanks and armored vehicles, while Russian and Syrian warplanes dropped incendiary explosives, cluster munitions, and massive barrel bombs on a population that included over a million people who had already fled from other parts of Syria and found, temporarily, refuge in the province. The bombs targeted schools and hospitals in neighborhoods thought to be rebel strongholds, neighborhoods now reduced to rubble, blood, ash, and the streams of people fleeing.

Earlier that winter, Abu Yassin and his family piled onto a motorcycle and joined the hundreds of thousands running for their lives and dying on the cold mud road packed with trucks, cars, handcarts, motorcycles, bicycles, animals, and whatever they could carry of their homes—a limping exodus heading north toward

Turkey in search of safety. But the hundreds of thousands of refugees were brought up short at the border wall: Turkey wouldn't let them in.

Abu Yassin's family was left without shelter in the miserable cold of a northwestern Syrian winter, blocked by Turkey's border to the north and "bombing, bombing, bombing," as he described it to me, to the south. The temperature frequently dropped below freezing at night, so people took to burning whatever they could find for warmth. One frigid night that February, in their floorless tent, Abu Yassin noticed that something was wrong with his 18-month-old daughter, Iman Leila. "Around three o'clock in the morning, I tried to move my little girl, the child," he said. "But she was really blue and not moving, and then her body became hot, and we didn't know what to do."

Little Iman Leila went limp, unresponsive, and then cold. Terrified, Abu Yassin took her in his arms and, along with his wife, searched for an ambulance or car that could transport her to a hospital. Finding no vehicle to help, they set out on foot along the frozen mud road. On the way, as Abu Yassin carried his daughter close against his chest, Iman Leila died.

I dream, he said, of being warm. After his daughter's death, Abu Yassin's family remained trapped in Syria, blocked by not only concrete and rebar but the impregnability of an idea, a fiction, the figment of sovereignty and territorial integrity, the concept of a nation: and the concept and the wall was not only Turkey's but backed and bolstered by the whole force of the European Union behind Turkey; and not only the EU but, as US diplomat James F. Jeffrey told an interviewer on Turkish TV, "the United States totally agrees with Turkey on the legal presence and justification for Turkey defending its existential interests against the refugee flow."

As the temperature dropped and the bombs barreled behind them, the refugees pounded on the wall and against Turkey, against the European Union, against the United States and against the concrete and rebar. The trapped refugees sought and forged

what shelter they could, draping olive trees with tarpaulins, weigh-
ing whether or not to use sticks for fires or for makeshift lean-tos,
burning anything and everything that wasn't immediately useful:
their extra clothes that couldn't fit on top of all they already wore,
their spare shoes. Those with cars, trucks, and handcarts who had
brought pieces of their homes with them—old front doors, window frames, bed frames, whatever furniture they had stacked and
strapped on in hope for the future—burned these too, along with
the hope that they would be able to return and rebuild their homes
in Turkey or build them in Germany or Sweden or wherever they
would end up. As geographer Tahir Zaman writes: "Home becomes
migratory." During the long, freezing nights from December to
February, they burned what remained. Still it was cold, shelter now
a dream, warmth a dream, and the wall, its cold integrity, "The
United States totally agrees with Turkey," and in the floorless tent,
18-month-old Iman Leila—shiver, heart stop, stillness—the little
girl wrapped frozen in her father's arms: suddenly hot, and then
cold again out on the road, and then dead.

Why? What are Turkey's "existential interests," and how does a
"refugee flow," or Iman Leila, threaten them? Why wouldn't Turkey
let Iman Leila cross the border?

Anthropologist James C. Scott described the state as the enemy
of "people who move around." Poet and activist Wendy Trevino
has referred to the state implementation of borders as a "cruel fiction." And political theorist Wendy Brown describes the bravado of
bordering as "heavily theatrical," also noting that "political theater
is never merely theater."

The *never merely theater* is what killed Iman Leila.

"Walls," Brown writes, "constitute a spectacular screen for fantasies of restored sovereign potency and national purity. They function brilliantly as icons of such potency and protection, even when
they fail."

Let us now question those spectacular fantasies and flip on the
lights in the darkened theater of national bordering.

The wall that day when Abu Yassin couldn't find warmth for his daughter, the wall that Turkey was defending with support of the European Union and the United States, was not impermeable. Others could pass. Turks could cross the wall in either direction. Foreign dignitaries, American citizens, Germans, reporters, anyone with enough luck to be gifted the proper passport could pass, flash their papers and cross, and cross again—they could do a triumphantly slow two-step back and forth to the rhythm of their national anthem: Syria to Turkey, Turkey to Syria, back and again. But anybody born in Syria, Afghanistan, Iraq, or any African country would be blanketly barred, left to burn their front doors for warmth.

That discrepancy defines much of our contemporary world. Not only are some free to traipse the globe while others are immobilized by walls and visa controls, but the very difference is the fulcrum point that drives the worldwide inequality regime—not only financial inequality but an inequality of rights, prospects, security, opportunity; an inequality of life.

The only way to live with such a violently discriminatory reality is to diabolically embrace it or to ignore it—ignorance is key to how borders function—or to be crushed by it. "Borders associated with fixed national territorial communities are responsible for nonemergency boundaries of compassion"—writes political theorist Jacqueline Stevens—"the limits for empathy." And yet, from here, as removed readers, we feel compassion. That is what hearing "I dream of being warm" does: it drives a pang of tenderness through us, maybe even guilt. But it is *because of the border* that we are rendered nearly helpless to act on any such feeling: its elaborate and extravagant technology, its ontology and its radial, near-ubiquitous modes of being skew our vision and impose their potent reality. The existential interests of the state outweighed the existential interests, and the bodily warmth, of Iman Leila. Because to Turkey, 18-month-old Iman Leila is more than she was. More than a little girl, Iman Leila is a flow, a flood, a million—she is a threat.

Borders thus act simultaneously through and against the individual. The border refracts the view of a single person into a mass; at the same time, the border, specifically and deliberately, violently acts upon, and *against*, the same individual it deindividualizes.

* * *

Over three million Syrian refugees were already in Turkey by the time Iman Leila was refused—a large portion of them received at the behest of the European Union, which applied a sharp diplomatic elbow into Turkey's side—along with a 3-billion-euro payout and visa-free travel for Turks wanting to peruse the Union—in exchange for Turkey's agreement to block more asylum seekers from touching European soil. The European Union was, in effect, "externalizing" their borders, pushing the border of the Union beyond the Union's border.

As recently as 2005, the Syrian government still considered Reyhanlı, where many refugees were hoping to cross into Turkey, part of their national territory. The small region bordering the Levantine Sea has been in dispute for centuries, making up part of various Akkadian, Amorite, Hittite, and Assryian kingdoms for millenia. It was then was subsumed by the Byzantine and finally Ottoman Empire in the twentieth century, when a secret agreement in 1916 between Mark Sykes, a British diplomat, and François Georges-Picot, representing France, divided the massive empire into five separate British and French spheres of influence, or mandates—a decision Vladimir Lenin called "an agreement of colonial thieves."[1] What is known as modern-day Syria was deemed part of the French mandate and extended to the coast. It wasn't until the beginning of

---

1   The mandate was based on a contractual concept from Roman private law, in which somebody must act upon somebody else's instructions. Given that the mandate system was enshrined under the Covenant of the League of Nations, its institution signaled that the people of the mandates were not quite capable of self-rule or independent statehood.

World War II that France staged a referendum in the Hatay region that includes Reyhanlı. The idea was that gifting the chunk of land to the Turks would convince them to turn against Hitler. (They remained neutral until the last months of the war.) However, France didn't want to presume to entirely gift one part of another country to a third country, so they staged a referendum, but not before helping Turkey ship tens of thousands of people into the region to vote and turn the land Turkish. In the late 1920s, the modern-day Turkish–Syrian border was established. As recently as 2010, the border at Reyhanlı was mostly open, and there were plans to build a Friendship Dam along the Orontes River, but then the Syrian war broke out, tensions resurfaced, and the border was fortified.

A century earlier, in 1915, Sykes allegedly claimed, "I should like to draw a line from the 'E' in Acre to the last 'K' in Kirkuk," and, standing in front of a map at 10 Downing Street, the home of the prime minister of the UK, used a grease pencil to trace that new border into existence.

In 2014, an Islamic State fighter standing at the border shouted, "We've broken Sykes-Picot!" Then a cartoonishly large bulldozer with a bucket dozed its way through a berm of sand, pushing away the dirt that separated Iraq from Syria. "When we crossed the borders, we didn't cross them using our passports," another fighter proclaimed. "These were our passports," he said, brandishing a scimitar. Another fighter, a Kalashnikov on his shoulder and bandoliers X'ed across his chest, stamped the recently cleared ground with his sandaled foot and pointed to the sky, repeating, "We've broken Sykes-Picot!" As soberly or as flippantly[2] as they are drawn,

---

2   See the probably apocryphal but nonetheless revealing story of "Churchill's Hiccup," about Winston's insouciant creation of Transjordan "with the stroke of a pen, one Sunday in Cairo." Supposedly, the remaining northwestern-pointed dent in the border between Jordan and Saudi Arabia is the result of a flinch when Churchill was singularly sketching the boundary. Such late nineteenth- and early twentieth-century population sorting, land divvying, and border drawing by distant statesmen laid the groundwork for conflict and slaughter that continues today.

as violently or as desperately as they are transgressed, borders foment and inflame more than keep safe or keep out. The border
itself is the incursion, inciting the scimitar to swing and the drone
to drop its hellfire.

I got in touch with Abu Yassin about a year after his daughter
had died. When we connected, he and his wife and three other
children—now five, nine, and eleven—had just relocated to Afrin, a city in northern Syria about a dozen miles from the Turkish
border. Turkey was then occupying Afrin, with the Turks holding
de facto control over the territory; Abu Yassin and his family now
effectively lived inside of Turkey but were considered foreigners in
their own land. They were still unable to cross the border.

Abu Yassin and I spoke by cell phone through an interpreter—
between Afrin and Brooklyn—which at first largely consisted of
me staring at his frozen face while he searched for a better signal,
until we took to exchanging WhatsApp audio messages. His profile picture was a photo of Iman Leila: the toddler was propped on
blankets and a pillow, wearing a loose-fitting T-shirt with a pink,
apple-cheeked cartoon animal.

In 2015, the world was momentarily aghast when images went
viral of Alan Kurdi: a three-year-old boy drowned in the Mediterranean and washed up on a Turkish shore, face down in the
tidal slick, his tiny shod feet neatly aligned behind his lifeless body.
Kurdi, who was from Kobanî, Syria, and who died along with his
mother and brother while trying to make the perilous journey
across the Aegean from Turkey to the Greek island of Kos, prompted the world to confront the humanitarian crisis millions of Syrians
were suffering. Politicians in the West were briefly held accountable
for having gutted refugee policies and for failing to respond ade-
quately to the crisis. As Kurdi's family had reportedly been trying
to ultimately reach Canada, the child's death became a major issue
in that country's national elections.

But by 2020, a half a decade after Kurdi's death, when another young Syrian boy drowned in the Aegean (his name was not

publicized), the world hardly noticed. (The Greek Coast Guard had earlier been seen nearly ramming the dinghy in which the boy was traveling, with officials repeatedly shouting, "Go back!") Was Iman Leila another example of the Syrian War superseding the limits of the world's attention, superseding empathy itself?

"And now we are here, in Syria," Abu Yassin said. He and his family had lived through yet another winter in a tent. He told me he was done running:

> As for crossing into Turkey, we tried to cross into Turkey, but the border guards are intensively guarding the borders and they would shoot at people approaching, so we gave up on that idea and stayed in Syria. We thought about where would we go. Our monetary conditions did not allow us to leave legally through the borders, and we tried to cross through smuggling, but it was not possible. This is what happened to us. Now we are in Syria and we are not thinking about leaving, because we are tired from moving around, and we are waiting for God to make things better for us. We want to teach the children and have them go to school. We want this situation to end, and we do not want anything else.

2

The Historical Argument

There is convincing evidence that the modern term "territory" does not, as widely assumed, find its etymological roots in the word "terra," but rather derives from the Latin "terreor"—to frighten, via "territor"—one who frightens, to "territorium"— that is, a place from which people are frightened off. It is indeed somewhat disquieting news that, in all probability, the word territory must hence be considered as a close etymological relative of the word "terrorist."

—Daniel-Erasmus Khan

Where does the authority to draw or enforce a border come from? On what grounds does a border guard justify blocking the path of someone walking across the land, or does a president issue an order to deploy troops to the border, build a wall, or arrest, detain, and deport migrants? On what moral grounds is any of this—the elaborate and extravagant border industrial complex abundantly proliferating across the world—justified? On what grounds does the United States require someone to "earn" their citizenship?[1]

---

1   The simultaneously heralded and excoriated US Citizenship Act of 2021, proposed by President Biden on his first day in office, would have allowed certain people living in the United States "an opportunity to earn citizenship."

According to the International Covenant on Civil and Political Rights, a United Nations resolution signed and ratified by almost every country on earth, "All peoples have the right of self-determination." Many liberal thinkers assume that such self-determination includes the right to exclude. As famed liberal stalwart Michael Walzer puts it, "The primary good that we distribute to one another is membership in some human community." Such thinking, however, is limited by a static, zero-sum view of society. "The world," Walzer writes, "is the political community, whose members distributed power to one another and avoid, if they possibly can, sharing it with anyone else." This view of power sharing and community membership, reminiscent of the social contract theory famously espoused by the philosopher Thomas Hobbes, is a pretty accurate reflection of the modern nation state, in which those holding power seek to maintain their exclusive grip on it (even if that power is achieved through a partially democratic process) and exercise exclusive authority (or authoritarian exclusion) by denying entry or expelling and deporting others. That presumed right, however, especially in regard to forcibly displaced people, bars migrants from their own self-determination.

And what such state-backed self-determinative monopolies produce is an oppressed minority (or minorities) living within the nation state and a migrant population suffering detention, deportation, and death.

Membership is not a token of which there is a limited supply. Rather, national membership is a method, a way of being in the world, an approach toward others. Membership in a small group may indeed be limited, but on a national scale, membership is better understood as simply acknowledging someone's humanity and basic human rights, of which there is no limit.

And yet, Walzer famously claimed that nations must maintain a "community of character" and thus be allowed to deny entry to migrants. Otherwise, he fears, citizens will become "radically deracinated" from their territory and culture. Political theorist Sarah

Song, in her book *Immigration and Democracy*, similarly claimed that "the right to control immigration derives from the right of the *demos* to rule itself."

But the "character" of those violently forged communities—nation states—is typically formed by oppressive majority rule: those in power dehumanizing and/or killing Indigenous and minority populations, forcibly assimilating intractable subjects, or establishing an *esprit national* through erasure and selective historical celebration and idolization. Historically, the demos (the "we" of "we the people") has been forged through some groups' exclusion of others. Another gaping blind spot in liberal thinking about borders is the presumption of who *already* belongs in the community. Walzer writes about membership: "We don't distribute it among ourselves; it is already ours. We give it out to strangers." But how is it "already ours"? Why does Walzer get to count himself amongst those who have the authority to bestow—or not—that invitation?

The manner in which most populations have gained the ability to exercise such self-determination is by violently wresting it from others, namely Indigenous peoples. The nation itself (in almost all cases) was founded on exclusionary principles: Song's "demos" and Walzer's "community" are not innocent associations of people seeking to maintain peaceful cultures but inherently discriminatory groups founded on and often perpetuated by cultural genocide.

There is no exact point of origin, but looking into history, you see surges of such misanthropic effrontery (strict border controls) following the rise of nations and nationalism. Study of the origins of some of today's most vigorously guarded borders reveals how borders have been turned into a political tool, serving as a whip, rally-round-the-flag, and moral blindfold. Such study also reveals how borders are *increasingly* used to economically exploit and immobilize populations already marginalized and racialized in an *increasingly* mobile world, all while shoring up power for the global elite. Exposing the origins of border enforcement mechanisms, like revealing the etiology of a disease, also exposes the means by which they can be inoculated against and abolished.

If you look into the past of almost any country today, you will encounter a history of violent conquest. This history is important to understand how borders and immigration controls are used to wrest, assert, and maintain control of the land, subjugate or exterminate the people living there, as well as keep access to that land restricted to a certain racialized subset of the ruling class. Key to this history are the idea of nation states, the genocide of Indigenous peoples, and the double standard and often-linked policies of colonization and the implementation of border controls. When interrogating them together, the legitimacy of today's borders comes into serious question—and then that legitimacy falls to pieces.

* * *

Somewhere around sixty thousand years ago, humans first moved through the Sunda and Sahul landmasses in the southwestern Pacific Ocean—establishing settlements, hunting, foraging, decamping, and dispersing as they went, in a slow migration which took about a thousand years—crossing short stretches of the Timor Sea or walking across low-lying woodlands that are now inundated by the Arafura Sea,[2] as they began to populate the land that would become known as Australia. By the seventeenth century, fifty or so millennia later, when the first Europeans converged on the continent,[3] an estimated 1 to 1.5 million Aboriginal people were living in Australia. This Aboriginal culture is among the oldest of any still-evolving cultures in the world.

To the diverse groups of Aboriginal people in Australia, land has always had immense spiritual importance (along with, as always,

---

2   As recently as eight thousand years ago, New Guinea and Australia were still one landmass.

3   Dutch Captain Dirk Hartog first sailed into what is now Cape Inscription in October 1616.

social, cultural, and economic importance). Aboriginal scholar Larissa Behrendt describes how custodianship of Australian land—a biodiverse array of ecologies ranging from rainforests to vast deserts, eucalypt woodlands, acacia forests, and extensive prairies and scrubland, many with sui generis flora and fauna, including the marsupials—was passed on to younger generations through storytelling. The children who listened learned to take responsibility and care for both the land and the stories themselves. "Knowledge," Behrendt writes, "created an obligation to protect the land, respect the past, to not exploit the land's resources, to take the responsibility of passing the country on to future generations, and to maintain the religious ceremonies that needed to be performed there." Land was communally cared for. Instead of owning it, one looked after it. "Other people's land had no meaning to someone who was a stranger to it, and there were rarely conflicts over boundaries."

Even in "desolate" stretches of Australia's inland desert, a stone, a bush, and a water hole could be regarded and remembered. Every trail had its own caretaker and sacred significance. "Our history," Nganyinytja, a Pitjantjara Aborigine woman explained, "is in the land, the footprints of our Creation Ancestors are on the rocks."[4]

But in the eyes of the English and the Dutch who first came across this land in the seventeenth century—at least forty-three thousand years after the Aboriginal people first inhabited it—this meticulously cared-for land was empty. The European invaders claimed that they had discovered it. And not only did they bandy this blatant falsehood; they vehemently espoused that lie and, over the following centuries, wielded it to justify their violent conquest.

On August 22, 1770, after landing near present-day Point Hicks in the southeast of the continent, the ransacking British flag-planter Captain Cook wrote in his diary:

---

4   Palmer Valor, a 92-year-old White Mountain Apache man living in the state of Arizona, commented in 1932: "All the mountains around here had names and now they have none." Quoted by Rachel St. John in *A Line in the Sand*.

[T]he Eastern Coast from the Latitude of 38 degrees South down to this place I am confident was never seen or visited by any European before us, and Notwithstand I had in the Name of His Majesty taken possession of several places upon this coast, I now once more hoisted English Coulers and in the Name of His Majesty King George the Third took possession of the whole Eastern Coast.

And so, a huge tract of land—tens of thousands of square miles—was claimed by Captain Cook. To stamp that claim, Cook "fired three Volleys of small Arms which were Answerd by the like number from the ship."[5]

"From the appearance of these People we expected that they would have opposed our landing," Cook had previously written of his first contact with the Aborigines, "but as we approached the Shore they all made off and left us in peaceable possession of as much of the Island as served our purpose." Elsewhere, he writes, a fellow officer "did all in his power to entice them to him by offering them presents &c but it was to no purpose, all they seem'd to want was for us to be gone."

Despite the conflicting descriptions of the "welcome" the invaders received, their prevailing view remained that the land was empty. It was no man's land, uninhabited—they officially called it "terra nullius." Here be dragons.

What happened afterward followed the same illogic: they did all they could to stop select others from being able to cross into what they now considered *their* land. While the justification for that near-simultaneous mobility and denial of mobility can basically be boiled down to a tautological "because we say so," it's important and, indeed, illuminating, to dissect the legal and philosophical sinews of that tautology.

---

5   *Ego sum custos et inventoris. Victus es et plorantium.* I am the finder and the keeper. You are the loser and the weeper (or, more familiarly, *finders keepers, losers weepers*).

The Discovery Doctrine—the notion that land unclaimed by White Christians was legally available, basically signaling open season for the slaughter and subjugation of the Indigenous[6]—impulsed and guided the invaders' self-conception as explorers and rightful owners of land they were stealing. Though mostly put into practice during the "Age of Discovery"—roughly from the fifteenth to the eighteenth century—this dogma can be traced back as far as the fifth century CE, when the Catholic Church invented, out of whole cloth, the idea of worldwide papal jurisdiction, claiming that any land that was "discovered" by White Christian European men was, by both moral and religious duty, theirs to claim, occupy, and legally possess. The idea was integral in spurring the Crusades, the series of Middle Ages religious wars waged in northern Europe, the Iberian Peninsula, and the Middle East, and that led to the Reconquista, the mass expulsion and violent forced conversion of Muslims and Jews[7] from the Iberian Peninsula—an early head-rearing of religious nationalism and ethnocentric ideas of bordering.

The Discovery Doctrine was easier to justify legally, and apply practically, when lands that were being "discovered" were seen and described as empty, even if they obviously weren't. Terra nullius was effectively welded to the Discovery Doctrine, with Europeans automatically and immediately granting—to themselves—property and political rights over Indigenous land and inhabitants.

A planted flag, a declamation, Captain Cook's "three Volleys"—and the whole east coast of Australia was suddenly British. The official date of the establishment of British sovereignty over the continent of Australia was January 26, 1788. By the 1850s, the

---

6   James Baldwin captures this sentiment with haunting poetic force in his *The Evidence of Things Not Seen*: "*We* thought that the nation was sacred, as sacred as the land. *They* thought that the nation was plunder. *We* thought that we belonged to the nation. *They* thought that the nation belonged to them."

7   Expropriated Jewish money, frequently in the form of forgiven loans from banished Jews, was a significant source of funding for Columbus's first voyage.

entire landmass—nearly three million square miles—was legally
draped in the Union Jack.[8]

Though it is a rather simple observation, both terra nullius and
the Discovery Doctrine—the first enables the other—take as a giv-
en the idea of open borders: that for the British "explorers," the land
was empty and no border could get in their way (the concept of a
closed border being anathema to discovery) as they took official title
and began dispossessing, slaughtering, enslaving, and deporting the
natives—then drawing borders around those same lands they had
just claimed and despoiled. In other words, they were throwing shut
behind themselves the open border they had just waltzed through.

By 1901, when the British colonies on the continent joined together to form an independent Australia, one of the infant nation's
first acts was to pass immigration controls, making the border unpassable for Asians and Pacific Islanders. These immigration laws
were part of the official "White Australia" policy, a series of statutes
that targeted everybody except Europeans. Meanwhile, the government and private actors set in motion a campaign to exterminate
the Aborigines.

Australia's first prime minister, Edmund Barton, justified the racist motivations of White Australia and its closely interlinked immigration policies, explaining, "There is no racial equality. There is that
basic inequality. These races are, in comparison with white races—I
think no one wants convincing of this fact—unequal and inferior."

---

8   Between 1815 and 1914, about ten million square miles of territory and four
    hundred million people were added to the British Empire. During that time,
    especially in Asia, the British facilitated a massive campaign of transporting
    human labor: the "coolie" trade. That was also the period when the UK's
    first immigration controls were instituted: in 1835, the British Council on
    the island of Mauritius passed two ordinances to regulate Indian laborers
    who were transported to the island. Nandita Sharma writes: "Imperial
    states simultaneously *facilitated* large-scale movements of people as
    laboring bodies for rapidly multiplying colonial ventures while passing laws
    restricting people's mobility to create a ready and increasingly disciplined
    supply of exploitable bodies."

Accordingly, they enforced those inequalities by drawing and enforcing the border. This is what sociologist Nandita Sharma describes as "nationalizing sovereignty"—defining and often militarizing the boundaries of national self-conception and territorial control to justify genocidal dispossession of Indigenous people.[9] "No nation-state, and no nationalist project," Sharma writes in *Home Rule*, "could imagine itself without immigration controls to 'protect' itself from the figure of the migrant."[10] In Australia, that protection was violently enacted against Aborigines.

Nation building, in other words, is not the cohesive realization of a people inside a territory as a political force, but the *setting apart* and *setting above* of a select group of people over another or other groups. The domination and extermination of the other creates a *limit*—inside of which "the nation" continues to dispossess and *define itself against* the minority or outsider. (To return to the line from Hegel cited in the preface, "Something only is what it is in its limit and through its limit.") Historically, nations target and seek to eliminate what they are not. Even the United States, which rhetorically—and sometimes actually—celebrates its diversity, has never been without an other who is severely oppressed, excluded, or worse.

---

9   The concept of genocide does not only apply as an adjective here, but in its strict legal sense: according to the 1948 Convention on the Prevention and Punishment of the Crime of Genocide, the term means "any of the following acts committed with intent to destroy, in whole or in part, a national, ethnical, racial or religious group, as such: a, Killing members of the group; b, Causing serious bodily or mental harm to members of the group; c, Deliberately inflicting on the group conditions of life calculated to bring about its physical destruction in whole or in part; d, Imposing measures intended to prevent births within the group; e, Forcibly transferring children of the group to another group." Clearly, the term also applies to settler colonialists' treatment of America's Indigenous population beginning in the fifteenth century and continuing, at least, well into the twentieth century.

10 Part of the United Nations' very broad definition of sovereignty is the "right of each country to determine the number and categories of international migrants to be admitted into its territory."

As part of the 1901 Immigration Restriction Act—a key element of the "White Australia" policy—any potential immigrant who could not write out a passage of fifty words recited to them in a European language was automatically denied entry. If the person was not white and *could* write out the passage, customs officers sometimes resorted to forcing them to write out passages in less common languages, such as Gaelic. Meanwhile—in a show of how their literacy had civilized them—colonizers ripped Aboriginal children from their families to "reeducate" them, white police officers sometimes hunted Aborigines for sport, and white "explorers" of the outback slaughtered, studied, theorized about, imprisoned, and raped Aborigines, whose graves they also desecrated and robbed. By the end of World War II, the Australian government was pushing a "populate or perish" policy, hoping to flood with white people land that was still, by official decree, considered terra nullius.

In the process, various aboriginal tribes were utterly extinguished, and tens of thousands were murdered, infected, enslaved, corralled, or deported. One group, the Pitjantjatjara, was forcibly removed from their ancestral land as Australia built a rail line in the 1930s and promised that the new territory granted to them would belong to them "in perpetuity." Ten years later, with the Australian government offering their "open spaces" to the United Kingdom for nuclear test sites, their reservation, including an area that would be known as Maralinga, was reappropriated, again, and used to detonate atom bombs (momentarily borrowed by the US Air Force). The territory is not far from the site where an immigration detention center would eventually be built—a convergence of Indigenous dispossession and immigration enforcement that is rarely so direct.[11]

Other Aborigines were moved to make way for yet more military testing sites, or to make space for cattle grazing and mining

---

11 The word "exterminate" comes from the Latin *exterminatus*, *ex–* meaning out, and *terminus* meaning boundary: to drive out, expel, or drive beyond the boundary; to push across the border.

operations. Displaced Aborigines were trampled on and overlooked, as was their land, and it was not until a 1967 referendum that they were included in the Australian census. Today, a single woman, Gina Rinehart, heiress to the country's largest iron-ore mining fortune and one of the largest landowners in the world, has approximately twenty-nine million acres of Australian land in her name.

In 1992, the Australian High Court declared the concept of terra nullius null, finally ratifying Aboriginal land rights and officially stating that the very premise of Australia as a nation was built on a fiction, acknowledging that the land claimed by the British had long been inhabited. It was too late. The land was taken. The borders had been conjured and weaponized. The fiction of the border had taken on, and was living, a life of its own.

One hundred years after the founding of White Australia, in 2001, 433 asylum seekers in a battered fishing sloop were rescued by a Norwegian freighter in the Indian Ocean, due south of Java. The nearest bit of land was Christmas Island, which was officially part of Australia, though still about a thousand miles away from the mainland. When the freighter carrying the asylum seekers, mainly Afghani Hazaras, entered Australian waters and prepared to dock, the Australian government refused it harbor. Their reasoning was as simple as it was odious: if the asylum seekers were to set foot on Australian territory, the government would be legally obligated to process their claims. Therefore, instead of offering them refuge, or even being willing to hear their asylum claims, Australia dispatched troops and rerouted the freighter about a thousand miles east, to Nauru, where they threw the Afghanis into a makeshift prison. By that point, having spent so much time stranded at sea, the asylum seekers were suffering from dehydration and dysentery, and for days had barely eaten. Those on board seeking safety included four pregnant women and forty-three children.

An oppressively hot former phosphate mine, hazed in white guano dust, Nauru is a tiny island nation that has been strong-armed by Australia to construct and manage a carceral hellhole. After

Australia deflected those asylum seekers to Nauru, the government decided to preempt any future asylum seekers from reaching Australia by legally lopping off Christmas Island, as well as other remotely accessible islands, from the domain of national territory. In other words, the country literally redrew the border and remade the national map—excising its own territory—to protect its border. The hypocrisy reveals a fundamental truth of the border: it can be moved to ensure its immovability; it can be violated to prove its inviolability; it can be crossed to prove its uncrossability.

The detention of asylum seekers on Nauru, at first stopgap and ad hoc, was soon made permanent. The Australians had a model to follow: the United States' establishment of Guantánamo Bay, Cuba, first as a temporary holding center for stranded Haitian refugees, then as a permanent detention center for asylum seekers in the 1980s, and finally as the hellish gulag where so-called enemy combatants continue to be held and tortured outside the selectively protective reach of the US Constitution. After Nauru, Australia soon opened other offshore detention centers where they could deflect asylum seekers and their claims.

Kurdish-Iranian poet and refugee Behrouz Boochani spent nearly five years locked in a squalid, abusive, death-dealing detention center on the Papua New Guinea island of Manus—another offshore Australian black site, where he smuggled off bits of a memoir, *No Friend but the Mountains*, via WhatsApp texts written on a contraband cell phone. "My life," Boochani writes, "has been mainly fear, stress, starvation, and displacement."

Detailing the self-harm that had turned into a sort of "cultural practice" among the prisoners, Boochani describes fellow detainees sitting on toilets in the only bit of partial privacy they were afforded (the stalls were half walled), where they sliced and clawed into their bellies with their fingernails. Children locked in the archipelago of Australia's offshore detention centers developed "resignation syndrome": losing the will to live, they contemplated and attempted suicide.

One girl, Sajeenthana—who had fled with her family from Sri Lanka when she was three years old, and was detained and remained on Nauru until she was eight—took to cutting herself. "One day I will kill myself," she told a reporter for *The New York Times*. "Wait and see, when I find the knife. I don't care about my body."

Boochani, Sajeenthana, and thousands of others suffered or continue to suffer years of miserable privation, humiliation, sexual abuse, and psychological and physical torture on the islands—all for daring to ask Australia for protection, for *almost* stepping across the line and onto territory claimed by Australia. And still, Australia's conception of their border has never been neatly or ultimately defined. Rather, their border—as are all borders—was and is mutable, permeable, and selectively *wielded* to exert control, to steal land, to build power and capital, and to keep out or expel those they don't want. "The border is elastic," writes activist and organizer Harsha Walia, "and the magical line can exist anywhere."

Or, potentially, it can exist nowhere.

"In the dead of night, at the peak of darkness, one is reminded more than ever of the power of the fences," Boochani writes. He later asks, simply: "What is a border?" He doesn't offer a precise answer, but notes that his "whole life has been impacted by this concept of 'border.'" He is not alone.

* * *

The history of the US border is full of even more hypocritical duplicity than the shifty Australian border.[12] Even before the Unit-

---

12 The history of the settler-colonial states of the United States, Canada, Australia, and later Israel follow the same pattern. In about 150 years, from around 1800 to 1950 alone, over sixty-two million Europeans moved to colonial territories throughout the world. Given the concerted conquest of the territories and extermination of native residents, such mobility cannot be understood within the framework of migration. From 1492 to 1600 alone, about fifty-six million Indigenous peoples in the Americas were killed or died from disease or famine directly tied to colonization. The

ed States came into being, its border had been invoked, dismissed, drawn and redrawn for over a century: from the hastily defined and competing imperial claims by the British, French, and Spanish empires, the "wall" of the Appalachian mountains, to the Proclamation Line of 1763, as set by King George III when he declared that it was "essential to our interest, and the security of our colonies, that the several nations or tribes of Indian with whom we are connected, and who live under our protection, should not be molested or disturbed." The proclamation set the then-westernmost border of the colonies.

The king's demarcation of the border was one of the principal but often-overlooked sparks of the Revolutionary War: the colonists' desire—their "destiny"—to push west and fill the land with white people ("populate or perish")—their refusal to be hemmed in, to be beholden to any border. Indeed, one of the charges against the British in the Declaration of Independence was that the king was *restricting* immigration: "He has endeavored to prevent the population of these States; for that purpose obstructing the Laws for Naturalization of Foreigners; refusing to pass others to encourage their migrations hither, and raising the conditions of new Appropriations of Lands."[13] The colonists valued freedom (for some) over and against the idea of borders and territorial limits.

Instead of respecting borders that they often themselves drew and defended, the invaders released their invasive hogs into Native hunting grounds, clear-cut forests, plied Natives with liquor, tempted them with baubles, infected them with diseases, and, when that

---

magnitude of human slaughter was so great and rapid that huge swaths of the continent regrew their vegetation, carbon emissions went down, and the temperature of the earth dropped.

13 Nick Estes calls the Declaration of Independence a "clever inversion of history where aggressors become victims and where colonialism looks like self-defense." As the settlers decried King George's tyranny and longed for the ideal of freedom, they laid the justification for the genocide of—in a less quoted passage from the Declaration of Independence—"the merciless Indian Savages."

wasn't enough, formed mobs or militias and went on the attack, always pushing beyond the westward-creeping border—land-grabbing and resource-gobbling as much as they could along the way.

After the colonists bucked British rule and established the new nation, they further loosened the belt, expanding, opening, and redrawing official borders multiple times: Vermont, Kentucky, Tennessee, then past the Appalachians and into Ohio. The Jay Treaty of 1794 drew the boundary with British Canada along the thalweg of the St. Lawrence River—a line that was later, with much confusion and controversy, dragged slowly and jaggedly west until it hit the Pacific. This was followed in the next six decades by the massive Louisiana Purchase (made possible by the Haitian Revolution pushing France against the ropes), the incorporation of Texas, the conquest of Mexico, the rush into Nebraska, and bleeding Kansas to impose slavery. [14]

The borders, as they shifted and feinted ever outward, acted in two capacities: as conciliatory offerings to Natives, and as territorial markers. Borders marked not the end of the nation, but, much like foreign military bases today, launching points to build new forts, establish new or control existing populations, and prepare military sorties.

The imperial settlers of the United States—much like the settlers of Australia—justified their genocidal pillage on two grounds: the Discovery Doctrine (with its myriad licentious legalisms) and sheer military might.

Christopher Columbus, to pick on one of many terrorizing slave-drivers subsequently heralded for "discovering" long-inhabited land, wrote back to his Spanish benefactors, the monarchs

---

14 The bitter and bloody fight over whether or not the new territories would be slave states was not betweeen pro-slavery proponents and abolitionists, but between slavers and "free-staters," the latter of whom not only didn't want slaves in the territories, but wanted *no Black people at all* in the territories. (The fight was mostly over where the slaves should go, not *if* people should be enslaved.) Following settler-colonial rather than abolitionist logic, they wanted the land for themselves and *only* for themselves.

Ferdinand and Isabella, that he found "nothing of importance" in the lands he had "discovered." The claim is hard to account for, especially given that Columbus wrote voluminously of the possible material benefits to be stolen from the Americas. However, one clear way of underscoring the importance of the Americas—where around one hundred million people were living at the time—to the Spanish Crown, and geopolitics writ large, may be to recall that the United States Constitution, along with its federal system of government, was at least partially cribbed from the Haudeno-saunee Constitution. Also known as the Great Law of Peace, the document begins, according to one translation, "We, the people, to form a union, to establish peace, equity, and order," and details the separation of governmental powers and individual liberties—still radical ideas at the time in European thought.

The settlers thought that Natives hadn't put the land to agri-cultural use because they didn't recognize, or simply didn't un-derstand or ignored, non-European agricultural techniques. The invaders described the Indians as betraying the laws of God and na-ture, that they and their lands needed to be corrected—on which grounds they undertook an elaborate and centuries-long scheme of skullduggery, terror, and mass murder. As Captain John Smith, settler of Jamestown, wrote, "[F]or a copper knife and a few toys, as beads and hatchets, they will sell you a whole Countrey." Indig-enous people sold no such thing. Squamish leader Chief Sealth (for whom the city of Seattle is named) laid bare the presumption much later, in 1854: "The President in Washington sends word that he wishes to buy our land. But how can you buy or sell the sky? Buy or sell the land? The idea is strange to us."[15]

---

15 Sealth's comment echoes what author Simon Winchester reports in his book, *Land*: that to a Matabele chief interviewed in Zimbabwe, the idea of buying or selling land was unimaginable: "You might as well buy the wind." The sea has largely remained unpossessed, *res nullius* or *res communis*—no one's property, or property in common. Seventeenth-century Dutch thinker Hugo Grotius famously wrote that "the sea is a thing so clearly common to all, that it cannot be the property of any one save God alone." Why such

In reality, they didn't even "buy" the land. They simply told the Indigenous peoples they were taking it, and then took it. In 1513, the Spanish monarchy instituted a "requirement," often referred to simply as the *requerimiento*—a legal text that invaders were obligated to read aloud in order to officially inform the Natives that they had two options: accept the colonizers' impending rule and become subjects or slaves, or face "just war" and annihilation.

Due to the obvious language barriers, as well as the absurdity of such a pronouncement, colonizers took to reading the requerimiento to the trees, intoning it to nobody as they stood on the prow of their ship, or, as historian Lewis Hanke puts it in *The Spanish Struggle for Justice in the Conquest of America*, muttering its "theological phrases into their beards on the edge of sleeping Indian settlements": "On the part of the King, Don Fernando," they proclaimed to the leaves and to the sea, "and of Doña Juana, his daughter, Queen of Castille and Leon, subduers of the barbarous nations, we their servants notify and make known to you, as best we can" that their Highnesses "are kings and lords of these islands and land."

The requerimiento also states that Natives should accept the news and their new lords "in the way that subjects ought to do, with good will, without any resistance, immediately."

If they didn't—if they were to "maliciously make delay" in accepting their new masters and handing over their ancestral land—the invaders assured them,

> I certify to you that, with the help of God, we shall powerfully enter into your country, and shall make war against you in all ways and manners that we can, and shall subject you to the yoke and obedience of the Church and of their Highnesses; we shall take you and your wives and your children, and shall make

---

thinking doesn't apply to the land has much to do with the legal primacy of trade (the sea is more a byway for commerce than a harvestable or inhabitable resource, such as land) and human insincerity.

slaves of them, and as such shall sell and dispose of them as their
Highnesses may command; and we shall take away your goods,
and shall do all the mischief and damage that we can.

It was a stunningly forthright admission. And as they warned, so
they did—making mischief and, to this day, doing unfathomable
damage.

"The government can do whatever we want with our own land.
The government can even destroy the land completely." The quote
rings as if from a seventeenth-century colonizer, but it was spoken
in 2021 in a federal courthouse in Tucson, Arizona, where I was
covering the trial of Amber Ortega, a Hia Ced O'odham woman
who protested the construction of the border wall that was stead-
ily cleaving her land in two and devastating a sacred spring, the
Quitobaquito Springs—now part of the Organ Pipe Cactus National Monument, along the border between the states of Sonora
and Arizona—which have been an oasis for Indigenous people for
possibly as long as sixteen thousand years. Ortega was arrested for
trespassing on her ancestral land as construction crews extended,
bollard by bollard, the thirty-foot-tall wall across the desert. First
taken to a for-profit immigration detention center, then prosecuted
over the course of two presidential administrations, Ortega defended her actions in court by claiming that the wall was impinging on
her religious freedom: the springs and surrounding areas contained
burial sites, where O'odham people performed religious ceremonies, and where salt runners who travel from present-day central
Arizona to the Gulf of California stop to rest.

Now that the wall is erected, O'odham salt runners have to
file applications to the Department of Homeland Security so that
giant doors in the wall will be opened for them to pass through.
Throughout their lands, the O'odham are frequently stopped and
questioned, sometimes hounded and harassed, by Border Patrol.

The assistant US attorney, Vincent J. Sottosanti—who in court
said, "The government can do whatever we want with our own
land"—declared Ortega's religious beliefs to be immaterial to

whether or not she was trespassing. The southern Arizona land in question officially became property of the federal government in 1853, after the Gadsden Purchase. As revealed by the initial indecision of the judge (who first ruled that her free exercise of religion had not been restricted, but then finally reversed course and ruled in her favor), the actions of Ortega, and the seemingly nervous desperation of the prosecutor, the actual owners or custodians of that land remains unclear. Who can inhabit that land, who can cross it, is still very much contested.

In the 1920s, Chief Rickard, founder of the Indian Defense League, wrote:

> A border has been set up, separating Canadians and Americans, but we never believed that it was meant to separate Indians. This was our country, our continent, long before the first European set foot on it. Our Six Nations people live on both sides of this border. We are intermarried and have relatives and friends on both sides. We go back and forth to each other's ceremonies and festivals. Our people are one. It is an injustice to separate families and impose restrictions upon us, the original North Americans, who were once a free people and wish to remain free.

One hundred years later, when Sottosanti was cross-examining Ortega, he asked: "You're aware that that was federal land?" Ortega's response recaptured the spirit of Chief Rickard's words: "It will always be Hia Ced O'odham land." As Ortega and other O'odham activists have repeatedly pointed out, in their language there is no word for "wall."

* * *

In the seventeenth, eighteenth, and nineteenth centuries, as the invaders crept mile by mile across the continent, they drew the borders closed behind them, like ashamed ne'er-do-wells drawing curtains on their misdeeds. They built forts that served as borderland security, demonstrating and insisting on their control: they would remain and expel any who were here before them, and any—depending on their race and provenance—who came after them.

"The anti-Indian campaigns of the Revolutionary War enacted the brutal logic of the Paxton Boys"—a murderous anti-Indian mob formed in 1763 in response to the government's hesitancy to exterminate the natives—"on a devastating scale," writes historian Kevin Kenny in *Peaceable Kingdom Lost*. "Now the violence was systematic rather than sporadic." The Paxton Boys, the most notorious of many such mobs, explicitly defended their usurpation of Indian territory in what is now Pennsylvania, operating between Philadelphia and Harrisburg, by citing the "right of conquest," that those who forcibly take the land get to keep it. "During the Revolution," Kenny continues, "waging total war against Indians became an act of patriotism." Both the Militia Act of 1792 and the Insurrection Act of 1807 mandated, as Indigenous scholar Roxanne Dunbar-Ortiz explains, "a genocidal policy against the Indigenous nations of the Northwest Territory, allowing for federal troops to eliminate the resistant communities in order to allow settlers to occupy the land."

Total genocidal war, quotidian slaughter and exultant knavery, along with presumptions of innocence and superiority, all folded into the budding spirit of patriotism: it was, in poet Wendy Trevino's phrase, "Violence no one can confuse for / Anything but violence." Nation building is based on not only ideas or principles, but also on—from a description of the 1637 Mystic Massacre in what is today Connecticut—Indians "frying in the fire."

Penobscot tribal members and researchers for the 2021 documentary film *Bounty* found that there were at least sixty-nine government-issued scalp edicts between 1675 to 1760 in New England, an area previously known as Dawnland, and at least another fifty scalp edicts issued elsewhere in the United States until 1885. Some of the edicts targeted specific tribes by name, offering, in today's dollars, up to $12,000 for a male scalp and about half that for a female scalp.

Frederick Jackson Turner, a founder of frontier scholarship, described this murderous land theft as "manufacturing civilization." Clearing out the natives and then barring the "other" from soiling newly claimed territory was how the nation was seeded and nurtured.

Invaders relied on and cited biblical decree to justify their encroachments: "Be fruitful and multiply, and replenish the earth, and subdue it." The religious and philosophical justification came, in part, from the English Enlightenment philosopher John Locke, who wrote,

> God and his reason commanded mankind to subdue the earth, i.e. improve it for the benefit of life, and therein lay out something upon it that was his own, his labour. He that, in obedience to this command of God, subdued, tilled, and sowed any part of it, thereby annexed to it something that was his property, which another had no title to, nor could without injury take from him.

By rapaciously "subduing" and effectively destroying the land was how settlers claimed title over what Locke described as "some inland vacant places of America."

Locke's writings, frequently citing the conquest of America as the paragon of mankind's prowess (and he was indeed discussing men), were an elaboration of Pope Alexander VI's blessing of the discovery doctrine in 1493, when he issued three papal bulls reaffirming Spain's title to newly "discovered" lands. The "inter caetera divinae," as they were known, stated that the lands claimed by Columbus, since they had been "undiscovered by others," now belonged to Spain.

The decrees are connected to what social scientist Mahmood Mamdani sees as the very origin of the nation state. While often described as rising out of the Peace of Westphalia in 1648, Mamdani, rather, sees the rise of the modern nation as coming from two simultaneous campaigns of ethnic cleansing: the murder and expulsion of Jews and Arabs from the Iberian Peninsula, and the Castilian monarchy's ethnic cleansing of Indigenous peoples across the Atlantic.

* * *

The Westphalian theory claims that nation states were born in response to decades of bloodshed during the Thirty Years' War, with a call to respect the territorial sovereignty of neighboring states: a "buffer-line dividing states from each other," as scholar Matthew Longo puts it in *The Politics of Borders*. That understanding, however, glosses the rise of nationalisms that took place in previous centuries. It's revealing to spend a bit more time unpacking the rise of nation states, the key political entities behind the projection and enforcement of borders.

In 1648, delegates from over one hundred empires, republics, palatinates, and confederacies gathered in Osnabrück and Münster (modern-day Germany) to end the Thirty Years' War by mutually recognizing both territorial sovereignty and the inviolability of borders, roughly drawing borders around states in an attempt to pacify and untangle a continental knot of bitter enemies. They basically promised to recognize each others' land claims. But the Westphalian version of the origins of nation states and borders lends a peace-building veneer to the concept that overlooks not only the thirty years of war that immediately preceded the treaties, but the tension fostered from the previous 150 years of imperial conquest playing out in the Americas. Mutual sovereignty and respect for borders in Europe rose out of violent *dismissal* of claims to land by Indigenous peoples, as well as the presumption that there were no borders that could get in the way of the Europeans' homicidal transoceanic adventuring. During the "Age of Discovery," imperial powers needed to recognize each other's territory in their bid to sweep up lands whose inhabitants, or "owners," they were *not* recognizing. As Mamdami notes, the mutual recognition between nation states was "not so much a respect for existing European borders, but the need to deal with the newly conquered territories."

"Frontiers are established by power," writes historian Elie Kedourie in *Nationalism*, "and maintained by the constant and known readiness to defend them by arms." It wasn't the Westphalian principle of mutual recognition, popular sovereignty, and respect for boundaries (as nation states are so often mythologized) that guided the political concept; it was the massive campaign of scalping, rape, and extermination.[16]

Political modernity, Mamdani writes, is "less an engine of tolerance than of conquest. Tolerance had to be imposed on the nation-state long after its birth in order to stanch the bloodshed it was causing."

In 1558, Queen Elizabeth I sent Sir Humphrey Gilbert to the Americas[17] with the instruction to "encounter, expulse, repel, and resist" all persons with whom he came into contact and who had no "special license" to inhabit the lands. Expulsion, of course, assumes a boundary or border, and such expulsions served as a nationalizing maneuver, a way to filter populations, and an early forging of a nation state.

Bacon's Rebellion of 1676–1677 exemplifies the pattern, pitting colonizers against each other in their mutual efforts to dispossess and control Natives. The conflict began when colonial governor William Berkeley refused plantation owner Nathaniel Bacon's plea to drive Indigenous people out of land in the Northern Neck of Virginia. The deeper into the continent the colonizers marked their ground and reaffirmed their sovereignty, the more land they sought,

---

16 The etymology of "nation" is *natio*, or birth. But countries (and their borders) are more death-states than nation states. The etymology of "politics" is also telling in this context. Related to "police," or *polis*, city—the deep roots of the word are connected to the Sanskrit term *pūr*: a wall or rampart.

17 Gilbert was a brother of more renowned Sir Walter Raleigh and veteran sacker of Ireland, where he was known to terrorize the Irish by publicly brandishing the decapitated heads of his victims.

and the more desperately they protected it. At the end of the rebellion—further fueled by grievances over the coastal elites pressing
their political agendas over smaller, more rural farmers (a dynamic
familiar today)—Bacon tellingly did not declare victory over Governor Berkeley, against whom he was supposedly rebelling, but, in
a show of selective unity, called for Virginians to "defend ourselves
against the common enemy."

The common enemy, of course, were the Indigenous. War, as it
is so often, was a brandishing of power, a coming-of-age and reaf-
firmation of authority more than an attempt to redress a specific
grievance. The losers of Bacon's Rebellion were—decidedly—the
natives, especially the Susquehannocks, who were almost entirely
wiped out in the conflict. These sorts of casualties on the fringes
of the imperial wars were not collateral consequences, but rather
defining aspects of westward expansion, establishing precedent for
how land was acquired, how natives were trampled or exterminat-
ed—"ruined" and "extirpated," to use Bacon's own words—and
how the colonizers shifted and refortified the border. In other
words, how the nation was forged. (The Mexican–American War
in the mid-nineteenth century is another such example.)

Roxanne Dunbar-Ortiz calls the settler-colonial invaders the
"shock troops of the 'westward movement' in North America."
These shock troops were not only taking the land from the natives;
they were planting their flags contra other imperial states. If you
look at a map of the North American backcountry settlements in
the late seventeenth century, the areas of European control were
mere slivers and blips along the coast, concentrated around Bos-
ton and Plymouth, hugging the shore up into modern-day Maine,
some settlements around Chesapeake Bay, a few flares around the
sounds of what would be called North Carolina, and dots of populations around Charles Town and St. Augustine in South Carolina and Florida. Along the coast and deep inland across the continent—all the rest—the land was held, monitored, managed, sometimes fought over by hundreds of different tribes and peoples. Just

a hundred years later, the land along the entire eastern coast and pushing hundreds of miles inland would be claimed by the United States. The colonial population ballooned over that same period from a few thousand people in 1625 to around 2.5 million by 1776.

¡Pasaremos! was the colonizers' trilling refrain. Then, looking behind them, it turned into *¡No pasarán!*

The musket, the fort, smallpox—followed in short order by the three branches of the United States government—reduced the population of natives suddenly enclosed by the new nation in what Mamdani calls "the first genocide in modern history and ... probably the most brutal and most complete ever undertaken." Much of that genocide was achieved by what could be termed the flexing of the border—using newly drawn borders and any trespass across them to justify violent outlash. Those bloodbaths, as one of many crests, culminated in the middle of the nineteenth century.

Though examples of brazen and bunker-mentality bordering abound in the United States—as well as in the rest of the Americas and in Australia—the incalculable destruction, violence, and hypocrisy driving the Indian removal campaigns that took place in the first half of the nineteenth century are as damning as they are revealing of how border and proto-immigration policies set the tone for the country's contemporary border politics.

While the "Indian Question" in the nineteenth century has been compared to the "Jewish Question" that cracked open civilization the following century in Europe, historian Claudio Saunt, author of *Unworthy Republic*, notes that there are "several striking similarities between the expulsion of Indigenous peoples in the 1830s and the state-sponsored mass deportations of the twentieth century in Turkey, Greece, Germany, the Soviet Union, and elsewhere." In fact, the United States was the first state in the modern era to undertake such a mass deportation.[18] The deadly expulsions, perfidi-

18 Mass expulsions had been carried out in previous millennia, such as the deportations of conquered peoples and untractable subjects in the Neo-

ous means of dispossession, and outright slaughter of natives from Florida to Ohio established and cemented central ideas around citizenship, sovereignty, and borderlands in the United States.

The motivation behind the Indian removal campaigns of the nineteenth century was not only hatred and fear of the natives (though it was also abundantly that) but a ravenous greed that saw natives' ancestral land as an opportunity to expand the slave-driven cotton industry. Especially in Georgia, Alabama, and Mississippi, white farmers and their mostly Northern financiers were desperate to plant more acres of the white gold. Politicians—local, state, and national, including President Andrew Jackson—did all they could to break through the recently established borders surrounding Indigenous lands and flood their territory with both slave drivers and their enslaved Black people. To clear those lands, they either outright killed or deported the natives across yet another concocted border, newly conceived just west of the Mississippi River.

The Supreme Court approved the measures of simultaneous encroachment and expulsion, with Chief Justice John Marshall writing in the 1832 case *Worcester v. Georgia*: "Power, war, conquest, give rights, which, after possession, are conceded by the world; and which can never be controverted by those on whom they descend." In other words, and quite simply, the Supreme Court was accrediting the idea that *might makes right*.

These early borders did not protect, but incited and served as excuse for further incursion and war—the primary elements of nationalism. Italian political scientist Maurizio Ferrera has referred to the dynamic as "internal bonding through external bounding."[19]

Assyrian Empire in the eighth and ninth century BCE. In fact, mass deportation—though it could be thought of as mass importation—was essential to Neo-Assyrian state-building efforts, during which, as James C. Scott writes, "entire populations and livestock of the conquered area were marched from the territory at the periphery of the kingdom to a location closer to the core, where they were forcibly resettled."

19 Consider NAFTA, the free trade agreement signed between the United States, Canada, and Mexico in 1994, which unleashed an unprecedented

By the mid-1830s, US troops were force-marching Indigenous people in chains across Alabama, hunting starving families from camp to camp in the swamps of Florida, with private mercenaries flocking into the dispossession business, turning—to paraphrase Roxanne Dunbar-Ortiz—sacred land into real estate. Much of the speculation and plenty of the political will was sparked by businessmen in New York investing in the clearing of Indian territory to make way for slave-driven cotton farming. Though the infamous Trail of Tears, and much of the rest of the mass deportation and murder, took place in the South, Native Americans were also similarly driven out of states in the North. In Ohio, curious white colonizers watched the forced deportation as if it were a spectacle, gathering around makeshift camps to sightsee as Indians limped past, carrying what few possessions they were permitted to take. (Sometimes they weren't allowed to take anything.) And it wasn't only entertainment: as the Seneca Indians were pushed west from Ohio, Saunt writes, "their white neighbors rushed in to dismantle their lodgings, carrying away windows and doors, disassembling and carting off brick and stone chimneys, and prying up and hauling away flooring and fencing. Some simply moved into the freshly vacated houses." As Dunbar-Ortiz puts it in her book *Not a "Nation of Immigrants,"* "Only with unlimited counterinsurgent war—destroying Indigenous towns, burning crops and food storage, driving inhabitants into peripheries as refugees—did the United States prevail, seizing most of present day Ohio." These removals were followed in subsequent decades with laws meant to spur European migration, especially the 1862 Homestead Act and the 1864 Act to Encourage Immigration.

---

corporate-backed invasion of goods into Mexico at the same time the United States militarized the US–Mexico border. The Zapatistas' declaration of war on January 1, 1994 was, in effect, a response to the US–Mexican–Canadian declaration of financial war (the implementation of NAFTA) against the Zapatistas, other Mexican Indigenous groups, and the millions of marginalized and exploited workers from Cleveland to San Cristóbal.

The forced-removal policies—intended to make Indians' lives so miserable that they would want to abandon their homes—resembles a strategy still in use nearly two hundred years later, calling to mind 2012 Republican presidential candidate Mitt Romney's reconception of self-deportation: making life in the United States so painful that undocumented migrants would supposedly leave of their own volition, or, as the senator hoped, "self-deport." It also resembles Border Patrol's policy of "prevention through deterrence," which deliberately makes crossing the border so dangerous that migrants would suffer and die in their attempts at finding freedom, thus dissuading others from attempting the crossing. (The problem is that, after nearly two centuries, such policies—a diverse gamut of intentionally brutalizing and dehumanizing tactics—don't work.) Prevention through deterrence, or deterrence by death, is effectively a method of corralling humans. In fact, human corralling is a function of nearly all modern border technology. "By forcing migration from Mexico and creating a funnel-shaped fence," writes political philosopher Thomas Nail in *Theory of the Border*, "the US-Mexico border effectively becomes the world's largest centripetal manhunting apparatus." None of this is happenstance or collateral. International legal scholar Itamar Mann, capturing the spirit of borders worldwide, described Australia's immigration detention complex as "cruelty by design."

President Andrew Jackson, who championed the Indian Removal Acts, wrote in 1828: "I have exonerated the national character from all imputation, and now leave the poor deluded creeks & cherokees to their fate, and their annihilation." In the same year, Georgia passed a border-enforcement law that prohibited Creek people from entering the state without a permit. Those caught illegally crossing into the territory were subject to ten days in prison.

Just in the decade of the 1830s, as colonizers feverishly killed and expelled natives, the number of enslaved people in Alabama doubled. By the end of the decade, nearly one out of every four enslaved people worked on land that only a few years earlier had belonged to the Creeks and other tribes.

Saunt calculates that the federal project of removing people from their homelands cost the government the equivalent of about a trillion dollars today. In the year 1836 alone, more than 40 cents of every federal dollar went to the deportation effort. Bordering costs a lot, but it can also pay a lot: in the Indian-removal decades of the 1820s and '30s, the government raked in extravagant profits, more than enough to cover expenditures, by selling lands expropriated from the Indigenous.[20]

But it wasn't just the border that garroted native necks; it was also citizenship itself. The concept of citizenship has always been a mercurial one. Consider, for example, how citizens were, according to the Naturalization Act of 1790, first defined in the United States as "free white persons" ("persons" meaning men) "of good character."[21] In the lead-up to the Trail of Tears, Southern states appealed to the federal government to extend citizenship to various tribes, not out of benevolence, but as a threat of incorporation: after they'd been long and repeatedly promised self-determination and sovereignty, Native Americans as citizens would be subjected to laws, taxes, and the full jurisdiction of federal and state governments. Southerners were, in effect, brandishing citizenship as a weapon. As Mahmood Mamdani writes, "The very policies that, on paper, were most straightforwardly intended to foster Indian citizenship, were in fact tools for turning over Indian land to white settlers."

---

20 See chapter 4. Though the number varies, independent watchdogs have calculated that ICE spends over $200 per day per person to lock up migrants in detention centers. With a high of over fifty-five thousand people detained every day in the summer of 2019, that's $11 million a day spent on keeping migrants behind bars. And with about 62 percent of detention beds run by private, for-profit prisons, corporations are making just under $7 million a day in the business.

21 Though it wasn't in continual practice, that provision stayed on the books until 1952.

In his autobiography, *Fighting Tuscarora*, Chief Clinton Rickard explains:

> By our ancient treaties, we expected the protection of the government. The white man had obtained most of our land and we felt he was obliged to provide something in return, which was protection of the land we had left, but we did not want to be absorbed and assimilated into his society. United States citizenship was just another way of absorbing us and destroying our customs and our government. . . .
>
> We feared citizenship would also put our treaty status in jeopardy and bring taxes upon our land. How can a citizen have a treaty with his own government?

The Indian Citizenship Act of 1924, which unilaterally bestowed citizenship to all noncitizen Indians, was signed just one week before the Immigration Act of 1924, which imposed racially motivated quotas on immigration, intending to filter out people from eastern and southern Europe. (Asians were completely barred.) The seemingly diametric folding into the nation (extending citizenship to the Indigenous) and excluding from the nation (denying entrance to certain foreigners) are two sides of the same coin of nation building: flexing the boundaries to assimilate the recalcitrant foreigners within and deflect the foreigners without. The nearly simultaneous moves had devastating effects on Indigenous people currently outside of the recently drawn US borders, even if Indigenous land in both the north and south of the country extended across the borders. "This was a violation of our sovereignty," Chief Rickard writes of the Indian Citizenship Act. "Our citizenship was in our own nations."

Another blatant use of the border not to block passage but to facilitate selective movement for the slaughter of Indigenous people is revealed in the 1882 treaty between Mexico and the United States, which established that "regular federal troops of the two republics may reciprocally cross the boundary line of the two countries when they are in close pursuit of a band of savage Indians." The treaty was signed to help kill off the last of the Apaches, who used the border as a shield to duck behind as they fought for their survival against both Mexican and American colonizers.

Of course, the despoiling land grabs of the nineteenth century weren't the end of the story. The dispossessions—which included attacks against culture, language, history, and daily life practices—continued long after legal title was obtained. In Canada—another nation with an obscene history of extirpation and extermination of the natives—the government began forcibly assimilating children through the Indian residential school system, which operated from the late nineteenth century until 1996, when the last school was closed. Over 150,000 Indigenous children were forced to attend the schools, where they were pushed into unpaid manual labor, had their hair chopped off, were fed starvation diets, were whipped for speaking their own languages, were sexually preyed upon, and were told that their traditions, ceremonies, religions, and world-views were satanic. Already torn from their parents and communities, it was revealed through a series of Truth and Reconciliation Commissions that they were also killed. In 2021, the Tk'emlups te Secwepemc First Nation and the Cowessess First Nation found the bodies of over one thousand children in unmarked graves at a former residential school in British Columbia and in Saskatchewan, respectively. The tally of children known to have died while attending these schools is now greater than five thousand, though many suggest the number of dead children is at least three times that. The schools were a way to "take the Indian out of the child," in the words of former Prime Minister John A. Macdonald—a practice that Canada's Truth and Reconciliation Commission report called "cultural genocide." (Legally, it's also simply genocide.) The report adds: "The Canadian government pursued this policy of cultural genocide because it wished to divest itself of its legal and financial obligations to Aboriginal people and gain control over their land and resources."

Indigenous leader George Manuel, as reported by Peter McFarlane and Doreen Manuel in *Brotherhood to Nationhood*, said that the residential school he was forced to attend was "the laboratory and the production line of the colonial system." Journalist and activist Naomi Klein referred to the schools as "rape mines," noting, in a 2021 article for the *Intercept*, "The torture at the schools was not sadism for its own sake but sadism in the service of a broader, highly profitable purpose—land theft on a grand scale. The schools cleared the land more effectively than any bulldozer could."[22]

In the United States, nearly four hundred such boarding schools were similarly tasked with the forcible assimilation of Indigenous children. Historian and activist Nick Estes explains, in a 2019 article for *High Country News*, that the US schools played a key role in pressuring the "most intransigent tribes to cede and sell land by taking their children hostage." In 2020, House Representative Deb Haaland (who became interior secretary in President Joe Biden's cabinet) sought to establish a US version of Canada's Truth and Reconciliation Commission with the introduction the Truth and Healing Commission on the Indian Boarding School Policy Act. The bill did not pass.

* * *

As with the "White Australia" policy, the first immigration policies implemented in the United States—once the natives were sufficiently pushed out of the way or murdered—were explicitly racist. The first federal immigration law, the Page Act of 1875, specifically targeted Chinese women. The subsequent Chinese Exclusion Acts—a series of laws that prohibited Chinese people from immigrating to the United States or, if they were already in the country, from naturalizing—was on the books for sixty years until finally

---

22 The land claimed by Canada on which the schools enacted their terror is unceded. There has never been a treaty, purchase, or land agreement—ever.

being repealed in 1943. But such virulent anti-Chinese policies weren't always reflective of the government's stance. Indeed, until shortly before the Page Act, Chinese people had been welcomed and even encouraged to migrate to the United States.

The treatment of the Chinese under US immigration law perfectly, and tragically, exemplifies the dangerously fickle stance of border and immigration policies. Before the acts barring any Chinese people from immigrating or naturalizing, a series of treaties sought to welcome Chinese migration: the 1844 Treaty of Wangxia, the 1858 Treaty of Tientsin (both of which sought to open and promote commerce with and immigration from China), and the 1868 Burlingame Treaty. The latter treaty clarified that both the United States and China "cordially recognize the inherent and inalienable right of man to change his home and allegiance, and also the mutual advantage of the free migration and emigration of their citizens and subjects, respectively, from the one country to the other, for the purposes of curiosity, of trade, or as permanent residents"—basically an open borders monograph. However, these treaties were followed, just a few years later, by laws barring all Chinese laborers, under penalty of ten years' imprisonment, from entering into the United States.

What explains the tergiversation? Once again, border and immigration policy was driven not by the inherent needs or rights of a nation, but rather by the vicissitudes of politics and shifting demands for labor. The laws were complemented by an extraordinary spate of murderous state-sponsored anti-Chinese conniptions, which incited massacres of Chinese people from Wyoming to Washington State, with dozens of Chinese people murdered and their houses and bodies burned in pogroms. In 1871 in Los Angeles, anti-immigrant zealots staged what remains the largest mass lynching in US history. Prompted by years of anti-Chinese legislation and hateful local propaganda—the Chinese were "barbarians taking jobs from whites," as one *Los Angeles News* editorial put it—when a fight broke out in a Chinese neighborhood and a white saloon owner

was killed, a mob went on a rampage, hanging at least fifteen people. According to one account, white Angelenos used pickaxes to
chop holes in the roof of one apartment building so they could aim
their rifles into the rooms and fire. Among the bodies left swinging
from the neck that day was a fourteen-year-old boy.

In Seattle, in 1886, a coordinated, city-government-backed mob
of around fifteen hundred people knocked down doors of Chinese
residents, threatened them, dragged them out of their homes, and
entirely purged the city of its Chinese population. One scholar
counts nearly two hundred American communities that expelled
or tried to expel all their Chinese residents between 1885 and 1887.
San Francisco banned Chinese children from attending public
schools or any Chinese people from going to the city hospital. California went so far as to amend its constitution to emphasize that
"[n]o native of China, no idiot, insane person, or person convicted of
any infamous crime . . . shall ever exercise the privileges of an elector
in this State." The 1892 Geary Act required all Chinese-born people living in the country to carry a resident permit—the first-ever
internal passport requirement in the United States—with a punishment for failure to do so of one year of hard labor or deportation.
The law was upheld by the Supreme Court in 1893, just twenty-five
years after the cordial recognition of "the inherent and inalienable
right of man to change his home and allegiance" signed between
the United States and China.

The neck-snapping policy change reveals how truly malleable
borders are. They are inflicted, not natural. They are weaponized
tools, not inherent edges. Borders are as mobile—and as vulnerable—as human beings.

* * *

Let's return to the idea of terra nullius. Imagine a subaltern subject—a poor migrant, an asylum seeker, an Indigenous person
looking to walk freely through the land—making such a claim.

Imagine them saying, "Well, the border isn't really a fixed thing. It's selectively permeable, and this land you are now living in, where your families and homes and lives and dreams all dwell, we see as empty, *uninhabited*. And we're going to decide to move the border a few miles away, and now we will claim, by decree—because we value our own legal, religious, and cultural institutions and practices more than yours—who is allowed to stay, who is permitted to cross, and where the boundaries are and how they will be enforced." Imagine them saying, as did the government of Australia, that they must *populate or perish*. Imagine a Nigerien migrant landing on Italy's Lampedusa Island and claiming that she had discovered it. Imagine her spouting off the requerimiento. Imagine a Guatemalan woman saying that if the residents of Texas don't readily and completely submit to her ruler and become their subject, she will kill them, rape their wives, take their land by force, and enslave them. Imagine a Hazara refugee docking on one of Australia's islands, firing off three volleys, and saying the land is now his. Imagine the full power of the government's response.

But we don't have to imagine it. Every day we see the enormous anti-migrant and anti-human machinery of Italy, the European Union, Australia, and the United States, as their security forces crash down on and smother not invaders or colonizers, but asylum seekers and migrants.[23]

Territorial conquests are now illegal. The "right of conquest"— officially recognized up and through World War II—was replaced (and specifically outlawed by the 1950 Nuremberg Principles) in the postbellum reset with the concept of "territorial integrity"—which

---

23 It's important to underscore here that despite my hypothetical, the situations are not parallel. Migrants today are not colonizers rapaciously brutalizing people and claiming and conquering land. Nor were the colonizers during the age of discovery, even those settling in the United States, *migrants*, in the true sense of the word: instead of assimilating or entering into and becoming a part of the preexisting society, they sought to extinguish that society and build their own—not an act of migration, but an act of conquest for the sake of settlement and profit.

is a locking-in of the post-Westphalian system, cementing the status quo and permanently granting the spoils to the winners, however ruthlessly they may have been won. As philosopher Frédéric Gros writes, to decide at any moment to respect and uphold territorial integrity is to "suppose that an instant photograph of a specific historical balance of forces be considered absolute and untouchable." And yet history shows us, and the history of borders blatantly reveals, that nothing is absolute and untouchable. Borders are pushed, pulled, broken, set, and reset. They are conjured, abolished, violently enforced, or completely ignored. They rise up, they shout, they convulse, and they die—just as do nations and human beings.

"Where does the authority to draw or enforce a border come from?" we asked. The authority invoked to enforce the borders of Australia and the United States (or any other nation) is by no means "natural," morally justifiable, or historical. Such authority is, rather, based on and upheld by the gun of the border guard and the black robe of the immigration judge.

3

Shafa and Hard Kinetic Solutions

"**W**e were on our way," Shafa, a 14-year-old girl from Niger, said of the Algeria-bound journey. She was traveling her mother, her two younger sisters, and a hundred or so other migrants via caravan through the Sahel, the semi-desert band that stretches across Africa, dividing the continent between the Sahara in the north and the tropical savanna to the south. Crisscrossed by sand-beaten roads that have been migration routes for the people of Nigeria, Guinea, Ghana, Sudan, South Sudan, the Congo, Cameroon, and Burkina Faso, millions are fleeing war-ravaged states, genocides, drought, hunger, and all forms of privation, misery, and want on their way to northern Africa: Morocco, Libya, and Algeria. There they toil to send money home or continue on to the north coast and across the sea toward Europe, whose officials sometimes welcome them but more often expel, "process," or push them back, sometimes into the sea, towing them out in indirigible floating rafts and leaving them to drift and drown, or loading them into Libyan fishing-boats-turned-people-pluckers and floating immigration prisons—boats that take the migrants back to Africa where they are locked up or beaten or deported, or sometimes enslaved. That possible fate, fate itself and almost any recognizable landmark in that sea of sand was still hundreds of miles north,[1] and Shafa was still in the dry sea of the Sa-

---

1   The European Union directly finances the Libyan Coast Guard, which
    is not a formal governmental agency but a hodgepodge of local patrols
    with connections to militias whose "agents" sometimes sell migrants to

hel, crammed into a truck beside her mother and two sisters. They were all, dozens of them, hanging onto wooden poles ringing the truck bed or piled upon and packed into the seat-stripped cabin as they rumbled across the open, slanting expanses that hazed and burned at the desert horizon—routes that the Tuareg and the Toubou have long dominated to transport people (going back at least to the sixth-century slave trade) and all variety of goods, including cigarettes and cocaine from South America, illicit tomatoes from the more verdant south, plus other illegal vegetables and toxic contraband. Shafa covered her face against the dust, the sun, the hard cough of the heat.

And then—"Our truck broke down," Shafa said. As some of the guides worked on the engine, the migrants drank the last of their water. They were able to find a well, and one of the migrants dropped into it and dug and scraped with a makeshift axe, yielding enough muddy water for some of them to able to drink. "The rest of us went thirsty," Shafa said. "The guides told us to wait, but after a night and a day, the guides hadn't returned. Some fifteen of us died on that second day without water." Finally—first a flare of dust on the horizon, then a rumble she could feel more than hear—the sharp pinch of diesel in the nose and the second truck returned, *Dieu merci*, and some of the men finished the repairs. Then, the migrants stacked on top of each other again, they drove on, the sand kicking and pluming and seeming to never settle behind them. Shafa didn't realize they had crossed a border until, in the villages they were passing, she started hearing Arabic.

She saw men in maroon berets and golden shoulder braids: Algerian soldiers trained in insurgency (focusing on "hard, kinetic solutions," according to Algeria's Ministry of Defense). The guards were protecting the unmarked border between Niger and Algeria, drawn first in 1905 between French West Africa and French

---

detection-center black sites where migrants are kept incommunicado, brutalized, raped, murdered, and sometimes sold again.

Algeria and then carried over, at least on maps, through independence—a border imposed by mapmakers ignorant of cultural, tribal,
or linguistic shifts and blend, unfamiliar with the rivers or mountains of Africa but drawing nonetheless, sketching circles like Le-
sotho (completely enisled by the sea of South Africa), tracing the
Namibian strip over the back of Botswana, or arching Cameroon's
tantalized reach toward Niger. In 1860, Lord Salisbury noted that
Europeans "have been engaged in drawing lines upon maps where
no white man's foot ever trod; we have been giving away mountains and rivers and lakes to each other, only hindered by the small
impediment that we never knew exactly where the mountains and
rivers and lakes were."

Today, 44 percent of the international borders in Africa are
straight lines. Worldwide, 40 percent of national borders were
drawn by just two countries: Britain and France.

For every person dying in the Mediterranean, often declared the
deadliest migrant crossing zone in the world, another two people,
according to United Nations figures, are dying in the desert on
their way to the Mediterranean. "There is nothing you can do to
prevent it. It's too strong," Giuseppe Loprete, an International Organization for Migration (IOM) official who worked for years in
the Sahel region, told me about migration in the region. "It's not
even a calculation," Loprete said. "People have to leave."

As Mahmood Mamdani writes in *Neither Settler Nor Native*:
"Writers on African affairs often bemoan the artificial nature of
boundaries drawn by colonial powers—artificial in that they cut
across cultural communities. . . . This criticism reinforces colonial modernist ideology by suggesting that internal boundaries between ethnic groups territorialized as tribes were somehow natural."
"Tribe" itself, at least tribe as a territorialized group, exclusively tied
to a demarcated boundary, Mamdani and others argue, is itself a
colonial imposition, a border just as deadly as the constructed loops
around nation states.

The fluidity of state power—shifting regions of control and regulated use and habitation—followed the rise and fall of kingdoms in Africa long before colonization. The pull and stretch of nomadic life, the loose and shifting clustering of language group and custom, the rise of city and city-states along with trade and war—all mingled together, setting against and aside differences. What did not happen until European conquest was the territorial demarcation of peoples in Africa: *these people here and only here, those people there and only there.*

The edges of what would become African nation states—territories marked to define majority and minority within specific territories—were drawn into existence beginning with the so-called Scramble for Africa, when, during the 1884 Berlin Conference, Europe's empires divvied up the continent between France, Britain, Belgium, Italy, Germany, Portugal, and, to a lesser extent, Spain.[2] In the twentieth century, those same borders were liberated, lost, won, and then won back in the decolonization movements, all of which hardened borders anew. "The Zulus and the Xhosas had their differences long before they had ever set eyes on a European," geographer Tim Marshall writes in *Prisoners of Geography.* "But colonialism forced those differences to be resolved within an artificial structure—the European concept of a nation state."

Today, as more and more Africans than ever before take heel and head to Europe, to the United States, to Australia, or to neighboring countries, more lines are being drawn: in the past decade, fifty separate independence movements have sprung up across Africa, promising liberation and new lines of "control." But as we continue to see with, for example, the South Sudanese independence movement, ethnic separation and definition by borders—the "define and rule" strategy—is both impossible to achieve and irrepressibly

---

2   Prussian prime minister Otto von Bismarck justified the carving up of the
    continent for European domination because it would "bring the natives of
    Africa within the pale of civilization."

violent. About 4.5 million South Sudanese are currently displaced and cannot return to their homes, prompting Refugees International to describe the country as a "displaced nation." In short: nations themselves are acts of continual displacement.

Niger, where Shafa is from, is the last of the Economic Community of West African States (ECOWAS)—including Benin, Burkina Faso, Cabo Verde, Cote d'Ivoire, The Gambia, Ghana, Guinea, Guinea-Bissau, Liberia, Mali, Niger, Nigeria, Senegal, Sierra Leone, and Togo—a region where crossing borders between the states is often a matter of a bribe, a long bus ride, and a quick shakedown. Leaving Niger for Mali, Algeria, or Libya, all outside of the ECOWAS region, is more difficult, costly, and dangerous.[3] In 2015, the European Union pressured Niger into cracking down on northbound migration. In response, Niger passed Law 36, which declared bus drivers and migrant guides human traffickers, and pushed migrants into the arms of upstart smugglers willing to take ever more perilous routes across the desert.

Enterprising locals sell wooden poles to use as braces so migrants won't fall out of the trucks and get marooned in the sea of sand. They sell bags of water, cigarettes, heavy coats for the cold nights. They pass by uranium mines, US air bases where drones buzz into the sky to scan for rebels or spit out a missile. According to Samantha Reho, a spokesperson for US Africa Command, "The enemy exploits these borders—all the time." In other words, the "enemy" is doing exactly what borders are drawn to accomplish.

Soon after Shafa saw the maroon berets and shoulder braids, the trucks abruptly turned around and sped south again. After a while,

---

3   "The contemporary smuggling economy in northern Niger can be traced back to the 1970s," write Peter Tinti and Tuesday Reitano, "when networks emerged to facilitate the illegal flow of subsidized goods such as fuel and foodstuffs from Libya and Algeria into Niger and neighboring Mali, and livestock and labor flowed in the opposite direction, almost always evading official channels, and forming the basis for informal trade for the entire region." Long before that, traders in the Sahel used slaves to transport salt, which was once the region's most valuable commodity.

the trucks stopped "and the guides told us to get down and to hide in a trench," Shafa explained to the BBC. The guides play numbers—they know when to give up and when to flee, when a load is worth losing and when to up the bribe; they advertise on Facebook and WhatsApp; kids travel for free; pay when you arrive; as many as two thousand people a week, cocaine from Colombia into Guinea-Bissau and people from West and Central Africa northbound and on toward Europe. And if they don't make it, they wait. Another thirty-five dollars, head north again; another fifty, negotiating the bribes, finding a new crossing. Shafa hunched in the shallow trench with the guides talking fast and scowling into their cell phones, and when one of the women waiting in the trench couldn't handle it anymore and started complaining, the guides took out hoses and started beating them, whipping the men and women into silence.

Some of the children died that night. Their water had run out again. The guides said they couldn't go on, that they had to go back to Niger, and they ordered people back into the trucks, driving south now toward the dust-hazed horizon. Then one of the trucks went silent. It had run out of fuel, coasting to a crunched stop, and the guides told the people to get out again, that they would leave to look for more fuel, abandoning them again in the sea of sand.

In 2020, with funds from the Italian government and the IOM, Niger built a short border wall and border station where previously there had been a mobile border post.

Alarme Phone Sahara, an organization focusing on migrant rights and rescues, began reporting on "non-official" or illegal mass deportations from Algeria to Niger in the spring of 2020. Hundreds of migrants, sometimes a thousand a day, were packed into trucks, buses, and vehicles of all sorts, driven south across the border, and dumped into the desert—dozens of miles from any city or facility. During one such deportation, a bus accident left sixty migrants dead. In the same month, militants in the Tillia region launched a terror attack, murdering at least 161 people. As traditional migrant routes were blocked, the journey has become, somehow, even more dangerous. On Alarme Phone's website, they list points of advice for migrants about to set off across the desert: "We hope that this information will save your life, but already know that despite everything, your journey will be hard and dangerous!" The IOM estimates that in the three years from 2016 to 2019, they rescued more than twenty thousand people who had been stranded in the Sahara desert as they attempted to migrate north.

Shafa and the others waited two more days in the desert, dying and watching over the dead. "There were eight of us," Shafa said, "including my mom and my younger sisters. When we got tired, we sat under a tree, and that was where one of my sisters died. We buried her there. Then we continued walking and after a day, my second sister died. Then on the third day my mother died. I buried all of them myself." The bodies of the others were torn apart and eaten by golden jackals.

4

The Economic Argument

The word "economy" derives from the Greek, meaning "rule of the home." Borders and immigration policy are often thought of as involving decisions and rules regarding the home: letting people or goods in or keeping them out. Border controls are largely a question of economy.

"Ask yourself," prompts one anti-immigrant promotional video from the far-right Federation for American Immigration Reform (FAIR)—and many hard-liners have similarly uttered—"why do we lock our doors at night?" The proffered answer: "Among other things, to prevent uninvited guests from simply walking into our homes." "So why," the narrator poses, "should our approach to securing our borders be any different?"

One online troll wrote to me warning, after a long and mostly nonsensical invective, of an "illegal [sic] taking a nap in your spare bedroom."

First of all, I don't have a spare bedroom. Second, the analogy, while perhaps seductive, is both facile and false. Extrapolating the needs and management of a house into the management of a few-hundred-million-person nation state is about as apt as comparing a jellyfish to a human. There are some basic crossover mechanical similarities—jellyfish have bodies, react to stimuli, and ingest nutrients and expel waste, just like humans—but the overlap doesn't go much further than that.

A home is a private, sacred space—one protected by private-property laws and constitutional prohibitions against, for example, having to quarter troops in one's house. The home is not only mostly static (whereas countries often expand—both in terms of population and geography—and contract) but is typically designed to be a single-family dwelling (whether that's a few-room apartment or a few-dozen-room mansion). A country, meanwhile, is expansive and, despite a long history and current reality of minority oppression, is built for multitudes.

Homeowners, under the wide range of property laws that govern most parts of the world, are petty despots. They can refuse to allow into their houses people who disagree with their views, and can discriminate based on religion, gender, even skin color. They can do basically whatever they want in their home and on their property, as long as it doesn't physically threaten or hurt someone else, though such actions aren't uncommon behind closed doors. Homeowners may also promulgate rules guaranteeing freedom of speech and religion, but they have zero duty to do so. Allowing governments the same leeway as a homeowner is opening the door—pun intended—to totalitarianism.

It's a scary thought—extending the rights cherished by a homeowner to a government—but in terms of immigration, that's basically what happens. It is the economy, in the common financial sense, that provides a key means of understanding why nations leverage severe immigration restrictions, and why greatly liberalizing immigration controls would be an economic windfall for both natives and immigrants alike.

But there is a trap here, and it's an easy one to trip into. In working to convince someone that migrants are not a drag on economies, and that they are, rather, a boon to both local and national economies, we risk further commodifying them. And that—commodifying migrants, squeezing them for all their labor power and compensating them as little as possible, bringing them halfway into the fold of the national economy only to exploit them and spit them back out—is one of the principal drivers for closed borders and restrictive immigration enforcement.

Correction of the record—that migrants are "worth their fiscal salt," as journalist Jeremy Harding puts it, and not a drag on the economy—is important, and I'll do it here. However, it is equally crucial to look at the economics of borders not from a mere accounting perspective, but from that of labor and class. After all, admission of more migrants into a country isn't just a boost to GDP (though it is very much that) but also a way to better protect worker and human rights and build cross-border solidarity. All to say, we should open borders because it's good for people, and enjoy the secondary benefits (which include an increase in GDP, native wages, and employment, as I will show). We shouldn't open borders *because* of the GDP.

* * *

Money—either the painful lack of it or the prickling want of it—drives tens of millions of people to migrate. Money also drives nations to try to stop or control migration. And corporations make millions off of migration, by exploiting migrant workers—harnessing borders to employ them at lower pay and offer them fewer labor protections—or by raking in billions in border-militarization contracts. According to a 2021 study from the Transnational Institute, annual growth of the border-security market is likely to rise 8.6 percent by 2025, reaching a total of nearly $70 billion a year.

The roots of immigration enforcement in the United States were largely driven by economics. Towns and cities in Massachusetts and New York established a host of so-called poor laws beginning as early as the seventeenth century. One 1639 order from the Massachusetts Bay settlement granted townspeople the "power to determine all differences about the lawfull setting and provideing for pore persons," as well as the "power to dispose of all insetled persons into such townes as they shall iudge to bee most fitt for the maintenance of such persons and families and the most ease of the country." That is, they were asserting the right to push poor people out of their towns. By the mid-nineteenth century, many wealthy Americans on the East Coast, again in Massachusetts and New York, viewed incoming Irish migrants as a direct financial threat. Some saw the Irish as "leeches" and, in order to keep them out or kick them out, developed the first state-level deportation laws. The nativist anti-Irish sentiment laid the groundwork for federal immigration laws that continued the classist targeting of the poor and tacked explicitly racist and misogynist components onto such discrimination.

Up to the nineteenth century, the United States wasn't only a place for migrants to be deported from; people were also deported *to* the United States. People seen as "surplus labor" in Britain were involuntarily loaded up and shipped across the Atlantic. At least ten thousand so-called vagrants or convicted criminals were sent westward across the Atlantic in the eighteenth century—a practice the British called "shovelling out." The practice reflects a key way in which class discrimination was the seed of immigration enforcement, including deportation laws, in (as well as to) the United States.

The economic fear was—and remains—that migrants are helping themselves to scarce resources: housing, medical care, welfare benefits, education, employment, wages. Importantly, however, neither national economies nor job markets are zero sum. In a hermetic system, resources, money, and jobs are limited: if a dollar goes to one person, it does not go to another. But that's not how national economies work, especially as they are today so convolutedly tangled into global markets, and ever since money—the whole financial system—has been decoupled from the gold or any material standard.

In national economies, jobs create jobs, and dollars—like the magic brooms of the Sorcerer's Apprentice—hold the potential to create dollars.

In basic economic terms, the drawing of a border delineates not the edges of the community but three separate classes: one population is taxed and has services rendered to them; another population (noncitizen legal residents) is taxed but receives fewer benefits; and another population (undocumented migrants) is exploited, offered scarce benefits, and sometimes imprisoned and expelled. (An in-between category would be "guest workers," temporary migrants forced to toil for a single boss and afforded only the most basic rights, though even those are hardly guaranteed to them.)

In practice, borders are drawn not only to mark boundaries of political organizations but to maximize control and maximize profit, to exploit the minority—that third category—the undocumented who are taxed and not given any benefits.

At least eleven million undocumented people live in the United States, about five million in Europe, and as many as twenty million in India. On top of the undocumented, there are tens of millions of guest workers—a million or so in the United States and millions suffering under the hyperexploitative Kafala system in the Gulf states. These undocumented or temporary workers are often locked into unsafe or underpaid jobs, have limited (sometimes zero) labor rights, and are subject to abuse, unwarranted firing, sexual assault, harassment, and death.

Even clearer than the privation and precarity of undocumented migrants or temporary workers are the inequalities that borders enforce. Consider the wage gaps across the US–Mexico, Gaza–Israel, Morocco–Spain, or Nicaragua–Costa Rica borders. In 1960 citizens from the richest countries in world were thirty-three times wealthier than people in poorest countries. By 2000, they were 134 times wealthier. In this way, borders uphold what economist Thomas Piketty calls "inequality regimes."

Before we get to the positive arguments for why opening borders would be good for domestic economies and good for migrants, why opening borders would lessen inequalities, and why opening borders would help extend human rights and justice, we first need to dispel a basic misunderstanding about borders. Contrary to much popular rhetoric, an influx of immigration does not lead to lower wages or higher unemployment.

In 2016, the United States took in over 1.1 million legal migrants. The number of unauthorized migrants that year was also high, though harder to pinpoint. It was a big year for immigration, but no aberration. Indeed, the wage trends that year, and the subsequent years, were normal: that is, even as productivity continued to rise, wages barely eked upward. Unemployment soon dropped to near-record lows, and GDP rose more than it had in almost a decade. In other words, with near-record highs of immigration, the country saw no negative effects on job markets and wages. In 2022, after a five-year dip, another million-plus immigrants moved to the United States, most of them working-age adults. Despite fears of rising inflation and recession, the labor market continued to perform beyond expectations, adding more jobs than pre pandemic forecasts. As economist and *New York Times* opinion columnist Paul Krugman put it: "It's an exaggeration, but one with some truth, to say that immigrants are saving the U.S. economy."

A 2007 study by Giovanni Peri, a professor of economics at the University of California at Davis, found "no evidence that the inflow of immigrants over the period 1960-2004"—a period of huge immigration to the United States—"worsened the employment opportunities of natives with similar education and experience." In fact, throughout the 1990s, Peri found that "immigration induced a 4 percent real wage increase for the average native worker." As author and *Wall Street Journal* columnist Jason Riley put it, "immigrants tended to expand the economic pie, not displace native workers."

One 2011 study found that "[i]mmigrants have started nearly half of America's 50 top venture-funded companies and are key members of management or product development teams in more than 75 percent of our country's leading cutting-edge companies." Another study found immigrants founded over half of America's startups that were valued at $1 billion or more. While immigration affects economies and cultures in complex ways, one thing is certain: migrants, whether tech entrepreneurs, academics, home caregivers, or construction workers, are both catalyst and ballast to the market.

The Rich, Not Immigrants, Are the Problem

The United States is one of the least equal countries in the world, with the divide between classes growing rapidly. As of 2023, the top 10 percent of income earners in the United States have more than 48 percent of the country's wealth. There are 540 billionaires in the United States, while about 350,000 people in the US live in extreme poverty (on less than two dollars a day) and almost twenty million people live in deep poverty (an annual income of about $12,000 dollars or less for a family of four).[1] The COVID-19 pandemic saw the gap between super rich and poor grow even wider. As Harsha Walia put it to me: "In our struggle against capitalist austerity, we must emphasize that our enemy arrives in a limousine and not on a boat." If one were truly worried about the national economy and wanted to help, the minority class to scapegoat (or deport) is not poor migrants but the super-rich.

From the mid-1980s until the mid-1990s, when neoliberalism was infecting the minds of economists and policymakers, there was a fifteen-fold increase in cross-border trade and greater than 500 percent increase in foreign direct investment throughout the world. By the late 1990s, international trade had a value of about $6 trillion. As Nandita Sharma recaps the toll this trade took on poor countries: from 1978 to 1982, while around $80 billion in loans and investments flowed *into* the seventeen most indebted developing states, $130 billion flowed *out* in the form of service charges. By the end of the 1980s, developing states were paying out, in debt repayment, $40 billion dollars a year more than what was coming in as foreign loans and aid. The disparity between rich and poor is

---

1   Median annual personal earning for migrants, in 2018, were just under $32,000 a year, or $59,000 for families, which is right in between the official poverty line and the average income for natives.

growing, not only within wealthy countries but between wealthy countries and poorer countries—a gap that is a major driver of migration.

In the United States, as of 2023, the tax rate on the country's richest hasn't been lower in the preceding ninety years. That rate has ranged from over 60 percent in the early 1930s, over 90 percent throughout the 1950s, dipping into the 70 percent range in the 1960s and '70s, and then dropping precipitously beginning in the 1980s. By the second decade of the twenty-first century, the marginal tax rate has plummeted to 37 percent, while hundreds of American billionaires isolate themselves in enclaves of opulence.

In the first nine months of the COVID-19 pandemic, the world's billionaire class increased their wealth by more than a third, raking more than a trillion dollars into their already-bursting coffers. With massive spending on the military and border militarization and huge payouts to defense and police budgets around the world, nations across the globe are trading the welfare state for a police and border state.

It's tempting, especially in times of extended financial crisis, to foist responsibility onto already-targeted populations. However, a look at some historical examples proves that such desperate incrimination is both bootless and misguided.

Soon after the 1929 stock market crash, the United States launched the Mexican Repatriation Act, in which as many as two million people were deported from the United States, many of them US citizens. The logic was that jobs were scarce, and getting rid of a big chunk of the labor supply would help. However, recent studies on labor market effects of those deportations found that, especially in rural areas from which a lot of Mexicans and Mexican Americans were deported, wages for domestic workers actually decreased. Production levels decreased, farmers struggled to complete harvests, and shops saw fewer patrons.

"The repatriation of Mexicans, who were laborers and farm workers," concluded researchers Jongkwan Lee, Giovanni Peri, and Vasil

Yasenov, "reduced demand for other jobs, especially skilled crafts-man and managerial, administrative and sales jobs mainly held by natives." None of the promised labor market benefits came through for the native workers, and, on top of their wages dropping, their unemployment increased.

Now that worries about the negative financial impacts of immigration have been addressed, let us consider how and who immigration *does* help.

Migration Helps Immigrants

Studies show that migrants moving from Mexico to the United States increase their wages by a factor of two to six, while migrants from sub-Saharan Africa to Europe increase their wages by even more. Someone from Yemen moving to the United States would increase their wages for doing nearly identical work by a factor of fourteen. From Haiti, it would be a factor of more than twenty-three. If you could double, triple, quadruple, or quattuordecimuple your wages for comparable work, would you move?

Besides the clear wage benefits—significantly more money for similar work—migrants typically move to places with better labor rights, more worker protections, better infrastructure, and more freedom, security, and opportunity.

Moving somewhere where you can earn more and better protect your earnings is part of what is referred to as a "place premium": according to the Center for Global Development, in societies with greater resources and better political and economic institutions, workers can be as much as several times more productive. One of the clear takeaways is that labor mobility, more than almost any other policy or fiscal intervention, is the best way to reduce household poverty in many countries around the world.

Consider, for instance, that over 40 percent of Tajikistan's GDP is based on money sent back to the country from migrants living abroad; the same is true of nearly one-third of Nepal's GDP and over 20 percent of El Salvador's. Families and sometimes entire local economies survive on remittances in many countries. And while self-sufficiency might sound more appealing or sustainable, communities have long relied on distant forays to bring back needed wealth or resources. And, in today's global market, nearly every country already sends out its corporate scouts or corporate migrants to reap riches and ship them home.

Communities establishing themselves across borders is basically the inverse of outsourcing. Companies like Ford, Nike, and Apple migrate their production facilities and send home the profits to their CEOs. If we can accept those transnational corporations, why can't we imagine other such loose and creative figurations of identity and belonging that transcend legal international divides? Perhaps it is because, as Indigenous linguist Yásnaya Elena Aguilar Gil writes, state borders "colonized even our imagination."

The reality is that many communities have long been effectively transnational. Gil writes in an article for *The Baffler* about how a community, even a nation, doesn't necessarily align with the territory claimed by the nation state. She cites the example of how the Yumano territory, like that of other Indigenous groups, was divided in two—half in Mexico, half in the United States. On Mexico's southern border, Maya territory was similarly spliced. Today, Oaxacan migrants have established their own vibrant communities thousands of miles north of their traditional homelands. The myth of territorialized communities or nations (fixed to a certain and unchangeable land) belies both history and reality. And the Garifuna people, who currently live in Guatemala, Honduras, Nicaragua, and Belize, and on some of the Caribbean islands, see themselves as part of a common nation despite the fracturing of the Central American isthmus into separate nation states in the 1830s.

Despite the sharp economic downturn at the beginning of the COVID-19 pandemic, in 2020 remittances sent from the United States to Mexico actually increased. Remittances nearly doubled in two years, according to a report from the Inter-American Dialogue, to over $3.5 billion, emphasizing the strength of supra-national ties.

So-called brain drain—when people with high levels of education emigrate, allegedly leaving their home countries drained of intelligence—is less a reality than an unfounded xenophobic riposte. The most commonly cited example of brain drain is that opening doors to more immigrants from poor countries would empty those countries of essential doctors and health care professionals. While the argument is reductive, and health care workers' experience abroad can be hugely beneficial to their native countries' healthcare, there is cause for concern. As one study noted, "Africa bears over 24 percent of the global disease burden with only 3 percent of health workers to take care of the sick." But walls won't solve the problem.

A quicker and more sustainable solution is to end ongoing economic exploitation, pay reparations for colonial-era devastation, and invest in training and mutual exchange of knowledge and expertise. If a doctor or another educated professional wishes to relocate, barring them not only from entering the receiving country but also from leaving their home country presents another realm of moral scrutiny regarding mobility restrictions. After all, the same argument could be levied against professionals who depart rural areas of the United States or other countries, leaving health care deserts in their wake. The argument to close borders because of brain drain is a slippery slope and could be used to immobilize all sorts of workers if a government deems it expedient.

Migration Increases Wealth—for All

US immigration restrictionists, even if many of them are against welfare in general, have long blamed migrants for draining welfare coffers. In 2019, Donald Trump's presidential administration published a rule that ordered Department of Homeland Security (DHS) officials to block immigrants seeking to come to the United States if they were deemed "likely to become a public charge"—that is, to use certain public benefits like food stamps or rely on subsidized housing.

Trump justified the rule—a revival of a nineteenth-century means of selective exclusion—as a way to ensure that immigrants are "financially self-sufficient," claiming, "I am tired of seeing our taxpayer paying for people to come into the country and immediately go onto welfare."

The same year, the director of US Citizenship and Immigration Services, Ken Cuccinelli, offered a rewrite of the Emma Lazarus poem emblazoned on the Statue of Liberty: "Give me your tired and your poor who can stand on their own two feet and who will not become a public charge." He was roundly ridiculed, but his rendering reflected reality more closely than did Lazarus's aspirational verse.

In 2020, DHS tried to further weed out asylum seekers based on measures of wealth: adding a fee to apply for asylum and barring asylum seekers who remained in a transit country for more than fourteen days on their way to the United States. For the overwhelming majority of Central American asylum seekers, whose only hope of refuge is getting to the US–Mexico border, passing through Mexico in less than two weeks is financially impossible. (While, as of 2023, the fee and the fourteen-day bar never went into effect, other similar legislation has been proposed.)

The 2019 rule on "public charges," which went back and forth in the courts and was blocked by the end of the Trump administration, stems from the 1882 Immigration Act, which barred from entry into the country "any convict, lunatic, idiot or any person unable to take care of himself or herself without becoming a public charge." The law also charged a head tax of fifty cents for every immigrant. By 1903, "professional beggars" were also barred from entering the country.

However, as we have seen, the practice of blocking the poor—contrary to the nation's mythos—goes back to even before the founding of the country. In 1701, the Massachusetts colonial government passed a law with an exclusion charge, requiring ship captains to procure bonds for passengers who were "impotent, lame or otherwise infirm, or likely to be a public charge."

Almost three hundred years later, in 1996, President Bill Clinton signed the Illegal Immigration Reform and Immigrant Responsibility Act, making immigrants prove their capability of maintaining an income above the poverty level. IIRIRA also required sponsors of all family-based visa applicants to prove they could maintain the sponsored immigrant with an income at least 125 percent of the poverty level. But it makes little sense to bar those immigrants who can't (or whose families can't) meet those requirements, because the vast majority of migrants make enough not only to support themselves but to pay into the pot—a pot they will not be eligible to take from for years. That is, migrants contribute more than they take.

Migrants pay taxes, and elimination of barriers to migration would let them pay more. A 2016 study by the Institute on Taxation and Economic Policy found that undocumented immigrants in the United States annually pay over $11.7 billion in state and local taxes. Undocumented immigrants pay on average about 8 percent of their incomes in state and local taxes. The top 1 percent of taxpayers, meanwhile, pay an average effective tax rate of 5.4 percent. In other words, super-rich Americans typically pay a lower percentage of their incomes in taxes than do undocumented migrants.

Most of those migrant-paid taxes are service taxes dished out at the state and local level. But many undocumented migrants, an estimated 50 percent (and perhaps as high as 75 percent), also pay federal income tax through Individual Taxpayer Identification Numbers.

At the same time, the same study found that undocumented migrants use fewer government resources. In 2016, the average per capita value of public benefits consumed by immigrants was $3,718, as compared to $6,081 among native-born Americans.

Despite what fearmongers would have you believe, undocumented migrants are also ineligible for most federal welfare benefits: they can't access most of the acronymic help programs, including SNAP (Supplemental Nutrition Assistance Program), CHIP (Children's Health Insurance Program), TANF (Temporary Assistance for Needy Families), or SSI (Supplemental Security Income). They don't receive federal Medicaid or Medicare. They can't draw Social Security benefits. And while they can receive emergency medical care and, in some instances, receive some help from a supplemental nutrition program for Women, Infants, and Children (WIC), they are generally barred from all means-tested welfare. Even legal immigrants with green cards can't receive most benefits during the first five years they are in the country: the idea is that they first have to "pay in". For Medicare and Social Security, legal permanent residents (green card holders) need to pay in for forty quarters, or ten years, before they are eligible to receive any benefits.

In 2017, the Department of Health and Human Services commissioned a study on the fiscal effects of refugees and asylees in the United States. What researchers found was contrary to what the Trump administration was looking for, and the study was buried—though eventually leaked. From 2005 to 2014, the study found that the US refugee and asylee population paid $63 billion more in taxes than they received in benefits. And the per capita annual net effect of each refugee or asylee was positive by $2,205, compared to a national average of $1,848 over the same time period.

A number of state-specific studies report similar findings. In Arizona, immigrants pay in $2.4 billion a year and receive about $1.4 billion in welfare benefits. In Florida, immigrants—both documented and undocumented—contribute about $1,500 more per capita than they receive.

In Europe, various studies have recognized the same trend. In 2014, just two years before the Brexit campaign spilled a pool of lies about migrants across the United Kingdom, University College London found that migrants from the EU contributed over £20 billion more in taxes than they received in benefits. A 2017 study in Denmark found that EU immigrants made a significant positive long-term net contribution to the Danish welfare state.

Despite numerous and consistent findings that "noncitizens use every welfare program less than natives do, often by wide margins"—as one Cato Institute study put it—it's easy to come across research that reaches the opposite conclusion. Immigration restrictionists note that young undocumented people are eligible for free education, as well as for school lunch programs, and that all people present in the United States can receive free emergency medical care. Undocumented immigrants also use roads, benefit from the electric grid, and can call upon fire departments and even police services. All true. But, again, they also chip in on all of those fronts: undocumented immigrants build roads, lay and repair the electrical grid, fight fires, and call police departments far less. (They also commit far fewer crimes.)

Though how much they pay in is clear, how much they use less calculable services or infrastructure—such as roads—is much harder to measure. What we can measure, however, or at least describe, are the pernicious effects of being marginalized into the corners of society and living in legal precarity—which, in the long run, is incredibly expensive.

Researchers at the University of Connecticut found that "stressors faced by immigrant students can drain their coping capacities and leave them vulnerable to academic failure." Undocumented youth, the study found, deal with uncertainty, fear, and stress, leading to psychological issues including depression, anxiety, and an increased risk of suicide. The constantly looming fear of deportation negatively shapes self-image in children. They see themselves as less deserving than their peers when the government devalues and marginalizes them, hounding and threatening both children and parents.

In a shocking yet quotidian scene captured in the serial documentary *Immigration Nation*, a group of Immigration and Customs

Enforcement agents in tactical gear dupe a New York City family into opening their door. "We are the police," the agents say, and then proceed to arrest a man in front of his wife and family. One of the ICE agents permits the man's 3-year-old daughter, who is sobbing, to say goodbye. Her father hugs her, kisses her hands, and then is pulled away and stuffed into a van. "We're all parents, on my team," an ICE agent says after the arrest, "so we always take into consideration the children, you know, and the family . . . and we try to make, you know, this probably unpleasant situation, you know, just a little bit easier for everyone."

Though it is hard to do, forget for a moment the fact that ICE is effectively kidnapping the father of a family in front of his young daughter and wife; forget the severe and lasting trauma this will have on all parties (ICE agents likely included), and consider the economic effects. What will this family do? How will they survive in New York City, except through extraordinary hardship, reliance on handouts, or perhaps begging? And what of the daughter? How will the lasting psychological effects of what she witnessed, as well as the secondary effects of what her family will now suffer, hamper her ability to get through school, secure a job, and become a contributing member of society? And how much did that arrest and deportation cost? As of 2017, according to ICE, the average cost of identifying, apprehending, detaining, processing, and deporting a single migrant was $10,854.[2] The number varies widely, however, and can be significantly higher. It costs to deport someone. It costs much more to be deported. Tearing apart families is not sound economic policy.

* * *

---

2   A 2016 study calculated that deporting all undocumented migrants from the United States would tank the GDP by $4.7 trillion.

Nobel Prize–winning economist Milton Friedman famously said, "You cannot simultaneously have free immigration and a welfare state." Smart guy, but wrong on this point. Michael Clemens, a leading immigration economist, estimates that completely opening borders would double the global GDP, adding literally trillions of dollars into the global economy. Clemens writes in a 2011 peer reviewed article that estimates in how much money is lost due to immigration barriers "should make economists' jaws hit their desks." Clemens surveyed a host of studies that look at efficiency gains from eliminating barriers to trade, capital flow, and human mobility. Taking away all policy barriers to trade would increase GDP between 0.3 and 4.1 percent, he estimates. Opening up capital flow would bump GDP by between 0.1 and 1.7 percent. And allowing free migration would boost overall GDP by between 67 and 147.3 percent. Taking his calculations for granted, a welfare state, and even a largely expanded welfare state, is more than doable with open borders.

But Clemens has his critics. Harvard economist George Borjas, for one, details typically unreported costs in a hypothetical world of completely open migration, emphasizing that while there may be a surplus of GDP, there will also be winners and losers, and that corporations stand to gain the most. "The politically correct narrative," Borjas writes, "is wrong: immigration is *not* good for everyone. And we would do a much better job of figuring out what to do if we could drop the pretense that everybody is better off and instead try to address the problems created by the fact that there are both winners and losers." Borjas, too, has his critics, but his point stands. Opening borders is not a panacea to all our ills. We also have to deal with other profound problems that allow for the kind of corporate speculation that creates such winners and losers.

If policymakers aren't convinced of the economic, physical, and existential harms of closed borders, and still fear for their wallets, there's an easy last-resort fix: restrictions on services offered to new immigrants, or higher tax rates for new immigrants than for native residents. This could be a version of the "wall around the welfare state not the nation state" argument. The few people who may suffer because of increased competition from new migrants can be justly compensated—there will be more than enough extra tax revenue to go around. This is what is known as a keyhole solution, acknowledging that almost no national policy change is going to benefit everyone, and then compensating those who are negatively affected. If open borders overwhelmingly benefit the vast majority of a country, but negatively impacts a small portion of certain sectors of the workforce, some of the economic gains can be directed to those suffering that adverse impact. Though such a proposed system sounds complex, it's not much different than other targeted public benefits, such as welfare, child tax credits, or other ways governments dip into the general pool to help those who need it.

One of the most obvious benefits of increased migration to many countries in the global North is simply filling empty job positions. In 2019, 3,454 teachers were hired in the United States through the J-1 visa. In June of 2020, the Trump administration abruptly froze visas for temporary foreign workers, leaving teachers—even those with pending contracts—in limbo. The administration justified the ban by declaring that it would prevent foreign workers from taking American jobs during the COVID-19 pandemic unemployment crisis. The move was consistent with previous efforts of White House adviser Stephen Miller—the architect behind most of Trump's anti-immigration policies—who for years sought to eliminate foreign work visas.

Meanwhile, there has been an ongoing, and growing, teacher shortage in American public schools, especially in public high schools in high-poverty locations. As the US population continues to grow, the number of total teachers has dropped in recent years. A study from the Economic Policy Institute found that between 2012 and 2017, the gap between teacher demand and teacher supply grew from 64,000 to 110,000. When looking only at schools in high-poverty areas, the gap is even larger. By 2021, the shortage had become a crisis: public K–12 education was more than half a million teachers short. Reliance on temporary visas, however—especially when they are subject to the whims of politics—fosters volatile and unproductive workplaces not only in schools but in other industries that have come to rely on temporary, expendable, and precarious labor.

Wouldn't a teacher who is committed to a city or neighborhood, who knows the community, who learns and understands the intricacies of the culture, who feels secure and confident in their position and prospects, be much better suited for the classroom? With a significant teacher shortage in the United States, as well as in Italy, Britain, and Japan, allowing foreigners to come and settle comfortably instead of barring them or treating them as provisional and expendable labor would be better for both students and society.

Outside of exceptional circumstances, such as the pandemic and the Great Recession, most US states have for years been undergoing a jobs surplus—that is, they have more open jobs than people to fill them. In 2019, Pew Trusts counted thirty-nine states with an excess of job vacancies. Nationally, by the end of 2019, there were 7.1 million job openings across the country. Essential industries such as agriculture, technology, fishing, construction, meatpacking, and tourism heavily rely on guest worker programs. But such reliance makes life and work harder for both employers, who frequently have to meet burdensome visa requirements and applications, and the workers themselves.

There are, however, good ways and bad ways of filling job openings.

One example that disturbingly captures the destabilizing nature of guest worker programs is the backwards and bizarre disruption of the tomato industries between Italy and Ghana. One-third of Italian farmworkers are now migrant workers, most of them recruited through the *caporalato*, or "gangmaster" system, under which, Harsha Walia explains in *Border and Rule*, "their wages are often withheld, they are coerced to take performance-enhancing drugs, and they experience routine violence by employers and labor brokers." Moreover, they often live in segregated clusters of shacks outside of towns where they have limited or no access to running water, electricity, or health care. Many of those recruited to toil on Italian farms are poor Africans. In Ghana, which has become one of the world's largest importers of tomato paste, the tomato industry—once a staple of employment and producer of a key ingredient of Ghanian cuisine—has vanished. Many of the out-of-work Ghanian farmers are now harvesting tomatoes in Italy, then sending them back to their home country.

With all tomato-processing plants in Ghana closed, Italy and China are dumping tons of canned tomatoes into a country in which half the population lives by agriculture. And still the vegetable (or fruit, if you're a stickler), now mostly imported, accounts for 40 percent of vegetable sales in Ghana. Tomato imports increased by over 1,000 percent in less than two decades, between 1996 and 2015. Italian tomato production, meanwhile, heavily subsidized, gives canned imports a significant advantage over Ghanian-grown tomatoes.

Ghanian tomato pickers toiling not in their home country, but in Italy, are paid rock-bottom wages, which are further skimmed off by *caporali*, "recruiters" often affiliated with organized crime. One Ghanian man, summing up his work conditions, told German news outlet *Deutsche Welle*, "We sell our life." Another said, "Maybe it would have been better to stay home than come to this wilderness."

The upside-down relationship of out-of-work farmers growing and picking tomatoes in a foreign country came about after the World Trade Organization (WTO) pushed Ghana, through structural adjustment policies, to dramatically lower import tariffs, which dropped to 10 percent, opening space for subsidized foreign vegetables to decimate the local industry. Ghanian farmers soon started going hungry and were forced to leave the country to search for work. They found that work in growing industries—such as tomato farming—abroad. Some critics claim that the WTO has "breached its responsibility to respect the Right to Food" in Ghana.

Added up, such policies—between Italy, the WTO, and Ghana; or between Canada, the United States, and Mexico under the North American Free Trade Agreement (NAFTA)—create, as Walia puts it, "pliable labor." There are, according to the International Labor Organization, about 164 million temporary migrant workers around the world. Most guest workers, in Italy and elsewhere, are shackled to their work permits, which bosses can use as a form of blackmail, threatening revocation—which would also revoke their permission to be in the country—if they speak out against any abuses or are shorted on payments, or simply want to organize or advocate for themselves.

When I reported on guest workers in New York's Hudson Valley, I found a similar dynamic to Ghanian workers in Italy: mostly Mexicans uprooted from ranches in their home country laboring away on ranches in a foreign country. Depending on the year, about a quarter million guest workers in the United States are sweating at jobs Americans either can't or won't do. These foreign workers have permission to live and work, but only under certain constraining and often dehumanizing conditions. Farmworker Justice, an advocacy group, calls the program, which has been expanding rapidly over the past decade, an "exploitative model of temporary indentured workers"; indeed, some guest workers, especially if they have to pay high recruiter fees to connect with an employer, actually go home in debt. Contracts between employers and workers stipulate a variety of work expectations and conditions, but reports, including the Southern Poverty Law Center's exposé, "Close to Slavery," enumerate a litany of abuses: unpaid wages, dangerous—sometimes deadly—working conditions, squalid living quarters, lack of medical benefits for on-the-job injuries, and being "held virtually captive by employers."

Some of the workers I spoke with put in, during the busy seasons, fourteen or sixteen hours a day, and they were all living in cramped and decrepit trailer homes, had almost no down time, and suffered frequent injury. "All there is here for me is working and sleeping," one man, Omar García García, told me. He explained that he signed on to become a guest worker because he was poor; because he wanted to build a bathroom in his home in Mexico and send his kids to school, and there was no other way.

The 2018 Global Compact for Migration promotes this modern form of peonage, and many advocates cite the obvious benefits—cheap labor for wealthy countries, a safety valve for poor countries with high unemployment—but overlook the serious ills. As Walia puts it, "Migrant workers provide liberal capital interests with cheapened labor without altering the racial social order through permanent immigration."

The Bracero Program in the United States, which ran from 1942 until 1964, treated workers, as the name suggests, as mere field hands. (*Bracero* is derived from *brazo*, or arm in Spanish.) The US agriculture industry didn't want workers; it wanted their work. The approach, still championed today, reflects Swiss dramatist Max Frisch's observation: "We wanted workers . . . we got human beings instead."

In April of 2021, DHS announced that, in order "to ensure that American businesses are equipped with the resources needed to recover successfully and contribute to the economic health of local communities," it was adding twenty-two thousand visas to the H-2B temporary nonagricultural worker program. Meanwhile, the same department was deporting thousands of people a month, the Supreme Court was hearing a case about how migrants with Temporary Protected Status couldn't become citizens, and millions of people were denied the legal right to work.

It's not hypocrisy, but a well-functioning system designed to squeeze and exploit.[3]

---

3   The United States also takes advantage of guest workers abroad, mostly on its military bases, where private mercenary corporations such as Halliburton

The same dynamic is present around the world. In Malaysia, guest workers from other South and Southeast Asian countries make up a third of the country's workforce. And nowhere do more guest workers make up a larger share of the workforce than in the Gulf Cooperation Council (GCC) states—Bahrain, Kuwait, Oman, Qatar, Saudi Arabia, and the United Arab Emirates—as well as Jordan and Lebanon. The Kafala system, as it's known, was developed and implemented by the British.

"Because the system falls under the jurisdiction of interior ministries, rather than labor ministries, workers have no protection under the host country's labor law," notes a report on Kafala workers from the Council on Foreign Relations. "This leaves them vulnerable to exploitation and denies them such rights as the ability to enter a labor dispute process or join a union." Moreover, because workers' employment and residency visas are linked, and only employers can renew or terminate them, "the system endows private citizens—rather than the state—with control over workers' legal statuses, creating a power imbalance that sponsors can exploit."

In countries around the world, migrants face systemic pressure to make unbearable sacrifices, countenanced by legal norms and market forces. Domestic workers in the Kafala system face particularly dire circumstances, as they are sequestered in private homes and face sexual abuse and even murder. As a 2021 article in *Newsweek* summarized the system in Lebanon: it "excludes foreign workers from the country's labor laws, instead tying their residency in the country to their employers. This leaves domestic workers particularly vulnerable to entrapment, exploitation, and abuse." Lebanese employers have been known to confiscate migrant domestic workers' passports[4] and cell phones, sometimes imprisoning them in their homes.

---

are able to exploit tens of thousands of imported, low-wage workers who suffer extreme duress, discrimination, wage theft, sexual assault, and injury.

4   In the 1980s in Australia, various Indigenous peoples created their own "Aboriginal passport," which was not recognized by the Australian state.

Overall, migrant workers make up nearly 70 percent of the total workforce of the GCC states, with, as of 2017, a total of about thirty million people toiling in the system. Saudi Arabia, where 80 percent of the labor force is comprised of guest workers, offered some reforms in 2021, but they still required, for example, an exit visa, meaning that if a guest worker wanted to leave the country for any reason, including abuse, they first needed to petition and get approval from the Ministry of Human Resources, pay a fee (200 Saudi riyal, or about 53 US dollars), and pay all outstanding traffic citations. If a worker were to "abscond," they could be jailed or deported. A Human Rights Watch report found over 3.7 million domestic workers face "serious abuses, including unpaid and delayed wages, long working hours without a day off, passport confiscations, and on top of that, forced confinement, isolation, and physical and sexual abuse." And, in periods of economic downturn, these migrant workers are aggressively flushed out of the country. In 2017, 2.1 million migrants were arrested in Saudi Arabia.

"The construction of an exclusionary regime of national citizenship and legalized segregation of migrant workers from citizens," Walia writes, "acts as an effective firewall against solidarity." Walia's most striking work on the subject is in critiquing Canada's guest worker program, which temporarily and precariously employs migrant workers in dangerous or deadly jobs, and is also rife with wage theft. Analysts estimate that temporary farmworkers and domestic workers in Canada are robbed of $20,000 and $10,000, respectively, in each two-year employment contract.

To turn back to the United States, a 2021 court filing in Georgia described "guest workers" who "had their passports and visas withheld, faced beatings, threats of violence and deportation at

---

The Haudenosaunee, or the Iroquois, have issued their own passports since 1923 as a way of claiming a sovereignty that the United States does not recognize. And in Canada, in the first half of the twentieth century, First Nations people who wanted to vote in elections had to first renounce their Indigenous rights.

gunpoint, and were forced to work for little or no pay in agricultural fields in Georgia, Florida and Texas while living in crowded and unsanitary living conditions."

Democratic citizens, writes political theorist Michael Walzer, have a choice: "If they want to bring in new workers, they must be prepared to enlarge their own membership; if they are unwilling to accept new members, they must find ways within the limits of the domestic labor market to get socially necessary work done. And those are their only two choices." As Walzer explains it, the purpose of guest workers' status—temporary and barred from organizing, switching jobs, or defending their own rights—is explicitly to "prevent them from improving their condition." They are left effectively homeless and consigned to what Walzer calls a "self-imposed prison term." It may be self-imposed in that they initially agreed to the terms, or even repeatedly agree to the terms (for guest workers who renew contracts or return to the work), but that does not mean that they have true agency in the matter. The more accurate description would be a "system-imposed prison term." Or: a backbreaking and soul-crushing system of exploitation on which the Western world relies for fresh salad and pasta sauce.

The Case of Cubans Moving to Miami

But what happens when a lot of migrants come, and come quickly, as would likely be the case if borders were suddenly opened? You can't introduce a new variable into a closed system without expecting some change, right? One way to understand the effects of rapid mass migration is to look at so-called "natural experiments."

The 1980 Mariel boatlift, when about 125,000 Cubans arrived to Miami in just a couple months, is the most frequently cited natural experiment in migration, offering an illustrative lesson. But to understand any sociological phenomenon, you need to start with the historical context.

In 1959, when Cubans rose up to take back their country from US-backed despot Fulgencio Batista, who gained power in a 1952 coup d'état, US officials were unsettled. A placid Cuba had been a way for the United States to exert control in the Caribbean for more than half a century. That control began around 1897, when Teddy Roosevelt, feeling the itch for empire, declared that the United States "should welcome almost any war, for I think this country needs one."

When Roosevelt traveled to Cuba to wage that war, historian Daniel Immerwahr notes, he took with him "two horses, his black manservant, a revolver that had been pulled from the wreck of the *Maine*, and his copy of Edond Demolin's book, *Anglo-Saxon Superiority*." With Teddy literally leading the charge, the United States conquered the island and beat back imperial Spain, launching a new era of American colonial conquest.

When the dust settled, Spain sold the Philippines to the United States for $20 million and gave away Puerto Rico and Guam. Because of the 1898 Teller Amendment, the United States couldn't annex Cuba, but they could occupy it, maintaining control until a "suitable government" could be installed. How "suitability" was defined was up to the military governor of Cuba—an American named Leonard Wood—who wrote to President McKinley in 1900, "When people ask me what I mean by stable government, I tell them 'Money at six percent'"—that is, an economy ripe for US investment. Using the recent invasion and the promise of investment as leverage, the Cuban constitution in fact contained a clause that gave the United States the right to invade the island again—which it did, four more times in the following decades. It was in the same agreement that Cuba leased Guantánamo Bay to the United States.

To maintain the grip on power, US officials made sure the presidency remained occupied by acquiescent Cubans willing to do their bidding. By the late 1950s, Cuba was basically a US protectorate plagued by profound and deadly inequalities, both between the city and the countryside and between white landowners and the Black population. *Macheteros*—sugarcane harvesters who were employed only seasonally—suffered from persistent and crushing debt. Many of the country's peasants were malnourished and lacked education, literacy, and access to basic health care. As a PBS documentary elucidated, there were clusters of graveyards that dotted one of Cuba's central highways, "marking the spots where people died waiting for transportation to the nearest hospitals and clinics in Santiago de Cuba."

When Batista took power in March 1952, the stage was set for ongoing revolts and resistance. "Batista's coup opened a Pandora's box," explains exiled Cuban author and journalist Carlos Alberto Montaner. "Institutions no longer mattered. What mattered was audacity, the individual capable of violent action." Thus, when Fidel Castro and his lieutenant Che Guevara finally wrested back control of the island in 1959, the United States went to extraordinary lengths to undermine that control. One of the means of undercutting Castro's control and legitimacy—besides attempting to assassinate him—was to encourage Cubans to emigrate.[5]

Operation Peter Pan, Operation Free Ride, Freedom Flights, the Cuban Adjustment Act—four US policy pushes undermining the Cuban government and directly encouraging emigration. The result was bursts of people heading north across the Straits of Florida, including a very telling few months in the fall of 1980—the famous Mariel boatlift.

Before getting into the effects of the boatlift on Miami, a bit more detail will help explain not only what became of the migrants, but more about *why* they came. In the year before the boatlift, in

---

5   The context of imperial meddling and conquest cannot be overlooked in any history of migration. Undermining human rights and democracy, and engaging in extractive and exploitative control over a nation, has lasting effects that, while hard to pinpoint exactly, clearly include instability, weakened institutions, and emigration. Blindness or ignorance to history is one of the primary impediments to "solving" the immigration crises.

1979, almost the entire tobacco crop in Cuba was lost to blue mold, compelling the Cuban government to lay off 26,000 workers. It's easy to think of the island's tobacco industry as simply producing good cigars, but the industry is more than a smooth puff. In the late 1970s, Cuba was exporting 125 million stogies a year, which brought in around $100 million, or over 15 percent of total exports. The same year that blue mold spread over the tobacco leaves, brown rust creeped into Cuba's sugarcane, destroying a third of the year's crop. At that point, Cuba was sending almost eight million tons of sugar abroad and had become one of the world's leading sugar exporters. Under grueling, sometimes slave-like conditions, macheteros stood in swamps, swatting at mosquitoes and hacking and burning the cane.

The same fateful year, anti-Communist governments banished Cuba from traditional fishing haunts. Blue mold, brown rust, and restricted access to fishing waters: tens of thousands of Cubans were suddenly out of work, and many more were going hungry.

Without getting into the politics of Fidel and his ruling barbudos, it's undeniable that if you dissented from the party line, or strayed from the newly established cultural orthodoxy, you became a political target, making life extremely difficult—a reality that often incited dangerously hasty departures. Another aspect often forgotten about the late 1970s was that Castro agreed to allow Cuban exiles living in the United States to visit the island, and, in 1979, over one hundred thousand Cuban Americans took him up on it. The émigrés displayed their relative wealth, "making an implicit statement that their decision to emigrate had been the right one," as William M. LeoGrande and Peter Kornbluh write in their history *Back Channel to Cuba*.

After the Nixon administration suspended Freedom Flights in 1973, Cubans had just as hard a time as any other people getting into the United States. So if they wanted to make it to Florida, they had to paddle, sail, or motor across the straits. By 1979, desperate Cubans were hijacking boats, heading north, and being welcomed in Florida as heroes. After a group of Cubans took over a Liberian freighter and diverted it to Florida (the hijackers were not charged in the United States), a top Cuban official called in US diplomat Wayne Smith and told him, "Our patience is running out. If your government wants people in small boats, we can give you more than you bargained for." Soon, Cuba's neighbors to the north would see what he intended by the threat.

Around the same time, Cubans were jumping gates at foreign embassies in Havana in order to levy asylum claims. In April of 1980, six Cubans commandeered a bus and crashed through the gate of the Peruvian embassy. In the skirmish, a Cuban police officer was killed. In order to try to wield the incident as a lesson—by showing what would happen if a few hundred migrants rushed to the embassy to ask for asylum—Fidel ordered that the gates and guard posts (controlled by Cuban police officers) be removed. In just a couple days, over ten thousand Cubans stormed the Peruvian embassy, filling the buildings, the yard, and even climbing and posting up in tree branches. It would be the last precipitating event that led to the boatlift.

"Our heart goes out to the almost 10,000 freedom-loving Cubans," President Carter said of the incident playing out at the Peruvian embassy, basically extending an invitation for Cubans to come to the United States. Castro countered by writing in a newspaper editorial that Cuban Americans in Florida could sail south and pick up their relatives in the Cuban port city of Mariel.

And so they did. Lots of them.

In the following few months, around 125,000 Cubans sailed to Miami in what was soon dubbed the "Freedom Flotilla." Most of the newly arrived were granted status under the Cuban Adjustment Act of 1966, which allowed Cubans to receive a green card after just a year of being in the United States. The act also granted them work authorization, no matter how they arrived.

"There Shall Be Open Borders": Miamians after Mariel

It's important to consider not only what did or didn't happen to Americans in Miami—which is where the bulk of attention has been focused over the last four decades of research—but what happened to the migrants themselves. The fact that economists bickering back and forth on the issue give little attention to the actual migrants says a lot about the effect of borders: marking the limits of interest, concern, and empathy.

I tracked down a few Marielitos, and the response to my basic question—"Are you and your family better off for having migrated as part of the 1980 boatlift?—was an overwhelming and enthusiastic *yes*. Ana Rabel, who opened a restaurant, the Green Gables Café, with her daughter in southern Florida in 2007, told me about her and her family's journey, and what the move has meant. At first, she had mixed feelings about leaving Cuba. In 1980 she was only seventeen, and was in love with a boy in Havana. She adored the culturally rich hubbub of the island capital, but her family had been targeted as dissidents. Her father had spent time in prison, and both Ana and her older sisters, despite being at the top of their classes, weren't allowed to study in the prestigious and selective Lenin school. "We had to celebrate Christmas behind closed doors," Ana told me. "We always knew we needed to leave—that we couldn't make the life we wanted there."

After attempting to emigrate numerous times, as the boatlift began they were finally granted exit visas—little slips of paper the size of a notecard—and through a chain of amicable connections (a friend with a brother-in-law who had a friend), they secured passage on an American shrimping boat that headed to the port of Mariel to pick them up. They spent two days packed in a small cabin in the rocking sea. As soon as they disembarked in Miami, a volunteer handed Ana a Coca-Cola. She drank it down in a few gulps, and then, still roiled by the journey, promptly vomited. She chuckled as she recounted her first moments in America.

The boatlift was a "one-way ticket," Ana said. "We left everything behind. We even gave away the keys to our house." She couldn't imagine having stayed in Cuba, especially given everything she built in the United States—her restaurant, her family, her whole life.

The Mariel boatlift was one of the most rapid and massive permanent migrations in recent history. 125,000 new Miamians practically overnight (about 100,000 people arrived to the city in just six weeks, from April until June), and its effects on the city and its residents would become, as journalist and author Mirta Ojito writes in *Finding Mañana*, "a much abused point of reference in political rhetoric on both sides of the Florida Straits."

How the tens of thousands settled, lived, struggled, found work, ate, and recreated varied in all the ways humans vary.[6]

Looking back on those fateful few months a decade later, David Card, a Canadian economist, was the first prominent scholar in his field to analyze the fiscal trends. The conclusion he drew would be hotly debated for years to come.

Card begins his article by explaining that "one of the chief concerns of immigration policy makers is the extent to which immigrants depress the labor market opportunities of less-skilled natives." The Marielitos who permanently settled in Miami contributed a 7 percent increase to the city's labor force and a 20 percent increase to the number of Cuban workers in Miami. In the 1970s, Miami had more immigrants as a percentage of its working population than any other US city, by far: 35.5 percent of working Miamians were foreign born, compared to just over 22 percent of working Angelinos—Los Angeles being the city with the next-highest percentage of immigrants.

A slightly more specific fear is that an influx of migrants specifically threatens minority employment and wages. But Card found that over a five-year period, Black people in Miami actually saw

---

6   Tony Montana, the ruthlessly ambitious titular character of *Scarface*, played by a Al Pacino, arrived to Miami as part of the boatlift.

their wages increase, while non-Cuban Hispanics saw their wages remain steady. The only group that saw a slight decrease in wages, according to Card, were other Cubans who had already been living in Miami.

Employment numbers followed the same trend, remaining steady or rising slightly over the five years following the arrival of the Marielitos, with one exception: the Black unemployment rate more than doubled from 1979 (8.3 percent) to 1983 (18.4 percent), but within the next two years it dropped to 7.8 percent, lower than it was in 1979.

"The Mariel immigration had essentially no effect on the wages or employment outcomes of non-Cuban workers in Miami," Card concludes. He also summarizes that despite some temporary depreciation for Cubans who had previously been living in Miami, "Mariel immigration had no strong effect" on their wages. "The data analysis suggests a remarkably rapid absorption of the Mariel immigrants into the Miami labor force."

Decades later, in 2015, Harvard economics professor George Borjas fired back, claiming that what he called the "Mariel supply shock" *did* have a negative effect on a certain segment of Miami's labor pool. A Cuban immigrant himself, Borjas focused specifically on Miamians who were high school dropouts, finding that their wages dropped dramatically, by 10 to 30 percent.

Borjas's methodology was basically to define more narrowly the skill group of the Marielitos, noting that about 60 percent of them were high school dropouts. And while Borjas writes that, with his more specific comparisons, the average wage of male high school dropouts in Miami fell by about 37 percent between the four-year period of 1976–79 and the six-year period of 1981–86, the negatively affected group *only consisted of seventeen people.* Even while burying that critical fact, he claims that "the evidence is robust."

Another hole in Borjas's argument is technical. Government-run wage and employment surveys shifted in 1980 to try to count more Black men, a demographic that had been undercounted for years.

Once surveys began counting them, the pool of Black men grew, and cities' cumulative average wages dropped, mostly because of entrenched racism that continues to pay nonwhites less.

Michael Clemens, who, like Borjas, has dedicated much of his career to the economics of migration, re-reevaluated Card's initial study and concluded: "The evidence from the Mariel Boatlift remains as found in David Card's seminal research: there is no evidence that wages fell, or unemployment rose, among the least-skilled workers in Miami even after a sudden refugee wave raised the size of that workforce by 20 percent." The dispute lingers, but even if Borjas is right, and, after adjusting for the different statistical models, Black male high school dropouts were negatively impacted by the enormous labor shock, the precarious position they hold in the first place is due not to immigration trends but domestic discrimination. They should—and could—be treated better, and be more fairly compensated, by both employers and the government.

Summing up, Ojito looks at the big economic picture over the years: while the initial estimated total cost of the boatlift was around $2 billion, within 20 years the Marielitos had an aggregate annual income of $2.2 billion." "Today, Marielitos own restaurants and nurseries," Ojito writes. "They work at Disney World and the National Broadcasting Company. They tend to customers in supermarkets and make house calls as plumbers. They teach at prestigious colleges, receive accolades in the art world, and work abroad as engineers for oil conglomerates. They are poets, journalists, factory workers, bakers, soldiers, and even army doctors."

As the boatlift "natural experiment" shows, if a lot of people did migrate to a country over a short time span, there would likely be little to fear economically. Borjas warns, however, in his 2016 book *We Wanted Workers*, "The fact that immigration had this particular impact at this particular time in this particular place does not guarantee that the same will happen the next time we see a supply shock." He's right, of course: simplicity can masquerade as wisdom, and we can never be sure of the outcome of similar future events.

But Borjas's admission undercuts his own warning against future migration. Plus, we have other "natural experiments," besides the Mariel boatlift, to guide us.

Between 1989 and 1995, enough Soviet refugees moved to Israel to boost the country's population by 12 percent—years of growth that dwarf even the Mariel boatlift in terms of sheer numbers. In just six years, more than 610,000 people moved from the former USSR to Israel. Scholar Rachel M. Friedberg, who closely studied the rapid migration, found "no adverse impact of immigration on native incomes" within the Israeli job markets. Over that six-year period, overall wages increased and unemployment went down. That is, immigration was a net positive for Israelis.

A similar study by Jennifer Hunt, former chief economist of the US Department of Labor, looks at the effects on French wages and native unemployment after the 1962 arrival from Algeria of 900,000 people—in that year alone. Algeria's independence led a significant portion of the population, overwhelmingly of European origin, to return to France, along with about 140,000 Arabs and Berbers. Hunt found that the arrival of the repatriates, which represented 1.6 percent of the total French labor force, raised French native unemployment by at most 0.3 percent. Annual average salaries, meanwhile, decreased by around 1.3 percent in the year after the migration surge. The repatriates, in this case, had some help, in that they received benefits as they looked for employment and were given a lump sum to assist with housing. Still, the movement of nearly a million people in a short period resulted in a minimal effect on wages and unemployment numbers.

A reminder: we must be careful here to do the double work of both disabusing people of the common sentiment that migrants are a drain on the economy—or that they don't pay taxes (which they do)—and of not commodifying them. After all, how much better is it, really, if the corporate elite suddenly cozy up to the idea of open borders, but only do so in order to squeeze migrants all the harder? When, in 1984, the *Wall Street Journal* called for a five-word amendment to the Constitution: "There shall be open borders," were they writing from the goodness of their hearts and real feeling for migrants, or were they sharpening their corporate filet knives?

* * *

In November of 2020, after two major hurricanes hit Central America, causing massive flooding, landslides, and crop destruction, hundreds of thousands of people were forced to flee. Guatemalan president Alejandro Giammattei responded to the catastrophe, "If we don't want to see hordes of Central Americans looking to go to countries with a better quality of life, we have to create walls of prosperity in Central America."

It's a clunky metaphor. A wall does create a certain type of prosperity, but only on one of its sides. It is the wall itself, and the US and Mexican immigration enforcement regime, that has trapped Guatemalans, and others, into cycles of "debt bondage," exploitation, forced displacement, and deportation, fomenting poverty and precarity. It is the wall that lets US officials and corporations maneuver Guatemala into being an export-dependent country that descended into genocidal violence for nearly four decades and now hovers on a thin edge between authoritarianism and a failed state.[7]

Prosperity, or at least dignity, would come to Guatemalans by allowing free transit to those who need or want it. Ending the manipulation of markets and targeting grifting politicians who leverage one-sided prosperity and uphold the global inequality regime is a far better solution than a human barrier. The only wall of prosperity is one with an open door. Prosperity requires a robust, egalitarian, and democratic community. This is the kind of economy—the rule of the home—that the world needs.

---

7   In 2023, Bernardo Arévalo, against the fierce pushback and threats of violence from the ruling elite, won the presidential election in Guatemala on promises to rout corruption and restore the rule of law.

5

The Political Argument— Never Merely Theater

"An act of hospitality can only be poetic."

—Jacques Derrida

The most convincing case for me of the urgent need to open borders is that borders kill. Pro-border immigration restrictionists may worry that opening borders—by letting in potential terrorists or allowing unsustainable population growth or unwanted cultural change—will also kill. But excusing current harms (that borders kill) for potential future ones (that opening borders *might* kill, or figuratively kill) is meager justification, especially when there is little to no evidence that strict border controls offer either financial, physical, or national security. But that justification is exactly the basis for militarized border controls. This bizarre logic—guarding the future by killing the present—is neatly captured in the 2019 film *Terminator: Dark Fate*, one of a series of sequels to the 1984 blockbuster, in which a cyborg soldier anti-hero, in order to avoid the future the cyborgs don't want, carries out "orders from a future that never happened." While chronologically erratic, the series twangs on the same logic of potential fear justifying present violence that pro-border advocates wield. (It's also the same speculative policing and stereotyping that's portrayed in another dystopian sci-fi film, *Minority Report,* based on the 1956 novella by

Philip K. Dick. Migrants—as in the movie and novella, in which criminals are policed before they commit their crimes—are pre-policed, and even pre-punished, by the logic of closed borders.)

In the latest *Terminator* sequel, the monomaniacally murderous cyborg slips into the body of—unsurprisingly—a US Border Patrol agent, taps into a surveillance system, takes on the eye of a drone, and even authorizes the use of deadly force against border crossers in the hopes of protecting the pan-cyborgian future.

People flock to such movies, which draw in tens of millions of viewers and hundreds of millions of dollars—boundary contests being an ancient and reliable source of drama. And while territorial incursion today mostly takes the form of people fleeing poverty, climate disaster, or state-backed or state-dismissed violence, the incursion itself is typically portrayed as the act of violence, not the original and actual act of violence that pushed the people to flee in the first place. Borders, in other words, reframe human mobility to signify it as a threat, invoking the need for military-style protectionism and placing the supposed security of the nation over the security of a person.

The implausible and grossly exaggerated nightmare of a cross-border catastrophe translates into hundreds of billions of dollars spent on anti-migrant matériel, including drones, blanket surveillance, and excessively armed guards trained to chase down and sometimes shoot families searching for dignity or safety. (And while drugs are trafficked across borders, most of them are smuggled through ports of entry, and the most effective method to counter drug trafficking is to stem demand, which is not achieved with anti-tank vehicles or moats.)

The Terminator's vision disturbingly echoes the Defense Threat Reduction Agency[1]: "Threats against our country are evolving.

---

1   The DTRA is a sub-agency of the United States Department of Defense, which has played a critical role—along with private, for-profit contractor Raytheon—in helping Lebanon and Jordan secure their borders with Syria and Iraq by building infrastructure and conducting training.

Global adversaries seek to destroy our nation's security. They do not restrict themselves to borders, boundaries, or conventions," reads one online pamphlet celebrating the agency's importance.

Unsurprisingly, nowhere does the Defense Threat Reduction Agency acknowledge the border-busting of the US military's frequent incursions into dozens of countries where they terrorize, kill, and basically taunt terrorists into being.

Neither terrorism nor fear are stymied by walls, as much as defense contractors and wall builders may want you to believe. The threat of terrorism, however, and its terrifying specter, may very well be increased by wall construction. Not only does the presence of armed border guards and soldiers increase harassment and discrimination against locals; it also provokes the very fear it's meant to quell.

Terrorists, in fact, want walls; they want to see a nation's fear displayed. As terrorism researcher Brian Jenkins has commented, "Terrorists like to see a lot of people watching, not a lot of people dead."

A study from the Cato Institute found that in the forty-plus years between 1975 and 2017, a total of seven people who entered the United States illegally have been convicted of planning terrorist attacks on US soil. Not one of them crossed into the country from Mexico. Not one of their plots were carried through, and not a single person was killed or injured by any of the convicted men. The only known terrorists in the last half century who *did* cross the US–Mexico border—ethnic Albanians from Macedonia—were brought into the country as children in 1984 and were arrested over two decades after their entry for a foiled plot to attack Fort Dix, New Jersey.

The second most convincing case for the need to open borders is that borders are practically untenable. They require not only persistent physical demarcation—border guards, walls, detention centers—but also cultural reification through the politics of fear and othering, as well as nationalist mythmaking and extravagantly violent schemes to draw and defend borders. That is, borders don't last on their own. They need constant coaxing and sacrifice to last. "Walls rarely work," notes border scholar Reece Jones, adding, however, that they are "powerful symbols of action against perceived problems." The unflappable insistence on territorial integrity—a stance taken by nationalists the world over—supposes that the political map is organized as it should be. Historical forces, however, are and always have been mercurial. A constantly quivering, amoebic, picture-in-motion better represents the actual limits and sovereignty of nation states than any static snapshot.

It's easy (and facile) to think of the map as fixed. The way it hangs on the wall, the staid hunks of motionless countries, the simplistic vision of world order represented by squiggled lines and contrasting colors—as if representing divine decree. We recognize and often think of countries by their territorial outlines: the boot of Italy, the logo-map of the United States, the stamp of Australia, and the unmistakable rough blocks of western Europe. But what does the map really capture, and what does it miss?[2] How closely does territory align with the idea or the actual workings of a nation state? And what about the world's many contested borders, "failed states," or the numerous semi-autonomous regions of the world, such as Somaliland, Iraqi Kurdistan, Zapatista territory in southern Mexico, the territory of Naga people living between India and Myanmar, or the nearly six hundred Indigenous Nations spread throughout territory claimed by the United States? What about the nomadic Romani? Or the stateless people who fall between the cracks of nation states and yet, like the rest of us, live on land purportedly belonging to a recognized nation state?

Besides a few rocky or sandy outposts unclaimed by any country—such as Bir Tawil, a strip of terra nullius crushed between

---

2   As Benedict Anderson has it in his 1983 book *Imagined Communities*: "A map anticipated spatial reality, not vice versa. In other words, a map was a model for, rather than a model of, what it purported to represent."

Egypt and Sudan, or Rockall, a molar shaped, guano-covered splat of stone in the North Atlantic—every other spit, prairie, mountain, beach, and forest on the planet is claimed by one country or another. "Every map is a fiction, *a legend*," writes historian and journalist Frances Stonor Saunders. "It is no more the territory than memory is the past."

And while national outlines may seem relatively stable in the twenty-first century, such global cartographical stasis is an anomaly. Elie Kedourie, in his study on nationalism, writes, "What now seems natural was once unfamiliar, needing argument, persuasion, evidences of many kinds." Such argument, persuasion, and evidences take many forms.

* * *

The moustaches are important. So is the men's flexibility, their long legs, muscled arms, mean mugs.

The infantrymen stand en garde with peacocked helmets on their heads, puttees over their boots, Mickey Mouse gloves on their hands. At bugle call, they burst out of stillness to swing their arms like berserking clock hands, high-kicking khaki-covered legs above their heads as they jacknife into formation. Then the gates are swung open. The crowd, sometimes thousands large, hails the spectacle at the Attari–Wagah border gate—two parallel gates, one controlled by each side, India and Pakistan—applauding the brief moment of aperture, then the snapping shut of one of the most contentious borders in the world. Two of the soldiers (one from each nation) twist on their heels and goose-step fast-forward toward the other, dime-stopping when they're level and twisting face to face. Then, clasping hands in three quick, big up-and-down pumps of a handshake, they quickly twist and high-kick away from each other, back to their prospective sides. The gates swing swiftly shut.

The Pakistan Rangers and India's Border Security Force have performed the stomping pantomime of aggression and reconciliation every afternoon since 1959. You can marvel at snippets of it on You-Tube. After the handshake, separation, and gate-slamming, the in-fantrymen yell "Huzzah!" and drummers on each side accompany further kicks and heel-slams as two other infantrymen swivel back to the gate, again stomping, kicking, and flaring toward culmina-tion. In near-perfect synchronization, a guard on each side angrily yanks back open the gate. Two other soldiers, chests puffed, feath-ers trembling—one on each side, each in their respective colors—high-kicks into the middle of the road, facing off from about thirty feet away and, in time with a deep tom-tom of the drum, raise their arms, flexing, glaring, practically growling at each other. (It seems laughable, until one recalls that these are two nuclear powers whose shows of force do not always end peacefully.)

Then, with a few more histrionic feather fluffs, the gates are closed, again, the flags are pulled down, the border is reasserted, and the crowd trickles home.

All borders, the world over, bear or disguise such pageantry: it's what a border is. As much as a capitol, flag, or sash—a parade of synchronized goose-steppers or line of tanks—a border wall, or even a border gate, reveals a nationalist fiction based on a mythical-ly constructed present and an often-apocryphal past more than any geographic, cultural, or political truth. "The state border, although physically at the extremities of the polity," writes geographer Nick Megoran of the Uzbekistan–Kyrgyzstan border, "can be at the heart of nationalist discourse about the meaning of the nation."

In the 1930s, King Carol II of Romania proposed digging a 36-foot-deep moat along Romania's border with Russia. He wanted to fill it with oil and light it on fire to turn the border into a "wall of liquid fire." Over a millennium ago, China began building what would become a 13,000-mile crenellated monster that snaked over mountains and across a huge swath of Asia. The German Demo-cratic Republic, beginning in 1961, erected an Anti-Fascist Protec-tion Rampart and shot anyone who tried to cross it. More recently, Trump wanted a black, hot-to-the-touch, "beautiful wall"—even claiming it would be a gift from those he wanted to keep out. The above-mentioned walls were mostly about containment, about rallying against and even creating a foreign enemy. They all expressed an outward-facing aggression partially disguised as security infrastructure. But that's not how border walls function, or not fully function. (George Washington, in calling for a "Chinese wall or a line of troops" to "restrain land jobbers and the incroachment [sic] of settlers upon the Indian Territory," understood that a wall served to keep people in, to help achieve governmentality, more than efficiently keeping people out.) As US Border Patrol agents frequently admit, walls obviously slow people down, or redirect them, but they don't stop them. A wall protects the idea of a nation more than the nation itself.

While some walls are indeed more simply about keeping people out, such as the Gaza–Israel barrier, the act of "bordering" is most often a response to indigestion in the belly of the nation. And many borders across the globe have been imposed on nations rather than built by them. Such is the case with the so-called Line of Control between India and Pakistan.

* * *

In the summer of 1947, British lawyer Cyril Radcliffe found himself in charge of the fate of a subcontinent. As the freshly appointed head of the Boundary Commission, Radcliffe was tasked with dividing up the British India territories of Bengal and Punjab—and was given just a few weeks to complete the task. So it was that Radcliffe drew the border so theatrically defended and celebrated at Attari–Wagah.

After three and a half centuries of brutal and exploitative control of the region, with the last ninety years as official imperial overlord of the British Raj, the United Kingdom was officially abdicating colonial rule. Deeply in debt from two world wars, and facing pressure from increasingly militant anti-colonial movements, the UK was ceding official control of the crown jewel of the British Empire to its inhabitants. Radcliffe was left a task over which white colonists had been scratching their heads for a century: how to sort out borderlines in territory that was much less tidy jigsaw and more watercolor blur of ethnicities, religions, and community ties.

Despite the jagged and shifting complexity of relations between people and the territory, Radcliffe and his commission contrived to divide the subcontinent solely on the basis of religion: the so-called "Radcliffe line" would separate a Hindu-majority India in the center from Muslim-majority East and West Pakistan on its wings, with a smattering of independent princely states throughout. Neat division not being remotely possible, what resulted was a labyrinthine confusion of over one hundred enclaves (a portion of East Pakistan entirely inside India), counter-enclaves (an enclave within an enclave), and even one counter-counter-enclave, Dahala Khagrabari, in which a little pocket of India sat in a little pocket of Bangladesh, which sat in a bigger pocket of India entirely surrounded by Bangladesh. (The enclaves were a legacy from Mughal rule, which also imposed its own lacerating lines of control on the land. By 2015, most of the enclaves were abolished.)

The fear and reality of religious violence that immediately followed in the partition's wake displaced over fourteen million people and killed hundreds of thousands—some estimates range as high as two million dead.[3] And the decades since witnessed a series of wars between India and Pakistan; a genocide and civil war that created Bangladesh out of what was once East Pakistan; and an ongoing, violent stalemate between the two nuclear powers, India and Pakistan, over the status of Kashmir—a conflict that

3   In a revealing and repugnant episode that lays bare the motivations behind bordering, even as Pakistan and India tried to divvy up their populations along religious lines and the human sorting commenced, Pakistan passed the Essential Services Maintenance Act. The law barred Hindu sanitation workers—the Dalits or "untouchables" who performed society's dirtiest work—from moving to India. In other words, they carved out an exception to be able to exploit needed workers.

threatens, every few years, to erupt into cataclysmic nuclear attack and counterattack.

After a few weeks, with his carving done, and with the heat of the subcontinent disagreeing with him, Radcliffe returned to England. As poet W. H. Auden described Radcliffe's time in India:

> a bout of dysentery kept him constantly on the trot,
> But in seven weeks it was done, the frontiers decided,
> A continent for better or worse divided.

For the two million people dead, and the stability of the region, it was definitely for worse. Perhaps in a show of his own contrition, Radcliffe refused to be compensated for his work (he had been contracted for five thousand dollars), and he later burned all of his notes, referring to what would become known as the Radcliffe Line as "this bloody line."

The lines violently drawn would be violently redrawn, again and again, not only by border ceremonies but by deadly border enforcement. Today, the Indian Border Security Force deploys 245,000 agents on the Pakistani and Bangladeshi borders. They have a standing shoot-to-kill order against any people jumping the fence, and in the first decade of the twenty-first century Indian border guards shot to death about a thousand Bangladeshis. One notorious case was of a 15-year-old Bangladeshi girl, who was shot after her dress snagged in the wall's barbed wire. She was left hanging off the wall for hours, as she called for help and slowly bled to death. Just in 2020, Indian border guards killed at least fifty-one migrants crossing the India–Bangladesh border.[4]

Radcliffe was remarkable for not knowing about the region's history or current reality, not to mention his lack of personal stake in its future. But as an arbiter of international boundaries, he was hardly an anomaly. As a rule to which there are few exceptions, the globe's current borders are the result of imperial horse-trading,

---

4   The United States Customs and Border Patrol (CBP) has an attaché office in New Delhi to help with border policing.

wars of expansion and conquest, and ragged lines drawn clumsily through integrated communities. Whether carved up by colonialist patricians trying to cram notions into nation states, or the outcome of aggressive land-grabbing and score-settling, our current system of borders does not take into account local histories, realities, or the needs or will of the people that they divide.

It is in Kashmir where the Radcliffe line stops. The British left that disputed territory for India and Pakistan to resolve on their own, and they immediately went to war over it. Though the conflict was never completely settled, the sides came to a cease-fire and established the still hotly contested Line of Control, which is the current de facto border cleaving the region into two, though it is yet to be a legally recognized international border.

If you take the Radcliffe Line and the Line of Control together, the effective border between India and Pakistan is eighteen hundred miles in length, about the length of the US–Mexico border. It is, as writer and activist Suchitra Vijayan writes in *Midnight's Borders*, "one of the most complex, violent, and dangerous boundaries in the world." The length of it is illuminated by 150,000 floodlights, whose shine can be seen from space, and much of it is mined and heavily fortified. India has imposed severe restrictions on the area—in both of the contested and heavily militarized states of Kashmir and Jammu—including a years-long curfew and information blockade that began in 2019: blocking landlines, cell phone signals, and the internet. The Indian government clamped down on the region at the same time that they revoked the "special status" agreement, basically wresting more control from the states. The move effectively made India a settler-colonial power in Kashmir, Vijayan explains, as Kashmiris remain subject to detention, torture, execution, and disappearance in a disturbing cycle of violence. In this way, India justifies, both implicitly and explicitly, much of the repression with the border itself.

The Line of Control embodies what is inherent to all borders: creating "the crisis it's trying to avoid," as anthropologist Mohamad

Junaid explained to me. When the Line of Control was drawn, "suddenly everything became criminalized, illegal. Movement that had been happening for thousands of years was now illegal." Even in the last few decades, it was still possible, though difficult or even dangerous, to cross back and forth. Now, it's all but impossible. People are shot, detained, or disappeared. As long as the Line of Control remains, Junaid reiterated, the border "will remain a powder keg." There are lots of such kegs along the region's borders.

On the other side of Pakistan, the Durand Line, drawn in 1893 by Sir Mortimer Durand, marks the divide between British India and the Emirate of Afghanistan, as it was then called, cutting right through Pashtun and Baloch land. Three decades later, the Afghanistan government officially annulled the line, and as recently as 2017, former Afghan president Hamid Karzai reminded Pakistan, via tweet, that "#Afghanistan hasn't and will not recognize the #Durand line"—though it remains the internationally recognized border. Such militarized borders proliferate. Head north past Afghanistan to Uzbekistan, which has planted mines along its border with Tajikistan.

On the other side of Pakistan, too, on its edge with Iran, a wall is being raised. Head further east on the other side of Bangladesh, and you'll run into another wall as the Bangladeshis seek to keep out the stateless Rohingya people, who have traditionally lived in lands now claimed by Myanmar and suffered genocide in 2017. One of the largest refugee camps in the world, the Kutupalong settlement in the port city of Cox's Bazar, Bangladesh, is the provisional and precarious home to around seven hundred thousand Rohingya refugees. Its network of camps have seen deadly fires, and, for an extended period in 2021, Bangladesh cut off all internet for the nearly quarter million refugees.

As more borders around the world are raised, hardened, thickened, and sometimes mined, as countries seek to defend their "homeland" from "foreigners," it's illuminating to step back and ask a simple question: What is a country?

The colloquial term for a nation state describes an agglomeration of people and government simplified into a few ideas (typically based on self-conceptions of racial or religious community) organized by institutions and laws, and pasted over a territory marked by treaty or wall. "The essence of a nation is that all of its individual members have a great deal in common and also that they have forgotten many things," wrote Ernest Renan, one of the early scholars of the nation state. "Unity," he adds—essential for country-building—"is always brutally established."

France for the French (or so the common understanding goes), China for the Chinese, America for Americans. "The French," however, are composed of Celtic, Iberian, and Germanic peoples, as well as, more recently, Arab-Berber, Pied-Noir, Basque, and Fulani, among many other so-called races. "The Chinese" are Han, Uighur, Manchu, Hui, Tibetan, Zhuang, among myriad other ethnic groups. And "Americans"—despite melting pot claims and overt efforts to mask over disparities or suppress cultural difference through forced Americanization (whether Henry Ford's grading of his employees on their levels of embodying American culture or the brutal and coercive Anglicization and assimilation of Native Americans)—are a wide-ranging, polyglot, poly-religious, polyethnic collage of humanity.

Religion is another commonly cited national glue, but examples of so-called mono-religious nations are examples of nations that in fact ignore—more often, suppress—religious and atheistic minorities. The people of India, despite its modern religious conception and its repressive Hindu nationalist ruling party, are Hindu, Muslim, Sikh, Christian, Buddhist, Jain, and Zoroastrian, among many others. Even Italy and Saudi Arabia are religiously pluralistic, and have, often violently, imposed the facade of religious singularity. As Massimo d'Azeglio, one of the pioneers of Italian unification, put it in 1861, "We have made Italy; now we must make Italians."

Currently, India—often hailed as the world's largest democracy, and the country that sends more migrants abroad than any other in the world—is engaging in a frenzy of religious nationalism as its police forces target, detain, disenfranchise, and expel Muslims. In 2018, the far eastern Indian state of Assam—sequestered off from the rest of the country by an isthmus of national territory squeezed between Bhutan and Bangladesh—published a National Register of Citizens, in which they purposely left off nearly four million mostly Muslim people that the head of India's far right national party referred to as *ghuspetiyas*, or infiltrators. Anybody left off of the registry had to face a tribunal and bear the burden of proving their citizenship. Writer Siddartha Deb referred to the move as the "largest mass disenfranchisement project in the twenty-first century." The policies have been compared to Nazi Germany's Reich Citizenship Law.

Female Muslims in Assam have a particularly hard time proving their citizenship, as many women marry young, don't hold jobs, aren't educated, and are legally disallowed from inheriting property, leaving them without the necessary paperwork to prove their ties to the territory. One attorney who represents those newly rendered stateless referred to Assam's policies as "manufacturing foreigners." It is a tidy formulation of what all borders do.

* * *

Africa is rife with examples of the ungainly and consequential imposition of the nation state on territories that are in constant ethnic, linguistic, and religious flux. Take Angola—though most African states have similar, and similarly brutal, histories—a large multiethnic country in western Africa comprised of Ovimbundu, Ambundu, Bakongo, *mestiço*, and other ethnicities, as well as hundreds of tribes that spill over and across the country's borders, which Portuguese colonizers first established and officialized in the 1885 Berlin Conference. One of the troubling legacies of that colonial history is that the Bakongo people, whose traditional lands stretched from modern-day Angola into the neighboring Republic of the Congo and Gabon, as well as Democratic Republic of the Congo (where they are a majority ethnicity), are cut through by a crosshatch of borders. The Bundu dia Kongo, a separatist and irredentist movement, meanwhile, is seeking a unified state, challenging what the Congo is, who controls it, and who lives within it. Unsurprisingly, border tensions frequently flare, exposing the anxiety between ethnic consciousness and territoriality.

The story repeats itself throughout the continent: artificial states cutting community ties by imposing borders, pitting ethnic groups against each other as they jockey for national power. There's a pull, of course, a natural human need to belong together in a coherent and stable community—a need that was historically satisfied by the family, neighborhood, or broader community. In the last 150 years, however, writes Elie Kedourie, "such institutions all over the world have had to bear the brunt of violent social and intellectual change, and it is no accident that nationalism was at its most intense where and when such institutions had little resilience and were ill-prepared to withstand the powerful attacks to which they became exposed." Kedourie published those words in 1960. In the sixty-plus years since, the institutions he was referring to—traditionally organized religion and family structures—have undergone even more profound revolutions. No wonder the cry for borders in the form of nationalism is growing ever-screechingly louder.

Another argument for closed borders around nation states is based on geography. Landscape, however, has little to nothing to do with the drawing of borders. As historian Rachel St. John writes, the US–Mexico border was created by a "collective act of imagination." We've already seen examples of borders decoupled from geography in the heart of Africa, and Spanish and British holdings on either side of the Strait of Gibraltar are other exemplary cases of the geographic illogic of bordering. The British still claim a 2.5-square-mile spearhead at the southern tip of the Iberian Peninsula, land that was captured by the British during the 1701–1714 War of Spanish Succession, part of a long and bloody balancing act between European empires. Whereas referendums in the past fifty years show overwhelming support for the British citizens in Gibraltar to remain part of the United Kingdom, the control makes zero geographic sense. Similarly, about fifteen miles across the same straight, Spain keeps its grip on Ceuta, abutting Morocco on the northern tip of Africa. The small exclave has proven a tempting landing spot for thousands of Africans seeking to reach European territory (even if attached to the continent of Africa). Spain, meanwhile, has walled off the land with high fences topped with razor wire, which hasn't stopped migrants from storming the barricades. Regular, violent, and sometimes deadly clashes between Spanish border guards and desperate migrants bloody that particular line.

Even when borders are marked by natural landmarks, such as rivers, seas, or mountains, they are often denaturalized or "weaponized" by the act of bordering. The Evros-Meriç River between Turkey and Greece—which was dammed, rerouted, its banks clear-cut, and then speckled with guideposts, detention centers, anti-tank moats, fences, and walls—is one such example of a national boundary marker turned into a militarized hellscape.

What are all these boundaries describing? What are they protecting, or purporting to protect? Indeed, what—to return to the pertinent question—is a nation state?

The legal definition, as established in 1933 at the Montevideo Convention on the Rights and Duties of States, declares the nation state to "possess the following qualifications: (a) a permanent population; (b) a defined territory; (c) government; and (d) capacity to enter into relations with the other states."

A number of internationally recognized sovereign countries, however, don't come close to meeting these criteria, as writer and foreign policy analyst Joshua Keating makes clear in *Invisible Countries: Journeys to the Edge of Nationhood*. Following Russia's invasion in 2014, and again in 2022, Ukraine isn't in full control of large swaths of its territory. And yet it seems abundantly more of a nation state than some of its European counterparts today. Syria's population has been so widely displaced—nearly six million refugees having fled in recent years—that it can hardly be said to have a permanent population. And while Somalia, for nearly three decades, has had no functioning central government, the independent state of Somaliland, which does have a functioning government, remains internationally unrecognized except by Kenya and Taiwan.

Another enduring and oft-cited definition of a nation state comes from sociologist Max Weber, who defines it as "a human community that (successfully) claims the monopoly of the legitimate use of physical force within a given territory." The *claim* itself is important here. And it is what the scholarship of political scientist Benedict Anderson has proven: that a country, in many ways, is formed by its own rhetorical insistence. Of particular significance are the novel and the newspaper, Anderson argues, which provide "the technical means for 're-presenting' the *kind* of imagined community that is the nation."

Trying to refashion so much of the world along national lines has not led to more peace and stability. "On the contrary, it has created new conflicts, exacerbated tensions, and brought catastrophe to numberless people innocent of all politics," Kedourie writes.

Or, as journalist Francis Wade argues, it is genocide, pogroms, and other "organizing" techniques that continue to be employed by states "in their unending efforts to build more socially and culturally cohesive societies." "As long as the nation-state remains the defining institution of modern societies," Wade continues, "those forms of violence will persist as key means of political engineering."

The problem, as many observers note, is that most nation states do not even remotely come close to resembling the homogenous ethnic, cultural, linguistic, or religious qualities of a single nation. There is never any simple "us here, them there," to quote former Israeli prime minister Ehud Barak. Consider, to return again to the United States, the wide and often-irreconcilable differences between a rancher outside of Omaha, a white coastal Mainer, a Puerto Rican in Fajardo, a Black kid in Detroit, a stevedore in American

Samoa, a Somali American in Minneapolis, a cosmopolitan in Seattle, a white retiree in South Carolina, or a Latino shopkeeper in Brownsville. What do they have in common, except for the fiction of unity? They might all believe in the same "American" principles, such as democracy or a few specific individual freedoms. But let's go back to the shopkeeper in Brownsville. He probably has more in common with his neighbor in Matamoros, a stone's throw across the international line into Mexico, than he does with the kid in South Central or the coastal Mainer. And both the Brownsvillean and the Matamoreño may well believe in the same "American" freedoms. But they are not compatriots, because of an 1848 Treaty that drew the US–Mexico border along the Rio Grande River. The Brownsvillean can travel north for almost two thousand miles, cross five state borders, exploring wildly different cultures, languages, religions, and cuisines, but can't take twenty steps south without permission and a passport. And if he tried to go south without permission and a passport, he could be arrested, detained, and deported. Of course, the consequences would be much more severe if his Matamoros neighbor tried to go north. He might feel the full weight of the US government on him: arrest, possible prosecution, and long-term detention, which could include solitary confinement and psychological torture before deportation back across the line into Mexico.

Anderson details a similar paradox in the unlikely creation of Indonesia, forged out of tens of thousands of islands, over seven hundred separate languages, and over six hundred different ethnic groups. People on the eastern coast of Sumatra are only a few miles away from their neighbors across the Straits of Malacca, home to ethnically related populations of the western littoral of the Malay Peninsula with whom they share a similar language and a common religion and often intermarry. However, in the founding of Indonesia in 1945, those Sumatrans have come to understand the Ambonese—who live on islands thousands of miles east of them, with whom they have no common language, ethnicity, nor religion—as "fellow-Indonesians," while, flabbergastingly, the same Sumatrans regard the nearby relative Malays as foreigners.

Concocted nations are little more than agreements of what is agreed upon. They create boundaries that both bind (within) and distinguish (without). So, do they need to be closed in order to function? A quick glance within the Schengen Area of Europe reveals that the answer is no: borders can mark cultural or linguistic difference, they can serve as organizational political lines, but they need not be unpassable, militarized, dehumanizing, or exploitative to do so.

* * *

Another popular defense of borders is that, as Donald Trump has repeatedly claimed, "We don't have a country without a border." Similarly, Obama White House advisor Cecilia Muñoz said that "[t]here are policy decisions to be made about who should be an immigrant, and that includes removing folks who don't qualify under the law. That's, I think, just the reality of being a nation."

But how does a closed border legitimize a country? The US border is wide open to goods, money, the well connected, and the wealthy—so why is keeping poor people out important for maintaining a nation state? Though there are no formal financial requirements for Mexicans obtaining nonimmigrant visas to enter the United States, consular officers consider a person's finances and employment before issuing a visa, and poor people almost never get the pass.

In other words, the border is supposed to keep only *some people* out. Compare the triple fencing, watch towers, paramilitary Border Patrol, ground sensors, drones, and billions of dollars spent keeping people out of Southern California to the Derby Line in Vermont at the northern US border, where an opera house is literally divided down the middle between United States and Canada, where the international divide is marked by a strip of black on the floor of the town library's reading room. You aren't legally permitted to enter and remain in the United States from there, but unless you're looking down, your book-browsing could take you back and forth across an international divide without any notice.

Journalist Michelle García writes of the concept of "border theater," or what she calls the "collective performance of American identity." It is, as García writes, "a mythology that holds the nation hostage." While the mythology is of a cohesive nation, the reality is, in fact, division.

"The mutability of borders," write philosopher Edward S. Casey and psychologist Mary Watkins in *Up Against the Wall*, "reflects their status as cultural constructions endowed with meaning." Though it may be hard to remember under the weight of the status quo, if borders have any defining or lasting quality, it is indeed their mutability. Just since the beginning of the twentieth century, the US border has shifted a dozen or so times, taking on the territories of Alaska and Hawaii, as well as numerous tiny island chains, conquering and then releasing the Philippines, and subsuming Guam, American Samoa, and the Virgin Islands. In the previous century, the border was even more jittery. When nativists or jingoists want to "hold the line," we would do well to remember that the line is shifting and slippery, and that, if history is any guide, tomorrow the border won't be where it is today.

* * *

In Franz Kafka's parable *Before the Law*, a man from the country approaches "the law" and asks a gatekeeper to permit him entry. "It is possible," says the gatekeeper, "but not now." After the man peers into the law through the gate, the gatekeeper warns him: "I am powerful," he says. "And I am only the most lowly gatekeeper." From room to room stand other gatekeepers, "each more powerful than the other. I can't endure even one glimpse of the third."

The man from the country wasn't expecting this. The law, he thought, "should always be accessible for everyone." Plus, the gate is wide open. After looking at the gatekeeper again, he decides to wait for permission before trying to go inside.

Sitting on a stool by the gate, the man ends up waiting his whole life. As he is fading into death, he whispers to the gatekeeper: "Everyone strives after the law . . . so how is it that in these many years no one except me has requested entry?" The gatekeeper replies, "Here no one else can gain entry, since this entrance was assigned only to you. I'm going now to close it."

The parable might seem as impregnable as the law it describes, but it captures something essential about borders: that the border itself generates transgression. "After all, if there were no borders, there would be no migrants—only mobility," notes migration scholar Nicholas de Genova. The gate is simultaneously open and guarded, inviting and yet impassable. This observation echoes one made by Michel Foucault, who writes, "A limit could not exist if it were absolutely uncrossable, and, reciprocally, transgression would be pointless if it merely crossed a limit composed of illusions and shadows." State borders are merely and also more than shadows, and their crossings are both entirely natural and radically transgressive. That is, the law of the border provokes what it prohibits.

In a keynote address delivered from the immigrant prison camp of Manus Island for a workshop at Oxford University, Kurdish-Iranian poet and refugee Behrouz Boochani explains, echoing Kafka: "We are outside of any law. Humanitarian laws and international conventions are routinely and fundamentally broken. At the same time, we are victims of law. It is a new phenomenon, how we are living under law and at the same time outside of law."

"Wherever Law ends, Tyranny begins," John Locke wrote. And it is the border—the crucible of law and rightlessness—where Law and Tyranny meet.

6

The Case for Urgency, or
The Environmental Argument

The environmental case for open borders is one of the simplest to make: people are on the run from climate catastrophe; if we don't open our doors to them, many will die. In the coming decades, the cascading climate crises will force hundreds of millions of people to flee their homes. Many millions of those people will be crossing borders, no matter what wall, law, fence, moar, admonishment, or threat of imprisonment is thrown at them. In fact, the unprecedented population upheaval is already upon us, and, in coming years, it will touch us all—even those behind fortifications of wealth and privilege.

Working behind and within borders, we will not find a solution to, or a means to mitigate, the climate crises. Tail chasing international meetings and accords amount to nothing when the promises proffered are repeatedly reneged, when emission caps are hurtled over, goalposts are ever shifting, and nations leave the conferences only to hunker back into the blanket of short-term national interest. In that self-imposed darkness, the current project pursued by many Western nation states is to build fortresses of short-term and relative ecological stability. But those fortresses are already crumbling. Borders, in this regard, are not body armor for the climate catastrophe but blindfolds.

Pull almost any thread of climate science, and you will unravel a story about people on the move. According to the Ocean

Foundation, humans have contributed to a 30 percent increase in ocean acidification over the last two centuries, profoundly altering one of the key planetary resources for *all biological life*. The manifold and exponential repercussions of that acidification are impossible to calculate, but as more and more ocean life is dying out and migrating to the poles, enormous hypoxic "dead zones" are left behind, lastingly reshaping the interconnected ecosystems that cover seven-tenths of the globe and which forty percent of the entire human population—or well over three billion people—lives within sixty miles of. To find an analog for today's oceanic mass extinction, scientists had to go back about 250 million years, to the "great dying." But changes to the oceans are not only depleting a key resource; they are also leaving six hundred million people in vulnerable "low-elevation coastal zones," right on the edge of seas whose surges, hurricanes, and high-tides are already laying waste to cities and agricultural zones. Meanwhile, in 2016, the United Nations Convention to Combat Desertification estimated that within thirty years, there will be "a billion or more vulnerable poor people with little choice but to fight or flee" ocean extinction and rising seas, droughts and broadening deserts, creeping blight and thawing permafrost.

In just the five-year period from 2005 to 2010, around 8.5 million people migrated from South Asia because of drought and changing monsoon patterns. (The region, where nearly a quarter of all human beings live, will soon be the most food insecure region in the world.) By 2050, according to the World Bank, the number of climate migrants *just from South Asia* could be as high as 35.7 million. In some parts of India, it may soon be so hot that without air-conditioning humans won't be able to survive. Much of Vietnam, home to almost one hundred million people, could be underwater at high tide by 2050. Meanwhile, in Africa, unsurvivably high temperatures, droughts, and blight are pushing people from the Sahel region, such as Shafa, toward the coasts and north toward and across the Mediterranean. The worst locust swarm in nearly a century hit Kenya in 2020, with hundreds of billions of the insects darkening the sun "like an umbrella had covered the sky," according to one Kenyan man. Much like Vietnam, the Nile delta and a huge swath of southern Iraq could also be covered in water during high tides within a few decades. One study, published in *Nature*, concluded that coastal communities worldwide must prepare themselves for much more difficult futures than currently anticipated. In the United States, sea level rise this century may induce large-scale migration away from unprotected coastlines, re-distributing population density across the country. Worldwide in 2020, climate change displaced more than thirty million people— three times more than those displaced by conflict that same year.[1]

China, meanwhile, is currently implementing the world's larg-est state-sponsored relocation program, which it calls "ecological migration." By 2016, the program had moved over three hundred thousand people, though the goal is to relocate—by force if neces-sary—more than two million more.

Some climate projections estimate that over thirty million mi-grants will head to the United States in the next thirty years.[2] Many more will migrate internally, from the countryside to cities. In that same span, Mexico itself could see about ten million new migrants show up at its southern border.

World leaders and the corporate elite have been aware of the problem for decades, and the situation has significantly deterio-rated. Since the first international conference to combat climate change, the Conference of the Parties (COP) was convened in 1995, promises have repeatedly and exhaustively been made and broken. In 1995, the worldwide burning of fossil fuels spewed six gigatons of carbon into the atmosphere. By 2018, that figure had passed ten

---

1 In 2021, according to a *Washington Post* analysis, more than 40 percent of Americans lived in counties that were hit by climate disasters.
2 Thirty million sounds like a lot, but a million a year is typical for annual legal migration to the United States. The difference here is why these people will be migrating.

gigatons per year. As human ecologist Andreas Malm puts it: "The hypermobility of the rich, their inordinate flying and yachting and driving—is what frees them from having to bother with the consequences, as they can always shift to safer locations."

With locked-down borders and slow-choking immigration processing, the world currently struggles to resettle or receive just a few hundred thousand people—a tiny percentage of the number displaced by environmental disasters. For those in wealthy countries, this is not only a problem of what to do with foreign climate refugees. Hurricane Harvey, which struck Texas and Louisiana in 2017, forced sixty thousand people from their homes. Hurricane Irma, which pounded Florida the same year, resulted in the evacuation of seven million. Hurricane Maria, which devastated Puerto Rico and other Caribbean islands, caused $90 billion in damages, left half of the entire Puerto Rican population without access to fresh water, and sent, by some estimates, hundreds of thousands to flee—some of them permanently.

The warming globe is both exposing and exacerbating existing inequalities, deepening what journalist David Wallace-Wells has called the "climate caste system." Poorer countries, though they have emitted only a fraction of the greenhouse gases that richer countries have spewed, are suffering the worst of worsening weather. That's because, in part, more of the poor countries are in the tropical areas—already hot to begin with—where climate change will make life harder to live and crops much harder to grow. A lot of these nations also have extensive coastlines, which make them especially vulnerable to storms, flooding, and incremental sea rise. Compounding those vulnerabilities is the fact that poorer countries have fewer resources to build newly needed infrastructure, rebuild after storms or floods, or find new and more sustainable ways to cultivate food and alter ways of living for a hotter, dryer, wetter, and stormier world.

A 2003 Pentagon report noted that the United States and Australia[3] are "likely to build defensive fortresses around their countries" in response to climate change. The Pentagon researchers wrote that US borders must be strengthened to "hold back unwanted starving immigrants from the Caribbean islands (an especially severe problem), Mexico, and South America." Nearly twenty years later, that promise has come true—at least partially: while US borders walls have been raised and extended, the "starving immigrants" have not been effectively held back. Indeed, when it comes to keeping human beings out, an important fact goes often overlooked: borders don't work very well.

In the fall of 2021, a White House report noted, "The current migration situation extending from the US–Mexico border into Central America presents an opportunity for the United States to model good practice and discuss openly managing migration humanely, highlight[ing] the role of climate change in migration." What the United States is actually modeling for the 1.3 million Central Americans displaced by climate crises in 2020 alone, however, is a slammed door.[4]

A 2021 report from the Transnational Institute calculated that seven countries (the United States, Germany, Japan, the United Kingdom, Canada, France, and Australia)—together responsible for 48 percent of the world's historic greenhouse gas emissions—"collectively spent at least twice as much on border and immigration enforcement (more than $33.1 billion) as on climate finance ($14.4 billion) between 2013 and 2018."

---

3 Thanks are due to journalist Todd Miller's reporting on the topic.
4 There is legislative precedent for protecting climate refugees, though offering such protection is hardly a reality. A Kiribati man, Ioane Teitiota, attempted to apply for refugee status in New Zealand because of the impacts of climate change. When his application was denied, he brought his case to the UN, which, in 2020, found that Teitiota's rights had not been violated, while also acknowledging that it is unlawful for states to send people to places where the impacts of climate change "expose them to life-threatening risks or cruel, inhuman, or degrading treatment."

The United States spent eleven times more militarizing its borders than on helping poorer countries mitigate the effects of climate change. Canada, the worst offender, spent fifteen times more on border enforcement. In effect, those countries, the report concludes, are trying to build a "climate wall" to keep the effects of climate change—displaced people—out. Mohamed Nasheed, former president of Maldives, a country that is literally being washed away by rising seas, had a message for Western countries, as reported by writer Suketu Mehta: "You can drastically reduce your greenhouse gas emissions so that the seas do not rise so much. Or when we show up on your shores in our boats, you can let us in. Or when we show up on your shores in our boats, you can shoot us. You pick."[5]

Opening borders, it bears repeating, is not the solution to our climate crises, but it will help mitigate some of their worst effects. Opening borders will also prompt a reevaluation of the extractive/exploitative capitalist regime that is driving the hyper-carbonization of the atmosphere, the acidification of the oceans, the kindling of rainforests, and the general trashing of ecosystems. Ruling regimes rely on borders to paper over these egregious harms, find loopholes in protective legal systems, and leverage differentials in labor laws to maximize constant production and growth, the flip side of which is constant destruction and waste—or, to use a scarily apt neologism: ecocide.

In his remarkable, and remarkably frightening, book *The Uninhabitable Earth*, David Wallace-Wells describes the coming onslaught of climate-provoked destruction as a "'dream time' or 'everywhen'—the semimythical experience of encountering, in the present moment, an out-of-time past, when ancestors, heroes, and demigods crowded an epic stage. You can find it already by

---

5   To poignantly lay bare the unequal effects of climate change and migration, consider Somalia, which is responsible for 0.00027 percent of total emissions since 1850 but had more than one million people (or 6 percent of its population) displaced by a climate-related disaster in 2020.

watching footage of an iceberg collapsing into the sea—a feeling of history happening all at once."

Soon, much of the world will be rendered unrecognizable. Australian environmental philosopher Glenn Albrecht coined the term *solastalgia* to describe the feeling of homesickness when you are at home—the realization that everything is changing. The idea is closely linked to eco-anxiety, or the fear of what will transpire to the earth and its inhabitants in coming decades. The lethal cocktail of climate disaster and closed borders threatens to infect us all, migrants and natives alike, with a pungent blend of nostalgia and solastalgia—when home and abroad are reduced to displacement and denial.

In 1816, Lord Byron wrote about the "year without a summer," after a major volcanic eruption dramatically altered global weather: "I had a dream, which was not all a dream." With climate change, that dream/non-dream is already upon us.

* * *

During the unusually cold winter of 1949, a breeding pair of gray wolves crossed a frozen-over channel onto Michigan's Isle Royale, a narrow spit of land just south of the US–Canada maritime border in Lake Superior. Finding abundant prey, including moose, the pair had pups and started a small lupine clan. But over the next fifty years, without access to the mainland, the clan grew increasingly inbred, with over half the wolves developing congenital spinal deformities and serious eye problems. As the wolf population declined (scientists found one mother, with seven unborn pups in her womb, dead in her den) the moose population came thundering back, gobbling up and trampling the forest's buds and shoots. The ecosystem's food chain suddenly had a broken link.

The Isle Royale wolf population was saved, however, by a migrant. In 1997, a male wolf crossed the maritime border between Canada and the United States and swam his way across a narrow strip of Lake Superior to the island. Within a generation—a little less than five years—56 percent of the young wolves carried the newcomer's genes. In the years since, thanks to ongoing conservation efforts, more wolves have been brought to the island to provide enough genetic diversity, not only to save the wolves but to preserve the ecosystem's new balance.

As I have pointed out before, and will pound on again, there are now more displaced humans than ever—around 1 percent of the total human population. The climate crises, together with humanity's ceaseless creep, are driving an increasing number of nonhuman species to search for more welcoming and less volatile climes. That half of the story is popularly understood: the world—human and non—is on the move. What is less often acknowledged is the biological necessity of that movement. "Migration's ecological function extends beyond the survival of the migrant itself," writes science journalist Sonia Shah in her book *The Next Great Migration*. "Wild migrants build the botanical scaffolding of entire ecosystems." Besides spreading pollen and seeds—upon which the survival of many plants and animals depend—migrants also transport genes, thus delivering and extending genetic diversity.

We are only beginning to understand the importance of "movement ecology"—that ecosystems are not static or closed, but open and always in flux; that migration is not only a human fact but a biological one. But this understanding of migration's critical import—whether broadly biological or specifically human—has been a long time coming.

The idea that certain people or species belong only in certain places, that they are tied to their territory, has a deep history in Western culture. According to that conception, Shah writes, "Migration is by necessity a catastrophe because it violates the natural order." This so-called natural order is actually a construct that has been buoyed for millennia by a broad coalition of theologians, scientists, politicians, and other ideologically inflected cavillers. As for the word "migrant," it didn't even appear in the English language until the seventeenth century—when it was coined by the English polymath Thomas Browne—and it took another hundred years before it was applied to humans. The presumption and enforcement of stasis—people rooted to a place, and a place inherent to a people—symbiotically melded with concepts around racism and white supremacy. One stalwart migrant-denialist (not an immigration restrictionist but an actual denier of the idea that, historically, people or animals migrated) was Swedish-born naturalist Carl Linnaeus, most famous for formalizing binomial nomenclature, the modern system of classifying organisms as, for example, *Homo sapiens* or *Canis lupus*.

Along with his contribution to taxonomy, Linnaeus also sparred with competing theorists who were beginning to propose then-revolutionary ideas—for instance, that all humans originated in and migrated out of Africa. With the concept of the "Great Chain of Being," Linnaeus toadied to the reigning theological explanation for the world being as it was: that beings were hierarchically categorized, in ascending order, from matter to plants, on up to animals, peasants, clergy, noblemen, kings, and, finally, to God. The cultural backdrop to these wild speculations was the generally held view that migration was an anomaly, and that people and animals lived where they belonged and belonged where they lived—and always had.

Ignorance—deliberate, political, or simply true and profound—of the realities of even animal migration pushed scientists to hatch myriad and far-fetched theories to explain, for instance, where migratory birds went in the winter. Leading naturalists in the eighteenth and nineteenth centuries postulated that some birds hibernated in lakes—a theory first proposed by Aristotle—or hid out the cold season in remote caves. Driving such assumptions was, in part, the idea of a stable, God-created, closed-system "harmony of nature."

When, in the mid-eighteenth century, some thinkers began to question such fixed stability, Linnaeus doubled down, insisting that animals inhabited and remained in their specific climes. The implication for humans was not only that they had *not* migrated from Africa, but that Africans—as well as Asians and Native Americans—were biologically distinct and should, both socially and spatially, stay put. This kind of racial essentialism was an important structural component of what would morph into eugenics. Linnaeus specifically divided *Homo sapiens* into *Homo sapiens europaeus* (white, serious, strong), *Homo sapiens asiaticus* (yellow, melancholy, greedy), *Homo sapiens americanus* (red, ill-tempered, subjugated), and *Homo sapiens afer* (black, impassive, lazy), as well as *Homo caudatus* (inhabitants of the Antarctic globe), and even *Homo monstrosus* (pygmies and Patagonian giants).

Such prevalent conjectures of presumed autochthony and racial essentialism, which saw migration as aberrant and humans as fixed to both land and caste, were not confined to parlor rooms or academic journals. The ideas both were accepted and persist, as Shah explains, to provide "theoretical ballast for today's generation of anti-immigration lobbyists and policy makers."

Even before species were officially classified, by Linnaeus and others, however, they were first deemed either "native" or "alien." And the implications of that dichotomization have long been harmful to humans and nonhumans alike, setting the stage for xenophobia and white anthropomorphism that spread across the globe and inflected thinking for centuries. As a case in point, the son of author and conservationist Aldo Leopold recommended in 1963 that US national parks "preserve, or where necessary . . . recreate the ecologic scene as viewed by the first European visitors." The idea of pristine, precolonial habitats, however, presumes an ahistorical falsehood: that humans and other animals left no trace, or that those traces could be undone and the ecologic scene returned to some static and edenic idyll.

While many Indigenous cultures certainly live less disruptively with and within their environment, as with the case in both the Americas and Australia, the arrival of the first *Homo sapiens* (long before the settler-colonial invasions) to new lands heralded huge changes, including the swift extinction of scores of native species: in the Americas, woolly mammoths, giant sloths, saber-toothed tigers, camelops, and the dire wolf all quickly died out. While I'm sorry to miss out on the drama of dire wolves—the largest prehistoric canine, with teeth and jaws designed to crack through bones—still roaming present-day Los Angeles (a large collection of dire wolf fossils were found in the La Brea tar pits), it is not change itself that is to fear, but the destruction and rendering uninhabitable of an ecosystem.

Overall, the importance of centering Indigenous peoples in a fight for a livable future planet is impossible to overstate. Not only do they have the most experience fighting extractive and displacing technologies (as well as invaders who have been strip-mining, clear-cutting, and laying waste to their ancestral lands for centuries); while they make up only 5 percent of the global population, as the authors of the *Red New Deal* (which calls for "Indigenous liberation" and proposes decolonization as a means of climate resiliency) point out, they protect 80 percent of the planet's biodiversity. That constantly morphing biodiversity is something many Western policymakers have failed to appreciate or understand.

In 1999, President Bill Clinton established the National Invasive Species Council, tasked with repelling "alien species." The move was an outgrowth of the recently hatched disciplines of conservation biology, restoration biology, and even invasion biology—movements that tracked a resurgence of official anti-immigration policies in the United States and elsewhere. As a kid growing up in northern Ohio, I heard plenty of doomsaying about the horror and devastation that was coming from the zebra mussel's inexorable encroachment into the Great Lakes. Invasion biologists around that time had calculated that wild species freely roaming the planet would devastate ecosystems, resulting in the number of land animals dropping by 65 percent, land birds by 47 percent, butterflies by 35 percent, and ocean life by 58 percent. But while the globe is certainly losing species to extinction, blaming migration—or *vagility*, the term of art—is missing the mark, buoying up what Shah calls the "myth of a sedentary planet."

New studies on "spatial heterogeneity" find that organisms moving from a "source ecosystem" to a "sink ecosystem" bring nutrients, much-needed genetic diversity (as with the Michigander wolves), energy (in the form of food and waste), and regulation (for example, Pacific salmon returning to their natal streams deposit marine-derived nitrogen essential for riparian plants; and migratory wildebeests let vegetation grow when they leave the woodlands to the plains and then fertilize vegetation when they return).[6]

Nonhuman migration, much like human migration, can also offer temporary or permanent escape from climate change–provoked habitat loss. That is, across species, migration is a net positive. But with rising walls, shrinking habitats, and ongoing resistance to vagility, migration writ large is in peril.[7]

For millennia, humans had hardly any idea of how species spread. They had neither the perspective nor technology to understand that creepy-crawlies have always creeped and crawled—often extraordinarily vast distances—and that almost all species are, in the big picture, always on the move. Zebra mussels, for example,

---

6   A study on the wildebeests found that the influence of their migration on the Serengeti ecosystem is so strong that scientists predict migration loss would lead, first, to a decline in wildebeest populations; then, to a decrease in the populations of their carnivorous predators; and, ultimately, to the collapse of the Serengeti ecosystem as a whole.

7   While it is hard to protect a single habitat from climate change or encroaching development, it's exceptionally harder to protect the entire range of a migratory species. One suggested fix for conserving some of the ecosystems that wild migrants had traditionally kept healthy is to allow for migratory pastoralists and their herds to perform some of the same functions as the original species. And yet, one of the troubling ironies, as the authors of the study "Conservation and Management of Migratory Species" write, "is that human pastoralist migratory behaviour is also under dire threat, with forced sedentarization, enclosure or agricultural development of their lands . . . leading to the loss of unique cultures, knowledge, and the ecosystem services that these movements provide."

were not the only, or even the greatest, threat to native clams in the Great Lakes. Besides disrupting the local ecosystems, the mussels filtered water and became a new source of food for native fish and fowl. One surprising statistic is that since the introduction of European species to the Americas four hundred years ago, biodiversity has actually increased by 18 percent. As Shah puts it, "Nature transgresses borders all the time."

Nonhuman animals are not only good for ecosystems but, like humans, are threatened by a combination of closed borders and climate change. A 2017 study from the Center for Biological Diversity found that wall construction along the US–Mexico border is having "disastrous impacts on our most vulnerable wildlife," including ninety-three threatened species put at risk of extinction due to ongoing wall construction. The imperiled animals include jaguars, jaguarundi, Quino checkerspot butterflies, arroyo toads, California red-legged frogs, black-spotted newts, Pacific pond turtles, and Mexican gray wolves. Another of the endangered species, the cactus ferruginous pygmy owl, are low flyers and can't make it over the border wall; their territory is thus sliced in half by immigration policy.

Cryptobiotic soil, or biological soil crust, is also imperiled by wall construction. The rare "living soil" is a dynamic crust made up of mosses, microfungi, bacteria, and one of the earliest known lifeforms, cyanobacteria. Lacing parts of the desert landscape, the intricate organic ménage helps combat erosion by keeping soil stuck together and retaining water that roots can tap into to survive dry and hot conditions.

When cryptobiotic soil is driven over by vehicles, the National Park Service concludes, it "may never fully recover." Under good circumstances, a thin veneer of living soil may return to health in under ten years, whereas it can take fifty years for mature crusts to recover, and hundreds of years for lichens and mosses to integrate back into the soil. Meanwhile, "renegade roads"—at least ten thousand miles of tracks carved into delicate wilderness areas, mostly by Border Patrol trucks—have been scarring the cryptobiotic soil in the US–Mexico borderlands for years. The long-term, maybe permanent, effects of disrupting the soil or killing even one of these border-threatened animals profoundly alters an already threatened ecosystem.

Another effect from the border wall on overlooked species came to light in a 2021 article in the *Journal of Hymenoptera Research*, which described, in just six square miles of desert at the border of Arizona, New Mexico, and the Mexican state of Sonora, the discovery of five hundred distinct bee species. It is the highest known concentration of bee species in the world—far more than even in the tropics. A similar biodiversity study counted eight hundred species of moths within a small five-acre area along a nearby strip of borderlands.

I scouted in this exact area, bees and moths a-humming around rare desert rivers, isolated springs, and cottonwood groves where the Chihuahuan and Sonoran deserts, along with the western grasslands, the Rocky Mountains, and the Sierra Madres, all meet and blend. The area is a node of overlooked but bounteous diversity, a vast landscape dotted by an archipelago of sky islands where cooler, wetter habitats rise out of the bake of the desert floor. Here, a single turn in a cliff, a cut in a canyon, or a depression shaded by a rocky outcrop offers a unique niche habitat. Russ McSpadden of the Center for Biological Diversity described the area as a hypersensitive and sui generis ecosystem. And though the region is full of blend and creative clash—ecotones—"there is no dividing line," McSpadden told me, "no plant or animal up here that isn't also down there." The convergence of habitat is "why jaguars and bears cross paths, and how such an arid place can be so damn vibrant and wild."

McSpadden and I hiked up a series of remote canyons to review footage from his trail cameras, which capture jaguars and other wide-roaming animals who need vast habitats to flourish. Currently, the few jaguars, all male, known to be living in southern

Arizona and New Mexico are at least partially blocked by the border wall from heading back to Mexico to breed. Maintaining this corridor for the jaguars, as well as for bear, deer, ocelots, low-flying owls, and other animals, is essential for the ecosystem's survival.

Within that jaguar corridor, the San Pedro River is a resting area for half of all bird species in North America as they fly their migratory routes. Some of the area's astounding biodiversity can be traced to a series of artesian wells that slowly pump out fossil groundwater, water that trickled deep under underground and into volcanic rock between four and twenty-five thousand years ago. These natural wells are not refilled by rainwater, or at least will not be any time within the next few millennia. And yet, wall construction is fast sucking the water out of the aquifers. Myles Traphagen, borderlands program coordinator of the Wildlands Network, told me that he'd heard from construction crews that they were pumping up as many as 770,000 gallons of water a day from nearby wells to mix cement for the border wall. Meanwhile, dozens of water tanker trucks lined up to be filled, hauling water out to the cement mixers. And water trucks were continuously spraying the newly cut dirt roads to try to keep the dust down.

"This entire region," McSpadden said, "is part of an ecological alchemy that thrives on and nourishes migration and the convergence of disparate communities." That alchemy is fast being extinguished by the wall.

* * *

One form of nonhuman migration that's an obvious concern is disease. Certain dangers do undeniably exist, as evidenced by Europeans bringing smallpox to the Americas, or Rome spreading malaria to the outer regions of its empire. But migrants today are less threatening pathogenic vectors than are trade or transnational business.

Take the US–Mexico border. About 350 million people cross it every year, the vast majority of them local residents going about their daily lives: businesspersons, as well as tourists and the curious, all browsing *la frontera*. The number of migrants who cross the US–Mexico border varies by year, but it's typically less than one million. For the majority of the COVID-19 pandemic, standard cross-border traffic was not shut down along the US–Mexico border, but migrants and asylum seekers were barred from crossing, even when infection rates plummeted. Scientifically, the discriminatory cordon sanitaire made zero sense. To keep a disease behind a border would require a shutdown of the entire capitalist system, not just attempts to stop asylum seekers.[8]

Even as the pandemic raged, immigration detention centers were turned into viral petri dishes. Migrants were unable to socially distance, while staff denied them personal protective equipment, refused to test them, were slow or refused to vaccinate them, and contributed to the spread of the virus both inside and outside of the prisons. Within the first six months of the pandemic, as I reported at the time for *The Intercept*, almost 5.5 percent of total US cases were attributable to spread from ICE detention centers. In total, that was at least an extra quarter million cases and an unknown

---

8   In May of 2021, the International Monetary Fund published a "staff discussion note" titled "A Proposal to End the Covid-19 Pandemic," in which researcher Ruchir Agarwal estimated it would cost about $50 billion to vaccinate at least 60 percent of the population of all countries by the end of 2021. Agarwal figured the investment would reap a return of about $9 trillion. The $50 billion price tag is about 6 percent of the US annual military budget and about 1 percent of the total the US spent on COVID relief. Except for meager vaccine donations, neither the United States nor the EU decided to make the investment. That is, borders stopped nation states from keeping themselves safer because they refused to see beyond their own borders. As David Wallace-Wells writes, "Faced with the choice— between one future in which everyone in the world was better off through expansive protection and one of more limited vaccination in which the rich were somewhat protected and others remained much more vulnerable—the wealthy nations of the world didn't take the path that maximized overall protection and prosperity."

number of deaths. The health care systems in economic areas where ICE ran detention centers were burdened by thousands of additional COVID-19 cases.

To be sure, wariness of foreign pathogens makes sense, but to guide foreign policy on such grounds or let that wariness morph into discrimination or violent backlash is liable to become a fever that—like a cytokine storm—climbs to dangerous heights, leading to self-destructive seizures, delirium, or death.

Xenophobia is the much more significant threat to humans. As Shah told me, "The reflexive solution to contagion—border closures, isolation, immobility—is in fact antithetical to biological resilience on a changing planet."

Poet Carolyn Forché aptly captured this disturbing reality when I interviewed her as COVID-19 was first gripping the planet: "The contagion of lack of empathy is going to be more harmful to us in the long run than anything else, because it will have no bounds. If we lose our empathy, we lose our empathy for everyone, and we isolate and atomize our society until it dries up, until it has nothing left."

* * *

For much of human history, people have lived and adapted to live in places with relatively stable climates. There were floods and disasters, cold years and hot ones, but we were able to cope and rely on mostly predictable weather patterns to grow food, build housing and roads, and know that the crops would flower and fruit, that our houses and roads would remain, and that the rains would either eventually stop or come again. We assumed that a bad year, or even a few bad years, would be followed by a typical or even a bountiful year.

That has changed. Perhaps the most remarkable early disaster of anthropogenic climate change—and harbinger of many disasters to come—was the catastrophic Dust Bowl in the American and Canadian prairies in the 1930s. Though the intense yearslong drought and massive dust storms were partly the result of a natural

dry cycle, it was the intensive farming practices and the impu-
dent—and ridiculous—belief that "rain followed the plow," and
the concomitant upturning of millions of acres of grasslands to
plant wheat and other crops, that left the dirt to be gathered up
by the wind in massive swirling clouds, or "black blizzards," that
literally blotted out the sun.

About 2.5 million Okies—farmers from Texas, New Mexico,
Colorado, Nebraska, Kansas, and Oklahoma—were forced to flee
the region. Some of the descendants of these migrants, many of
whom settled in California, are themselves now practicing unsustainable farming methods in America's newest (temporary) bread-
basket: the Imperial and San Joaquin valleys, which have sunk
dozens of feet as farmers suck out groundwater at unprecedented
levels. (Similar to the reactions to forced migration today, in the
1930s Californians attempted to stop the Dust Bowl refugees from
entering their state by implementing "bum blockades" at the state
border line.)

I saw a similar phenomenon in Guatemala, where a small village
in the western highlands was, year by year, simultaneously sinking
and being washed away as periods of drought were occasionally
interspersed by heavy, drenching rains.

Being forced out of one's home by storms, floods, drought, rising
seas, and conflagrating forests is a symptom of climate change. The
cause of that sickness is extractive capitalism, and climate refugees
are, more accurately, refugees of late capitalism. Open borders are
not the cure, but they are a necessary palliative and lifesaving measure to take while we cut emissions and work toward climate justice
and financial and industrial sustainability.

* * *

In 2017, a solo Mexican wolf, known as M1425, loped northbound
through Mexico's Chihuahuan Desert, following a path that other
wolves and humans have traveled for thousands of years. Scientists

were especially interested in this loner as he came from a waning population of endangered Mexican wolves that were dispersing genes from a tiny pack in Mexico to a slightly more robust population in the United States.

Like the Isle Royale wolves, a New Mexico magazine reported, "If the two wild populations of Mexican gray wolves can find and mate with each other, the exchange of genetic material could boost recovery efforts for both populations." But the area where M1425 crossed the international boundary is now closed off by a border wall, and other wolves—bearing much-needed genes and doing what wolves in these parts have done for millenia—are blocked.

In November of 2021, a young male Mexican wolf, born north of the border, set off on his own through the desert scrub and grassland, heading south. When he reached the wall, he loped alongside it, flashing in and out of the shadows cast by the steel bollards. Finally, finding no gap, no way to head further south and into a breeding population, he veered away, north again.

"There is no more natural and fundamental adaptation to a changing climate than to migrate," writes journalist Abrahm Lustgarten. The maxim also holds for nonhuman animals.

* * *

A number of refrains were repeated in the first half of 2021 as the Biden administration explained that they were working to reinstate the asylum and refugee programs that the Trump administration had gutted:[9] "It takes time," "We're working on it," and, simply, "Do not come." The president, the vice president, the press secretary, and dozens of officials repeated the messages, primarily to Mexicans and Central Americans: *Stay at home, Quédate en casa.* But

---

9   This was before, in 2023, the Biden administration not only fell in line with the Trump administration's anti-asylum stance, but hardened it, implementing novel ways to deny asylum claims and push away those seeking safety.

you can't ask someone whose home was destroyed by a hurricane to stay at home. You can't ask a parent whose child is hungry to wait a few months. You can't ask someone running for their lives to slow down to a walk.

"We are now faced with the fact that tomorrow is today," said Martin Luther King Jr. on the steps of the Lincoln Memorial, back in 1963—words that ring truer than ever today, as the constellation of urgent crises facing us has only broadened to include those faced by climate refugees. "We are confronted with the fierce urgency of now. In this unfolding conundrum of life and history, there *is* such a thing as being too late." King was speaking about a different issue at a different time, but it's not hard to imagine him helping to lead the fight against climate change. As we begin to see the greatest wave of global migration the world has ever experienced, we must recognize that the crisis is already upon us, that we must act with humanity, and that we must open the borders.

How Do We Get There?

"There is no heart the state can constrain; dreams eat into its reason like acid."

—Joseph Andras

L et's say you're convinced. You recognize that the diverse harms of closed borders outweigh the material benefits they afford the global elite, and now you're ready to tear down the walls. That's a good spot to be in. But where exactly are those walls? Besides the scores of physical barriers and the hundreds of thousands of border guards around the world, what about the bureaucratic walls that people have to navigate to freely move around the world? What about the roaming immigrant police forces that lurk outside of courthouses and schoolyards, bust down the doors of businesses, or creep outside family homes before dawn? And, an important related question that could help stoke opening the gates: What would an open-borders world actually look like?

While "open borders" has long stood as both rhetorical cudgel and metonym for basically any reform to the increasingly cemented status quo of ever-tightening borders, few have taken pains to describe what "open borders" means. (The opposite extreme—total global lockdowns—may be easier to imagine, if also impossible to enforce.)[1]

---

1 The Secure Fence Act of 2006 mandated that the Secretary of Homeland

There are two diametrical answers to what an open-borders world would look like, and they are both right. The first answer is that it wouldn't look that different from how the world looks today; the second is that everything must be different. Let's walk through these contradictory responses to consider how they can both simultaneously hold promise and hew toward truth.

Things Wouldn't Be That Different

To understand why things wouldn't necessarily look that different, why open borders between nation states could look like the open borders within nation states (as within the United States), we first have to consider implementation: *How* would borders actually be opened? Because despite the allure of some regal decree setting the world aright, that's not how major reforms typically work these days. *Could* they work that way? Maybe. The plenary power doctrine grants certain branches of the US government near-absolute power to control particular issues. Congress has the sole power to institute and regulate commerce, and it also faces minimal judicial review for passing immigration laws. The executive branch, meanwhile, has wide-ranging power to *enforce* those immigration laws.

I asked Aaron Reichlin-Melnick, policy director at the American Immigration Council, if Congress could snap its fingers and do away with all immigration laws. His answer: "Yeah, they could." More likely, and more pointedly, they could do away with key provisions that criminalize migration.

But with Congress repeatedly proving itself to be wildly ineffectual at even piecemeal immigration reform over the last three

---

Security take "all actions the Secretary determines necessary and appropriate to achieve and maintain operational control over the entire international land and maritime borders of the United States." The act defined "operational control" as "the prevention of all unlawful entries into the United States." The goal is impossible to achieve, especially in that the very act creates the criminality it's portending to deter.

decades, recent immigration policies in the United States have largely been enacted by executive order. Many of those orders are subsequently challenged or enjoined in the courts, but plenty also go into partial effect. So, could a president issue an executive order decreeing that the border be opened effective tomorrow? Probably not, according to Reichlin-Melnick, but the president could minimize the degree to which unauthorized immigrants are criminalized, significantly narrow the scope of enforcement, withdraw all troops from the border, and grant temporary status to millions of people.[2] In 2021, President Biden issued a partial, one-hundred-day moratorium on deportations, which was swiftly blocked by a Texas state lawsuit. Any president would be similarly hamstrung in the pursuit of open borders (not that that's what Biden was after) by the 1946 Administrative Procedure Act, as well as by the "take care" clause of the US Constitution. Both of these basically hold the president to doing his job, which means executing the laws Congress passes, even if, like current immigration policy, they are inhumane, anti-immigrant, unpopular, or just plain awful.

So, if an executive order isn't going to get us there, what will?[3] There's always revolution, a usurpation of power by the masses and an unlocking of the gates—not a bad option.

Much more likely, however, is that we'll get to open borders in legal steps. Silky Shah, director of Detention Watch Network, told me that "infrastructure reduction should be the priority of any move towards open borders." Her first steps would be defunding immigration agencies, slapping a moratorium on all new border technology and infrastructure, and terminating contracts with military and private contractors. Simple awareness and increased

---

2 Granting TPS, or temporary protected status, to Mexicans, would temporarily block the deportation of millions of people currently living without authorization in the United States. A host of similar technical steps could have enormous real-life impacts.

3 I'm concentrating again on the United States, but the paths pertain to many other countries as well.

education, Shah also points out, would be key toward opening borders. "If people saw and understood the gravity of the harms the border enacted, we'd be opening them much more quickly." (Though for some, as journalist Adam Serwer has put it, the "cruelty is the point.")

Here, then, is a list of some initial moves that are not tweaks to the system of closed borders, but real efforts toward its dismantling and dissolution.

* * *

The billion-dollar business of making money by caging certain people because they cross certain borders is relatively new.[4] Though the state of California leased out a prison for private management as early as 1850, the experiment didn't work or catch on. Not until 1983 was the first-ever private prison company, Corrections Corporation of America (rebranded as CoreCivic in 2016), founded. Their first contract was with the Immigration and Naturalization Service to lock up migrants in a converted motel outside of Houston.

Part of for-profit immigration prison companies' strategy to ensure their bottom line always points skyward is to skimp on offering decent medical care to the tens of thousands of people it locks away. This practice ensures that detention centers—already

---

4   About 350 million people cross the US–Mexico border every year. In the United States, using 2019 as an example and counting the total estimated crossings just of the US–Mexican border, only about 0.03 percent of the people making those crossings were prosecuted for doing so. If you were to count all border crossings into the United States, including the US–Canada border, maritime borders, and the borders crossed by air travel, the percentage of crossings that are criminalized fade away into a horizon of zeros. My back-of-envelope calculation is 0.002 percent of people who cross the border into the United States each year are criminalized. If you have legal status, take a moment and imagine that you are one of those 0.002 percent of people who are not allowed to do what well over half a billion people do—and not only are you barred from doing it, but you will be arrested, humiliated, sometimes tortured, and imprisoned for doing so.

cramped, traumatizing, isolating, and bleakly depressing—are medically perilous places to be confined. These for-profit centers offer bland, rotting, insufficient, and non-nutritious food, and generally cultivate a spirit of high-anxiety malaise and sometimes suicidal anomie.

The guards who oversee the people they're caging are often underpaid, undertrained, and known to take out their own angst and discontent against those they're charged to lord over. If people stuffed into these hellholes stand up for themselves, or try to, they can be beaten, isolated, transferred, or have their few diversions (including reading material, fresh air, sunlight, or interaction with other humans) snatched from them. In recent years, there has been a spate of hunger strikes in private detention centers (so many, in fact, that even when dozens of people go on weeks-long strikes in protest of their severe mistreatment, it's no longer newsworthy). In response to such desperation, overworked medical staff resort to force-feeding, which is widely considered torture, as well as sometimes beating or threatening to deport strikers.[5]

One asylum seeker from India, Ajay Kumar, fled to the United States to seek safety and spent almost a year locked up in a detention center while waiting for a decision on his case. At one point, after he complained that he was being fed beef, which is against his religion, he was placed in solitary confinement. After being denied his request to be released on bond, along with three other asylum seekers, he began a hunger strike in July of 2019. After he went a month without eating anything, US Justice Department lawyers obtained a judge's order to begin force-feeding him. When the guards gave him a last chance to eat something before medical staff began stuffing a tube up his nose, Kumar refused: "You guys know the only thing I want: my freedom."

---

5 The World Medical Association considers it unethical for a doctor to participate in force-feeding, and the UN deems it a violation of international law.

He later told the *Intercept*, which obtained footage of the gruesome procedure, "At first I got scared seeing that tube—the tube that was almost as thick as my pinky finger"—about six millimeters thick—"which they were going to put in my nose."

As the staff started snaking the tube up his nostril, he remembered, "Right then, my mind stopped working. I was only thinking that I wish this tube would flip and go into my brain and the story ended there. I felt as if it was going through the throat, tearing the flesh. And blood started coming from the mouth and nose." The tube got caught in his esophagus, and staff had to pull it back out. "As soon as they started the second time," Kumar said, "it was more painful than the first time, because my nose was already injured and the tube was going inside, tearing it again."

Once again, the tube had coiled in his esophagus, and they had to pull it back out and try again.

During the COVID-19 pandemic, the already-dire situation in immigration detention centers further deteriorated. Along with José Olivares, I reported on a nurse whistleblower in Irwin County Detention Center, a privately run clink in Georgia, who described a panoply of vile conditions, including mold and bug infestations in the medical ward, staff lying about the prevalence of COVID infections, and staff ignoring requests for medical attention, even from people with COVID symptoms. Altogether, the facility became an incubator for the virus. Meanwhile, a doctor contracted by Immigration and Customs Enforcement who serviced that same facility was credibly accused of performing dozens of nonconsensual gynecological procedures, including hysterectomies, on detained women, sterilizing them.

Overall, for-profit detention is an invitation to abuse, faces negligible accountability, and relies on a perverse profit motive to further criminalize migration. There's also the nauseating revolving door between policymakers and migrant prison company boardrooms. To name just one example, former White House Chief of Staff John Kelly left politics (where he worked for the Trump administration, which was imprisoning migrant children recently separated from their families) to take a handsomely remunerated gig at a corporation that locks up those same children.

The states of California, Illinois, and Washington have passed bills to phase out for-profit immigration detention, and a number of other states are following suit. But even if they are government-run, services (such as medical care or food) are often subcontracted to for-profit corporations. Cutting out the profit motive (which results in dangerously skimping on basic provisions and medical care) is a good first move. Banning such gulags altogether would be better.

While immigration detention has a long history, the US government has not always been so zealous in its quest to lock away migrants. As recently as the 1960s, immigration detention was practically abolished. In 1970, less than 600 people in the United States were charged with an immigration crime. And as recently as 1993, less than 2,500 people were charged with immigration crimes. By 2018, the number rose to nearly 110,000.

Today, in the more than two hundred immigration jails in the United States, many of which are effectively black sites, migrants languish for weeks, months, even years. And before they are transferred to these sites, many are first crammed into freezing cold dungeons known by migrants as *hieleras*, or iceboxes, where fluorescent lights buzz 24/7, there are no beds, migrants are afforded little to eat, and they are sometimes mocked and gawked at like animals through the security windows.

Of course, it's not only in the United States that such abuse and neglect takes place. Besides the horrorscape that is Australia's offshore detention center, the notorious Siglo XXI in southern Mexico is an open-air prison that resembles a stockyard. In Libyan prisons where migrants are crammed after being pushed back from Italy, they are tortured, raped, sometimes forced to defecate in the corners of cells, and have been sold into slavery, as well as beaten to death. "It would be well not to forget that the first camps in Europe were built as places to control refugees," writes Italian philosopher

Giorgio Agamben, "and that the progression—internment camps, concentration camps, extermination camps—represents a perfectly real filiation."

Shuttering these places, worldwide, would be a huge leap toward ending gross injustices.

There are many ways forward. In the United States, local governments—cities and counties—contract with the federal government to open and keep these places running. Organizing at the city council and county levels to cancel these contracts could shutter many of the camps—as both Adelanto, California, and Williamson County, Texas, have fought to end their detention contracts with ICE. Although these and other detention centers in cities and counties cutting ties with ICE have remained open, states and more local jurisdictions in New York, Michigan, Illinois, California and elsewhere are limiting how and where ICE can lock people up. Allegations of serious abuse and public outcry have closed various such facilities in recent years. Movement on the federal side is also feasible, and while the Biden administration has perpetuated the immigration detention system in the United States, they campaigned singing a very different tune. As such, holding politicians to account to fulfill campaign promises is crucial to advancing a world where people can freely move.

Direct action and protest, as activists have already shown through successful sabotage operations against the US–Mexico border wall and interruptions of deportations, is also necessary. A personal example here is illustrative, as I've been a small part of a few actions that have temporarily stopped migrants from being deported or transferred between detention centers. Outside of the notorious Adelanto Detention Center, where a surprise inspection in 2018 found fifteen nooses, made out of ripped and braided bedsheets, hanging in cells, I once bike-locked a young undocumented woman's neck to the fence through which deportation buses depart the facility. The brave woman was arrested after firefighters sawed through the U-lock, but she was later released. For at least that day, nobody from Adelanto was deported. Making it difficult, cost-ly, slow, or impossible to do the work of migrant caging can help build momentum toward gumming up the system to the point of unsustainability.

Nobody should be jailed for seeking safety or dignity.

Abolition of ICE's immigration-enforcement duties, and the assignment of all ICE agents to their *other* tasks—such as stop-ping child pornography—would be a much better use of agents' time and public resources. The proposal to sever ICE's immigra-tion-enforcement duties from the rest of the work has been repeat-edly made by ICE agents themselves, as the agents working in the investigative units don't like the politicization or stigma its immi-gration work brings them; they say their jobs are harder because people don't trust them. As it turns out, you run a reputation when you're known for stalking parents as they drop their kids off at school, shackling women during childbirth, or staging mass arrests of people doing the honest work of building your homes, laying your roads, cooking your eggs, or butchering your meat. Trust in police more broadly has been undercut for, among other valid rea-sons (including rampant, overt, and deadly racism in police ranks), the association migrants rightly make between ICE and street cops.

If a US law enforcement officer comes across a person who is not authorized to be in the country, they could refer them not to ICE but to US Citizenship and Immigration Services (USCIS)—the agency (its own troubling history notwithstanding) that could help them straighten out their paperwork rather than drop them into a carceral pit. Processing migrants to grant them legal status rather than arresting and deporting them would be a positive half step.

Or, we could just abolish ICE completely, especially given that it is a neo-feudalistic, violently abusive, and frequently lawless police force. In an age that purports to hail both democracy and universal human rights, it's a wonder that it took until 2018 for "Abolish ICE" to become a widely referenced slogan. Like any political slo-gan, however, it is opaque, and to literally abolish ICE remains beyond the pale (literally, beyond the boundary) for many who heard and perhaps even chanted the phrase. Writing in the *Yale Law Journal* in 2019, Peter L. Markowitz noted that "[l]acking in the public discourse is a clear affirmative vision for a practical immigration-enforcement system that is not dependent on mass detention and deportation." Markowitz sought to offer "a vision for a new immigration-enforcement paradigm that is humane and effective, but that does not rely on the existence of ICE, or any immigration police agency." But that vision, for Markowitz and many others, means a re-jiggering reform with gaping exceptions to the concept of "abolish." Arguing for dialing down ICE's abuses, for example, he pushes for identifying "the optimal scale" of ICE enforcement, which, as seen above, includes ripping parents from their children, as well as shackling women who are seeking safety, and force-feeding asylum seekers.

Still, some mean the slogan literally: we want to entirely do away with the Immigrations and Customs Enforcement agency, which, since its inception, has earned a reputation as a dishonest, racist, and rogue agency that regularly bucks legal limits and balks at any whiff of accountability. The goal of the agency, as spelled out in the 2003 detention and removal strategic plan, "Endgame," was to achieve a "100% removal rate" by arresting and deporting all unauthorized migrants living in the United States. Not only has ICE failed to come even close to achieving that goal (the undocumented population increased by about 70 percent, from 7 million to 12 million in the first decade of the agency's existence) but the harms and costs of achieving that goal have been incalculably high.

As of 2023, ICE is only twenty years old. The country survived for centuries without this cutthroat immigration police force, and it can do so again.

But, you might ask, what about immigrants who commit violent crimes—shouldn't they be given the boot? It's a common counter-argument, and one that needs to be addressed. You might answer that an unauthorized immigrant convicted of such a crime should be treated as would any other person convicted of a crime; but in the United States, especially, any considerate or thinking person would hesitate to subject them, or anybody, to the dysfunctional, discriminatory, and wildly abusive criminal justice system. Mass criminalization and incarceration, especially of Black and Brown people, is a horribly failed national experiment, has not made society safer, and does a lot to make families, communities, and especially the people thrown into the system, miserable. Indeed, in the United States, prison does more to provoke crime and violence than it does to prevent it.

Even so, let us further unpack the scenario of an immigrant committing a crime. The logic of bordering would suggest they should be deported, or perhaps first imprisoned and then deported.[6] But deporting someone who has committed a crime is merely deflecting a problem, not solving it. To expect the migrant's native country to deliver justice is to misunderstand global interconnections and contemporary migration.

Consider, for instance, the cost-benefit approach to the police in the United States catching an unauthorized migrant from Mexico who has been caught driving drunk. Driving under the influence is certainly a dangerous act that is in society's interest to curtail. But what are the costs of a local police department issuing an ICE hold, ICE contracting a private transportation service to take the migrant to an ICE detention center, detaining the person there for weeks, perhaps months (or even years), flying or driving them to their country of origin, and then releasing them, where they will likely be emotionally distressed and without a job, money, or the necessary support to pick themselves up?[7] The scenario is primed

---

6   We should also note here, again, that migrants commit crimes at far lower rates than natives. One sweeping 2020 study in *Proceedings of the National Academy of Sciences* concluded, "Relative to undocumented immigrants, US-born citizens are over 2 times more likely to be arrested for violent crimes, 2.5 times more likely to be arrested for drug crimes, and over 4 times more likely to be arrested for property crimes."

7   Consider the rise of the MS-13 and Barrio 18 gangs, which were both

for pushing them back onto the barstool or to make a desperate journey back into the United States. A more reasonable option would be considering why the person decided to drink and drive in the first place. Were they working sixty-hour weeks in a low-paid, under-the-table job, trying to make ends meet and send remittance money home? Were they stressed about their legal status, feeling devil-may-care about driving after a few drinks when they're not even allowed to legally drive at all?

You can pick apart this specific scenario (What if the crime were worse? What if it was a repeat violation?), but the general point is that deflection of criminal justice across a border isn't a productive response to violent acts. Offshoring society's problems, or offshoring people who commit crimes, is not a long-term or sustainable solution. Assessing and addressing how society pushes people toward addiction, violent actions, and instability would be more beneficial than the superficial and ad hoc responses of locking up and deporting offenders.

* * *

In her book *Migra!*, historian Kelly Lytle Hernández describes Border Patrol agents' daily work as "bringing bodies to the abstract caste of illegality." The agents—about twenty thousand of them as of 2023—charged with tracking down people who have crossed a line and prosecuting them or pushing them back across that line (or both) strip migrants of their political and human rights. And the agents have little oversight in how they do it.

A look back at the formation of this infamous agency provides helpful insight into their ongoing and ignominious role in upholding the US border regime. The first iteration of the US Border

established in Los Angeles, but then, after years of mass deportations back to El Salvador and other Central American countries, took root there, proliferated, and moved back again to the United States. Deporting a problem is not solving it.

Patrol was as a mounted force specifically tasked, beginning in 1904, with keeping Chinese people out of the country. Initial recruits had close ties to the Ku Klux Klan or were former agents of the Texas Rangers, a force initially dedicated to hunting down Indians. One of the agency's earliest chiefs, Harlon Carter—the man who led "Operation Wetback"—was convicted of killing a Mexican teenager for talking too loudly. Long known for resorting to savage violence and even murder, and with a through line of white nationalism, the Border Patrol is an unreformable agency.

However, if outright abolition is out of reach, Border Patrol agents should be stripped of their weapons, especially the leadership, and the agency should submit to a serious independent review. Those agents who are not fired for abuse or misconduct could be retrained to conduct remote rescues, care for and restore ecosystems, and combat climate change. They could form part of a new Civilian Climate Corps, with a focus on flood control, soil erosion, and forestry maintenance, with a mission to enhance infrastructure to combat and alleviate the effects of climate change. Almost any public works project—rebuilding roads, the electrical grid, or retraining agents as health care workers, social workers, or simply transferring them into onshored industry jobs—would be much more beneficial to society.

Another easy step is to keep unauthorized-entry statutes in place, but to allow *all* immigration through ports of entry. This might be the most broadly palatable of open-border visions, as migrants would still have to present at official ports of entry, submit documentation, and register before they were granted entry—but *all* would be granted entry. People who tried to gain access between ports of entry could be turned around or sent back to come through an official port of entry. Once they arrive, a nonenforcement agency, such as USCIS, would be charged with getting their paperwork in order, but nobody would be forced to live off the books or under the threat of banishment. With such a system, the anti-immigrant quip to "get in line" would actually make sense. (Currently, for most people, except the well heeled and well connected, *there is no line*.) This approach would target the manner in which people come, not the people themselves.

But why criminalize migration at all? Again, a look back at the history of the US immigration apparatus is revealing. The "crime" of crossing the border without inspection is the most prosecuted federal offense in the United States, and was invented in 1929 after a focused effort by Secretary of Labor James Davis and South Carolina senator Coleman Livingston Blease, who Kelly Lytle Hernández characterizes as "a proud and unreconstructed white supremacist." Unlawful entry thus became a misdemeanor punishable by six months' imprisonment and up to a $250 fine; a second unlawful entry was deemed a felony, punishable by two years' imprisonment or a $2,000 fine, or both.[8]

Criminalization and punishment of people who migrate doesn't work as a deterrent. No study has been able to demonstrate that threats of punishment stop people from crossing or recrossing the border. In fact, "illegal reentry" prosecutions have gone up over the last decades, and show no signs of flagging. And while there is no specific crime for illegal *re*-reentry (or *re-re*-reentry), when people are driven by existential needs, family, or fear, the basic act of fulfilling that need—reuniting with family or moving out of harm's way—is natural. Criminalization of those acts won't stop them. The costs of incarcerating tens of thousands of migrants a year in the United States is over $1.3 billion. There are few policy moves that can achieve so much public good not by bureaucratic grit but by simply ceasing to do something. The pain and suffering can end—and justice and profits be had—by simply *not* considering migration a crime.

A key move—both symbolic and restorative—would be to pull down the wall itself—just as the dismantling of the Berlin Wall

---

8   It is *not* a crime to be in the United States without papers; it's only a crime to cross into the country without authorization.

in November of 1989 took on huge symbolic importance for Germans on both sides of Berlin, and for much of the world. While tearing down the wall didn't herald the end of history or a new Pax Romana, it did provide hope and serve as a key step toward the reintegration of Germany, along with much of Europe, and a cooling of global tensions.

The wall on the US–Mexico border, as we know it today, is about as old as the Berlin Wall was when it was taken down (though some major new segments, erected during the Trump administration, are much younger). Before the 1990s, there was almost no physical infrastructure along the US–Mexico borderline, even if some fence segments were raised in the first two decades of the twentieth century. There are now about 700 miles of fences and walls stretching along the 1,933-mile border. If the United States and Mexico survived without a wall for nearly two hundred years, they can do so again. "Who would have thought that a wall could be built!" muses Australian author Anna Funder about the Berlin Wall in *Stasiland*, "And who would have thought at the end that it might ever fall! That was also impossible!"

Politics is always limited by the possible—if politics erected these walls, politics can tear them down. We ourselves would do well to follow Ronald Reagan's 1987 imperative to his Soviet counterpart, Mr. Gorbachev, and "tear down this wall!"

Before coming to that more frequently quoted finale, in an earlier part of the same speech, Reagan observed: "As long as this gate is closed, as long as this scar of a wall is permitted to stand, it is not the German question alone that remains open, but the question of freedom for all mankind."

How do we take down the walls? A bulldozer can follow the passage of a bill. Or the reverse: the heart can follow the hand.

* * *

Pundits and politicians alike have proposed a plethora of technocratic fixes in order to deescalate decades of anti-migrant policies. One rather simple and technocratic proposal is not counting dependents toward immigration quotas.

Current US law limits annual immigration to 226,000 visas for family members of US citizens, 140,000 for employees, and 55,000 visas for "diversity immigrants" through the green card lottery. Beginning in 1990, the Bush administration started counting spouses and children against the cap. Soon, especially for employee-sponsored immigrants, the partners and kids of new hires were taking up the majority of delegated visas. By 2014, almost 60 percent of immigrants admitted for "employer-sponsored" immigration were actually the worker's family members. The law, however, contains no requirement to count family members against the quota. A simple and more accurate reading of the law—not counting family members toward the quota cap—would more than double the number of migrants allowed into the United States.[9]

The reinstitution of the Burlingame Treaty—the landmark nineteenth-century agreement between the US and China that inaugurated a new era of trade and migration between the two powers—would be a welcome advance and a reparative move for Chinese migrants in particular.

"Peace, Amity, and Commerce" was the official title of the treaty signed on July 4, 1868, between the United States of America and the Chinese Ta-Tsing Empire, which celebrated "the inherent and inalienable right of man to change his home and allegiance, and also the mutual advantage of the free migration and emigration of

9 The law itself, however, has its own problems, as those forty thousand visas are reserved for "(A) Aliens with extraordinary ability ... (B) Outstanding professors and researchers ... (C) Certain multinational executives and managers." This unfairly favors the wealthy and the well educated, further entrenching immigration policy as a way to divide the haves from the have-nots.

their citizens and subjects respectively from the one country for the other, for purposes of curiosity, of trade, or as permanent residents."

There's some martial gobbledygook tacked on after that, but *the inherent and inalienable right of man to change his home and allegiance . . . the mutual advantage of free migration*—that's an American tradition worth harking back to.

An obvious, and yet overlooked, move would be to establish a free-transit zone within the territories of the United States, Canada, and Mexico. The United States already effectively treats the southern Mexican border and the borders dividing Central America into separate states as the de facto US southern border, spending hundreds of millions of dollars on outsourced immigration enforcement, training foreign border guards, and applying diplomatic pressure and threats of sanctions to get those countries to police their borders. "The United States," as journalist Todd Miller observes in *Empire of Borders*, "has become a global border-building machine." An easy move here would be not to do any of that—allowing for free transit from Panama to Canada. The C-4 Agreement between Guatemala, Honduras, El Salvador, and Nicaragua already allows citizens of those countries free transit. Tacking the C-4 countries onto the NAFTA countries (United States, Canada, Mexico) and allowing people to follow the free transit of goods and capital would be a natural and just next step.

Why not just weld the concept of free migration to free trade?

Free trade should not be a means of lining the pockets of the wealthy and immiserating the working class. The devastating effects of NAFTA on both Mexican and US labor have been thoroughly catalogued.[10] The setup itself relies on the capitalist lever of

---

10 Author and activist David Bacon makes some trenchant comparisons. As of 2017, a US autoworker earned $21.50 an hour compared to $3.00 for a Mexican autoworker. Despite this, a gallon of milk costs more in Mexico than it does in the US. It takes a Mexican autoworker more than an hour of work to afford a pound of hamburger meat, while a worker in Detroit can buy it after ten minutes, even though the Mexican workers are equally efficient in their work. "The difference," Bacon writes, "means profit for

the free movement of goods and the exploitation of an immobilized labor force: shunting human beings into high-demand/low-pay sweatshops built in slums. If countries freely trade toasters and tomatoes across their borders, the people who make those toasters and who harvest those tomatoes should be free to move as well. (Or, if that's too unpalatable, we should reverse the equation and criminalize the toasters.)

* * *

Among other such border openings, the European Union could begin incorporating more countries into the Schengen Area.

Beginning in 1985, members of the European Economic Community (later subsumed by the European Union) agreed upon the gradual dissolution of passport and migration controls to separate the countries. As of 2021, nearly half a billion people in twenty-six different countries can travel freely within 1.6 million square miles without worrying about having to prove where they were born or contort their way through a bureaucratic tangle. (Given the Brexit flinch and the rise of hard-right anti-immigrant parties across Europe, by the time you read this, that free transit zone could have been considerably shrunk.)

While twentieth-century Europe saw both the steep rise and quick fall of immigration restrictions, by the 2000s, even while internal checks were abolished, the European Union began militarizing its external borders.

I've reported on the extraordinarily dangerous Turkish–Greek line, where the increasingly militarized border is blistered with detention centers, police stations, watchtowers, anti-tank moats, and minefields, and where European commando forces violently push

---

GM, poverty for Mexican workers, and the migration from Mexico to the US of those who can't survive." See the work of Justin Akers Chacón and David Bacon for more on the iniquities imposed by current "free trade" models.

back and disappear migrants. The too-simple-to-see solution would be, again, to simply stop. Demobilize, demilitarize, and tell the agents to do something more constructive with their time than hunting and disappearing humans.

After incorporating Turkey into the free-migration zone—and turning the strip of violent rightlessness along the Evros-Meriç River back into a river once again—former African colonies could be tacked on as well. Morocco would be the obvious first step, especially as Spain has ongoing land claims—the exclaves of Melilla and Ceuta—on the northern tips of Africa. The other four north African coastal countries, Algeria, Tunisia, Libya, and Egypt, are polyethnic nations with deep historical, cultural, and linguistic ties to Europe—including trade and back-and-forth colonization—all of which should ease incorporation. Algeria was a former colony administered by France until 1962. Allowing its citizens access to French territory would be as much an act of recompense or reparations as a natural organization of population and geography.

Other regional free-migration zones should also expand.

Throughout the world, such zones are more common than many people realize. The African Continental Free Trade Area, which includes Algeria, Libya, and Morocco, could extend its inclusivity. The Free Movement Protocol in the Intergovernmental Authority on Development (IGAD) region—a trade bloc consisting of Eritrea, Ethiopia, Kenya, South Sudan, Sudan, Somalia, Djibouti, and Uganda—includes specific provisions to enable those affected by disasters and climate change to move freely across contiguous borders.

Mercosur, the common market between Argentina, Brazil, Paraguay, and Uruguay (with Bolivia, Chile, Colombia, Ecuador, Guyana, Peru, and Suriname as associate members, and Venezuela currently suspended), represents a vast landmass where citizens of any member country can obtain residence and a work permit in other signatory states with no requirements other than a valid passport, birth certificate, and a background check. Temporary residence lasts up to two years, and people can apply to stay permanently. Adding the rest of the continent and reincorporating Venezuela (from which around six million migrants have fled in recent years) is an obvious move. (Next would be the northward incorporation of Central America.)

The Nordic Passport Union, which includes Iceland, Denmark, Norway, Sweden, and Finland, permits their citizens to travel to and reside within the zone in another Nordic country (including Svalbard) without any travel documentation whatsoever. (Since 2001, those five states are also part of the Schengen Area.)

The Trans-Tasman Travel Arrangement allows free movement between Australia and New Zealand. Tacking on Papua New Guinea, where Australia currently runs detention camps, would be a key next step, but so would the extension of the zone to other South Asian countries, against whose people Australia has long discriminated.

In 1950, India and Nepal signed what is effectively an open-border agreement with the Treaty of Peace and Friendship. Extending the treaty to India's other neighbors, Pakistan and Bangladesh, could ease long-simmering political tensions, save money from unnecessary and deadly border enforcement operations, and offer safety, reprieve, and opportunity to those forced from their homes.

Even the United States had, at least on the books, what was effectively a regional free-movement agreement until 1968. Part of the Immigration Act of 1924, the racially discriminatory act that set country quotas explicitly meant to make America whiter, also included exceptions to migrants born "in the Dominion of Canada, Newfoundland, the Republic of Mexico, the Republic of Cuba, the Republic of Haiti, the Dominican Republic, the Canal Zone, or an independent country of Central or South America."

Expanding these many open-border agreements would not, by itself, improve the global situation, for regional borders can be just as pernicious and deadly as national borders. For instance, Europe's Iron Curtain divided the Eastern Warsaw Pact countries from Western NATO countries for almost a half a century, even as each country's frontier was similarly guarded over. Today, the edge of Fortress Europe is, by far, the deadliest border in the world.

Still, every new territory added to free-migration zones expands freedom, promotes justice and economic equality, and is a step toward the liberation of people oppressed and victimized merely on the basis of where they are born.

* * *

Borderlands residents are already effectively subject to two states—one on each side of the line—with border regions increasingly under dual national control. Political scientist Matthew Longo thus suggests a "perimeter zone citizenship," which would give borderlands residents at least partial political control over border policies. Citizens in the zone would remain citizens of their own country but also "be afforded special rights and responsibilities unique to the perimeter zone itself." One basic such right would be protection, as Longo suggests the borderland zones could become "Human Rights Havens," in which asylum seekers would find safety and at least some freedoms.

This would be a quarter step, at best, but useful in turning borders away from rightlessness and violence and back into zones of interaction and exchange.

Perhaps the most convincing argument Longo makes for the unique form of citizenship is that residents on one side of the border directly, and often severely, suffer the consequences of policies emanating from the other side. The idea of giving these people some political control comes from the concept of *affectedness*: "the principle that those people who are affected by a policy should have a say in its formulation." (The concept obviously applies to the clandestini within countries as well, and offers self-determination to more than just the aggressors or boundary enforcers.)

And while granting borderlands citizenship rights would enable borderland citizens to cross freely between states and vote on shared issues, Longo suggests that it wouldn't enable the same privileges of residency. In this scenario, rather than erasing or opening the border, the line would become *graduated*. Longo cites legal scholar Ayelet Shachar's concept of *jus nexi*, or earned citizenship, which "derives its moral strength from the idea of rootedness in a community." People deserve citizenship and the rights that come with it, the theory goes, based on relationships they have with the communities and lands they live in.

For the lawmakers among us: you could start by unwriting anti-immigrant laws. To lawfully open US borders, Congress would have to do entirely away with the concept of authorized versus unauthorized migration, and the only real way to do that would be to undo immigration law, rewriting or simply nixing completely the Immigration and Nationality Act, which was first passed in 1952, substantially revamped in 1965, and has been tweaked and amended ever since.

Unwriting a law follows the same process as writing a law: a member of Congress introduces a revocation bill, it passes in both houses, and then the president signs it. A flurry of state laws in recent years, for example, have effectively unwritten laws criminalizing marijuana use. Bills can be passed within days: the Patriot Act, which expanded the surveillance powers of law enforcement dramatically in the wake of the September 11, 2001, attacks—and was part of a package of policies demonizing, denying, and detaining migrants—was brought to the House floor on the same day it was introduced, and then passed and signed three days later. There's nothing technically stopping an open borders bill from becoming law the day after tomorrow.

* * *

But, back to our original question, what would the world look like after some or all those steps?

An open-borders world might look like the United States or the European Union today. Both are incredibly diverse political bodies composed of states with varying degrees of independence that write and enforce their own laws, and whose populations practice their own customs and (especially in the European Union) speak their own languages.

In an open borders world, there will be room enough, even in receiving countries. The US, one of the world's largest nations, has a density of 86 people per square mile.[11] Meanwhile, France has about 350 people per square mile, Belgium 976 people per square mile, and South Korea 1,337. None of those countries has anywhere near Bangladesh's 2,980 people per square mile, or Singapore's 20,000. All to say, the United States could quadruple its population and still be less dense than France, which hardly feels crowded. Overall, only about 5 percent of America's land area is developed. Economist Thomas Sowell has noted that the state of Texas could house the entire current global population: all of us would fit in single-story, single-family houses with a yard. Even then, Texas would be less dense than Manhattan. (While this is perhaps not the rosiest picture of how we might work it all out, the point stands: we have room enough.)

Even Poland, a much smaller country than the United States, with a much higher population density (with a total population of less than 40 million, Poland has around 320 people per square mile compared to 86 people per square mile, respectively), was able to absorb over 3 million Ukrainian refugees in just a few months in 2022. Of course, such a rapid and massive influx was a strain, but the Polish economy was not devastated, and many of the Ukrainians quickly sought work to support themselves; meanwhile, there

---

11 Overall, about 75 percent of the US population lives on 3.5 percent of the nation's land.

were no reports of increases in crime rates, and only a few incidents of xenophobia. If Poland and Turkey (which dealt with previous rapid influxes of migrants) can effectively welcome millions, so can much wealthier Western nations.

Again, it's critical here to dispel fears that your country, whichever it is, would be overrun. The United States, currently clocking a fertility rate far below the replacement rate of 2.1 births per woman necessary to maintain a stable population, needs migrants. Preliminary data suggests the birth rate fell to 1.7 births per woman in 2020, meaning that without migration, the US population will begin to shrink and the average age rise—straining tax bases, health care systems, and all benefit programs. Any American who plans to get old should advocate for more immigration.

Crossing the border between the neighboring states of Arizona and California doesn't have to be so different from crossing the border between the neighboring states of Sonora and Arizona. Nor does walking from the Pakistani state of Punjab to the Indian state of Punjab have to be so much more regulated than walking between two Indian states. Some might worry that long-brewing animosity between Pakistanis and Indians would be a powder keg if the populations mixed. But that logic has it backwards: it is, rather, *because* of the border and all the border represents—including militant nationalism—that the animosity and differences between the two nations are stoked and exaggerated. The Partition of British India into racial/ethnic/religious states is what provoked and propagates the violence. Similarly, in apartheid South Africa, it was the separation of races that sparked conflagrations of violence, while the reunification movement calmed the political waters. And the US–Mexico border is predominantly *why* the borderlands have become crucibles of such economic disparity, exploitation, and suffering.

Crossing a boundary, as evidenced by the crossing between, say, France and Germany, or between Ohio and Pennsylvania, doesn't need to entail stripping people of their humanity. An open-borders world could look like a collection of independent and culturally/

linguistically/legally distinct states, with marked but crossable borderlines that serve to organize populations and state governments.
We can lose the fortress mentality, the extremes of nationalism,
and the human filtering and still keep—even restore—democratic
governance.

As political theorist Jacqueline Stevens puts it: "Borders themselves do not need to be changed, only their role in establishing
groups by birth and in restricting movement on this basis."

* * *

The other truth—the other goal and urgent necessity—is that
when borders are opened, *the world will be completely different.*

That's because the implementation of a border policy that is just,
moral, and fair requires a significant shakeup of the current world
order, including massive reparations and an end to postcolonial
capitalist exploitation.

It's important here to recall that migrants don't show up at or
cross borders willy-nilly, leaving their homes on a lark to inject
themselves into foreign populations. Rather, and in overwhelmingly large part, they are pushed and pulled by systemic forces:
the evisceration of traditional ways of life (including deculturation,
commodity dumping, industrial agriculture, and economic war-
fare) as well as political persecution and climate catastrophe.

As Harsha Walia explained to me in an interview for *The Nation*,
dismantling borders, in the true sense, is not just about opening
the gates but about developing and guaranteeing two key freedoms:
the freedom of movement, and the freedom to have a home and, if
so desired, stay in that home. "It's not only getting rid of the border," Walia said, "and then maintaining all of the social and state
violences that gives rise to forced displacement."

Leaving intact the global inequality regime and opening borders
would not end forced displacement: it would still be forced; the
displacement would just be a little smoother. "When I'm thinking

of a no-border politics," Walia said, "it necessarily is part of a larger project and vision of eradicating those relations of dominance. It's about eradicating the social organization of difference, about eradicating capitalism such that the division between the so-called North and South effectively collapses." But eradicating division does not, as social scientist Mahmood Mamdani writes, "require that we all pretend we are the same; far from it. It requires that we stop accepting that our differences should define who benefits from the state and who is marginalized by it."

If the United States, the European Union, and Australia were to defund the border enforcement and military budgets, they would free up enormous quantities of money that could be spent on job creation, school funding, climate change mitigation, reparations, and the arts, as well as responsibly bolstering foreign communities that people are fleeing.

In that vision, the need to emigrate because of repression or severe inequality is obviated. People might still move (especially when driven by the climate crisis), but migration would be more of a flow and spread. It would be less constant, unidirectional, desperate, and dangerous, and more occasional, multidirectional, dignified, and safe.

Open borders, in short, cannot be an isolated policy move. They must be part of a more profound readjustment of global politics that includes the abolition of the inequality regime set in place by postcolonial capitalism. A groundbreaking 2016 study from the Global Financial Integrity think tank found that, despite the common narrative, developing countries actually act as creditors to the rest of the word. Despite claims that development represents a transfer of wealth to poor countries, if you tally up all financial resource exchanges between rich and poor countries, there is an annual net outflow from poor to rich that has reached over $1 trillion a year. The study concluded that between 1980 and 2016, developing countries lost $16.3 trillion to rich countries. If we only open or knock down the borders, and don't stop the cycle of heaping debt on impoverished countries, building up export economies, backing authoritarian strongmen, and if we don't do all we can to minimize global climate change, opening the borders will be just a quick pump of the brakes as we continue careering toward the edge of a cliff.

One possible vision of how that world would look, espoused by Jacqueline Stevens, is "states without nations." That is, populations would still organize themselves by state governments, but we would drop the "nation" part of the equation, which creates a strained and typically coerced identity marked by exclusionary practices and a rapacious and proprietary attachment to territory.

"If the historical precedent of strongly and deeply felt anxieties about free movement among towns can become a historical oddity,"[12] Stevens writes, "then it certainly seems plausible to imagine that a similar dynamic might occur in the aftermath of eliminating birthright citizenship." Stevens makes a salient point that should help shake us out of our status quo bias. Looking back at today, even from only a few decades down the road, we may see our current medieval mindset of fortressing ourselves away according to passport color, of refusing the weary and afeard, as a shameful barbarism.

While the tight linkages of identity and territory may be inseverable, identity (national, regional, familial, or of any kind) is built over time, and is always altering and alterable. Would the national identity of the United States of 2023 be recognizable to the United States of a century earlier, when women had just been legally granted the right to vote, Jim Crow laws were still in full thrust, Catholics in public office were unheard of, gay marriage and even

---

12 See chapter 4, p. 68, on the poor laws instituted in colonial and early America in New York and Massachusetts. The English poor laws were especially draconian, as in 1388 under Richard II, when "beggars" were barred from leaving their town of origin. If they did, they were whipped at the first offense, had their ears cut off at the second, and, after the third offense, were hanged.

mention of gay rights was practically unthinkable, Alaska and Hawaii were not yet states, eugenics was popular science, the sale and consumption of alcohol was illegal, and there was neither any border wall nor Border Patrol? The bygone heyday can be both criticized and revered without becoming political—and moral—deadweight. Culture and identity are always in flux, and any tradition that depends on denial or exclusion, especially when that results in suffering and death, is not worth maintaining.

So, if state governments decoupled themselves from nationalism and that weakened attachments to some rituals, Stevens writes, "this seems a small price to pay for ending organized violence and freeing resources for more creative pursuits, for sustaining rather than suffocating impulses of empathy."

But, after all of this, after abolishing nativist oppression and eradicating the extremes of merciless capitalism, what would the world look like? "A map of the world," wrote the famed poet and playwright Oscar Wilde, "that does not include Utopia is not worth even glancing at." Given that the current world order has resulted in the immiseration of billions of people and the debilitating and sometimes deadly discrimination against hundreds of millions of others, it's worth not only thinking about a different system but working to support and defend those people who are crushed by this one. The best way to accomplish that aim is to open the border, either by legislation or by crowbar.

* * *

While straightforward enough in theory, following any of these steps in the real world may be scary, and a common knee-jerk response is that open borders would result in chaos. Given natural experiments such as the Mariel boatlift and other instances of rapid mass migration, it's clear that such fears are unfounded. And even if the initial resettling would be relatively hectic, what do you call the current situation along the world's borderlines—lines of death, disappearance, prolonged detention, and near-absolute rightless-ness—if not chaos?

A 2021 survey from the Cato Institute found that Americans es-timated that 40 percent of the US population were immigrants. In reality, the number is less than 14 percent. That wild misperception underscores that a common reaction to any new element or person introduced into a system may provoke anxiety, especially when the media regularly discusses that new element in apocalyptic terms: immigrants are referred to as waves, floods, surges; human mobility is seen as a breach or invasion. Migration, however, lest we forget, is a normal and natural act. People move, and they always have. Im-migrants are, at bottom, much like we are all. They share our needs, concerns, hopes, and fears. They want to live and prosper. Dif-ferences between migrants and natives are superficial, geographic, and hardly greater than differences between any neighbors. Even in countries where the percentage of migrants is significantly high-er—such as the United Arab Emirates, where nearly 90 percent of the population is foreign born—the prevailing culture successfully adapts *and* abides.

Another knee-jerk response is that the idea of open borders is simply too radical. But what is radical about not wanting to be ripped from your family and deported thousands of miles away? What is radical about granting people the right to seek dignity, se-curity, opportunity, and prosperity? What is radical about adding a necessary and overlooked component to Article 13 of the Universal Declaration of Human Rights, which affirms that everyone has the right to leave one's country? The obvious corollary, not stipulated in the declaration, is the *right to enter another country*. As political scientist Norman Finkelstein writes about the Israeli blockade of Gaza—an observation that holds true for much of the world in terms of asylum—"Is it 'effective' to post signs warning *In case of fire, use emergency exit*, if the building doesn't have an emergency exit?" The situation in terms of migration is not that there is no exit but that, with closed borders, the exit door is barricaded.

* * *

So how do we get there? We open borders by crossing them. We get there by helping and welcoming people on the move. We fight against the criminalization, imprisonment, and deportation of migrants. We support and protect our neighbors. We rally against the despoiling foreign wars and economic policies that uproot and unhome people across the globe. We aggressively ramp up the fight against climate change.

As Harsha Walia puts it: "I fundamentally don't believe that the current deathscape of incrementalism is somehow more 'practical' than radical transformation."

All good, all fine. But in concrete terms, what does all of this really look like in the end? Stay tuned for the novelistic sequel to this book, which is set in our open-borders future of 2030. (Or maybe, if we move too slowly, 2035.) As abolitionist trailblazer Mariame Kaba has responded about what a world without prisons would look like, "We'll figure it out by working to get there." Or, perhaps, we answer the question with another question: What better and more just world can we imagine?

Are blanket surveillance, state repression, a massive incarceration regime, walls, and the constant threat of deportations our answer to climate change, growing inequalities, and entrenched racism? Or can we imagine something better?

"It is time," Kaba writes, "to envision and create alternatives to the hellish conditions our society has brought into being."

Actually, it's long past time.

8

Josiel and Iron Obelisks

Outside of a migrant aid center in Nogales, Sonora—shattered concrete patio, blinding whitewashed walls, street vendor bells, the hard-shifting of buses pulling up the nearby hill—Josiel squatted on a cracked curb, pulled his hat brim down to his eyes, and told me how, a few weeks earlier, after having left Honduras, passing through Guatemala, and trekking by foot and by train north through Mexico—a trip that took over two months, during which he "lost everything"—he'd crossed the border into the United States with a group of three men and two women he'd recently met. They'd only spent a few days together, but already felt like friends, he said (he didn't tell me their names; he didn't want me to use his either—it's not Josiel). And after a cold night and a long morning on their second day of walking through the desert, they came across a dirt road and saw two Border Patrol trucks parked on the shoulder. An agent in one of the trucks, his window down, spotted them and opened his door, calling out *¡Párense!* The group dropped their packs and took off running, and then the agent got out of his truck and started after them, the other truck speeding away down the road. The two women in the group didn't want to run and soon stopped to give themselves up ("give-ups," the Border Patrol calls them; "bodies," they call them; "gotaways," agents lament). Another truck sped across the road, and then an ATV and other agents came, and there might have been a drone in the sky, or a surveillance tower nearby, or infrared cameras and klieg lights to burn away the night, an aerostat balloon like a pregnant kite looming fatly in the sky, motion sensors buried in the dirt, and the air-conditioned intel centers where agents monitor it all from far away: "operational control" is what they seek, to see everything, to stop everything except what they don't want to stop.

There were already other agents coming, Josiel said, but we just ran: cutting through the sharp bushes and weaving the brechas, not knowing if they would make it or get caught, not even knowing in which direction they were running. In another few minutes—had they escaped their pursuers?—already exhausted, they started slowing down, and then they came to another or maybe the same road and they realized that they'd run in a circle. Then they heard the gunning engine of a truck and they bolted back into the dry brush, pushing through the prick and pull of the thorns until they hit a clearing and kept running and Josiel's vision was blurring from the blood hammering in his head again and the sweat in his eyes. He and the two other men came to a short buffalo jump, about four or five feet high, almost running right off of the brink—it wasn't too high, he said, but the ground was uneven below, with rocks and scattered scree, and their legs were unsteady and their lungs burning and the agents on foot and at gun behind them. Josiel jumped, or fell, really, stumbled, and picked himself up to start running again until he heard, from behind, a loud snap of bone.

One of the men, a boy really, the new friend he had just met, landed wrong. His body pitched forward, his foot did not, his shin levering against a rock, snapping the bone like a piece of kindling. A bone shard tore through the skin, the boy sank into his calf, and blood gulped down his leg while a gasp of pain flashed up his spine.

It was bleeding a lot, Josiel told me. He pulled his shirt off and wrapped it around the kid's leg, but the blood seeped through, and the other man pulled the kid down to his side and gripped hard against him, as if he were trying to hug him, to brace him against the pain, and then Josiel took off his belt and wrapped it around his thigh to try to slow the blood. The kid was breathing so hard he didn't seem to be breathing at all, and except for the sawing of breath and the seeping of blood and sweat, the world had gone quiet. Josiel remembers thinking: *Now what?*

The agents hadn't found them, but they were still looking, and, he said, "I didn't want to leave him, but"—pausing—"I didn't want to get caught either."

The sun was dropping. Josiel tried to hear if the agents were close, but all he could catch was his own dry breath coming in and out, and the grunting pain emanating out of the kid at his side, the desert beginning to tick and sigh and hum in the evening, the arms and spindles of cacti silhouetted against the sky, coyotes yipping madness in the distance, predators on the hunt—and then he heard it, the hot acceleration and the dry spitting of tires against sand. And then a threatening cry, and Josiel told the injured kid that he was going to leave him.

The other man, too, stood up, ready to save himself. Give us a minute to run, Josiel said, and then scream as loudly as you can so they come for you. Let us get away first, and then scream and scream and scream, okay? Okay? He and the other man started running, and he doesn't remember hearing any screams. After getting separated from the other man, all he remembered was his pounding breath and the pain in his chest, the pain in his back and his legs. Then, still running, he saw the agents backlit on a nearby ridge holding binoculars to their faces, and he ducked down and pushed himself into the brush. "They didn't see me," he said. "I could see them, the agents, up on the ridge, about five of them, looking for me. There were trucks, too. I didn't move." It was almost dark. He pushed himself deeper into the scrub.

He was tired. Hurting. Scared. He couldn't move. He waited until the agents left and, he said to me, when I tried to get up again, I couldn't, I just couldn't, and so he hunkered back into his bush and finally, much later that night, almost into the morning, he got up, started walking, and at first he didn't know where he was going. He was in a daze—what had happened? What had he done? Why had he left the boy with the broken leg? Could he find him again?

He wandered, backtracking, looking for the boy, but nothing was familiar.

Eventually, Josiel walked back to Mexico, back across the line established in 1853 after the Gadsden Purchase shifted the border south from where it was drawn in 1848 in the Treaty of Guadalupe Hidalgo—the Treaty of Peace, Friendship, Limits, and Settlement—which officialized the US annexation of about half of Mexico.[1] It took Josiel almost four days to walk back across that line. He ate leaves, roots, anything he could find. He was almost dead, still walking, and then he was back on this side, or that side, the right or the wrong side of the border, depending on how you look at it.

The exact division between the two countries, on land that had been occupied and stolen from the O'odham, Apache, Pima, Jano, Cocopah, Maricopa, and other tribes in what would become the states known as Arizona and Sonora—the current split—was first marked by a series of stone cairns in the late nineteenth century, which were shifted and maneuvered one way and then the other by ranchers and prospectors seeking to maximize grazing land and mineral rights. The stone piles were eventually replaced by two hundred iron obelisks, costing $150 apiece, and placed along the 1,800-mile-long border, now marked by iron fences, vehicle barriers, surveillance towers, unidentified corpses, a US Air Force bombing range, open desert, and a river. "The region that was to become the US-Mexico borderlands was, in the 1800s," writes geographer Joseph Nevins, "a dynamic, multinational zone of fluid identities and porous and flexible social boundaries." No longer.

---

1   In the 1960s, groups led mostly by Hispanos (descendants of some of the original Spanish colonizers of New Mexico) led a fight to renegotiate the treaty, asking for a restoration of the land grants that were agreed upon in the mid-nineteenth century. Later, in 2018, a bill, H.R. 6365, was introduced into Congress to "establish the Treaty of Guadalupe Hidalgo Land Grant-Merced Claims Commission and other Federal policies for the restoration of land for hardships resulting from the incomplete and inequitable implementation" of the treaty.

As Rachel St. John puts it in her transnational history, *Line in the Sand*, "On the site of the western border there had simply been no there there before the Treaty of Guadalupe Hidalgo .... they drew a line across a map and conjured up an entirely new space where there had not been one before."

Josiel didn't know what happened to the kid with the broken leg. He didn't know what he was going to do next, either. We were squatting on the curb outside of the migrant aid shelter. He looked peaceful, tired, and very lost. His straight-brimmed Dodgers hat was pulled all the way down to his eyebrows, and I had to drop my head to look him in the eye.

One leaves their land, he explained to me, because of crime and poverty:

> In my land they pay me five dollars for a day of work. All day grunt-working without food. It's too little to pay rent, buy enough to eat—to survive. It's hard to cross the desert. One suffers a lot. You live through so much that nobody talks about, you can't understand it unless you live through it. If you break a leg and you can't walk and nobody is following you, you can do something, you can carry the person. But if somebody is chasing you, trying to catch you and you need to escape, and if your friend is hurt, like that kid who broke his leg—I wanted to help him, to carry him, but I didn't want them to catch me. It was hard for me to leave him lying there, to run away, because he's a human being, but, with all the pain in my soul, I had to leave him. I think he died. That's what I think really happened. I think he bled to death. There was too much blood coming out of his bone.

Josiel asked me to stop recording. He never wanted to have to make that decision. He wished he hadn't left the boy. He wished he hadn't done what he had done. "I wish . . ." he said—and then he didn't, or couldn't, finish the thought.

* * *

In the first two decades of the twenty-first century, the United States has spent more than $400 billion on immigration and border enforcement. In that same period, at least ten thousand people have died while attempting to cross the US–Mexico border (the actual number is likely two, three, or more times as high). Many have also died on their way toward the United States while traveling through Mexico and Central America, or trekking the jungle in the Darién Gap that divides South and Central America. Europe spends their own billions on border enforcement every year, and tens of thousands of migrants die on their way to its shores, drowning in the Mediterranean or succumbing to the desert, to bandits, or to the dust and jackals on earlier legs of the journey north through Africa. From 2005 to 2015, an estimated one hundred thousand migrants worldwide perished as they sought to cross a border. (What the subsequent ten-year tally will turn out to be is terrifying. Double or triple that number? Over a quarter million dead along the world's borderlines?)

"I crossed the border and I could feel it," a Salvadoran man told me about entering into the United States. "I was less human."

Why spend so much on a project of death and dehumanization? Proponents of immigration restrictions will tell you it is to safeguard the homeland, to maintain the integrity of the nation state, to upkeep sovereignty, to protect our own. "A country without borders is not a country at all," Donald Trump repeatedly said, echoing scores of others. But the more convincing formulation is the inverse: that a border without a nation is no border. It is the nation that provides the lights, the ushers, the bunting, and the curtain to put on the elaborate show of bordering. And a show is essential for a nation—it's what binds us in what Benedict Anderson has called "imagined communities"—the national link between distant and disparate citizens. The forged connection is why nations celebrate themselves in holidays, museums, textbooks, all the pomp and conversating in politics, media, and popular culture. Trump's familiar quip resembles a quotation commonly attributed to Ronald

Reagan: "A nation that cannot control its borders is not a nation." But what is control? Does control have to mean human filtering, detention, and killing?

"I just want my children to feel warm," Abu Yassin told me. "I don't want to lose them to the cold. I don't want anything except a house with windows that keeps out the cold and the wind." What is barring Abu Yassin from that house, from a home, is the border.

The borders that Josiel crossed, and crossed back, that blocked Abu Yassin and Shafa, are legal fictions. That is, they are not demarcated by landmarks or by clear cultural or linguistic distinction. It is a *Mauer im Kopf*, the term the East German Stasi officials once used—a "wall in the mind."

"If my dad was a different person, or a citizen, I think he would have received a different search," one young woman said of her father, who had disappeared into the same desert Josiel tried to cross.

Josiel's choice—his friend's life or his own chances—is not unique: humans living in the borderlands are forced to confront their own dehumanization, pushed to ignore the most basic pleas for humanity. Many who spend time in the world's borderlands are similarly morally cornered.

The enormous machine of the state, its antipathy and anxiety toward the other, its criminalization of basic acts of survival and humanity—of humans themselves—tears away at the good that civilization has afforded us. We don't act as we ought to act toward each other, we fail to act out of care and compassion toward each other not only because we fear the state but because the state has implanted its own fear into us: the fear of the other.

In 1951, the historian and philosopher Hannah Arendt—herself a Jewish German émigré to the US—wrote that what was unprecedented in the twentieth century was "not the loss of a home but the impossibility of finding a new one." In the twenty-first century, new precedents will be set on both counts: more people will lose their homes, and more people will have more difficulty finding new ones. The scale of uprootedness today is unlike anything humans have ever experienced. In 2023, nearly 110 million people, at least, have been forcibly displaced from their homes. And yet, the problem is not, and has never been, as Arendt identified, a lack of homes, but that the homes are out of reach—blocked by borders and immigration policing. At the same time, year by year, cross-border finance and trade increase. As of 2021, international trade accounts for over 50 percent of the global GDP, or nearly $50 trillion. How to solve the problem—the intentional disaster—of deracination, suffering, and the premature violent death of millions of migrants or those trapped behind borders?

One way is to open national borders and reenvision how to make life itself more accessible. It's hard to know what exactly would constitute a solution that is workable and fair—which are not always the same thing—but we have clear and abundant evidence for what is *not* working.

Increasingly imminent and realistic warnings predict that climate change will soon render huge tracts of the world uninhabitable. Despite that dire reality pressing in on us, the idea of open borders is consistently dismissed, the phrase itself becoming something of a slur, a sign of puerile idealism, political suicide.

Just one hundred years ago, for those who were not Asian, Irish, or poor, the United States effectively had open borders. The country had no walls. In fact, there were almost no border walls anywhere in the world. In the 1950s, the United States had effectively ended immigration imprisonment in the country.[2] As recently as 1984, as we've already seen, the conservative standard bearer, the *Wall Street Journal*, published an op-ed calling for a five-word amendment to the Constitution: "There shall be open borders." The *Journal* doesn't take the same position today. Instead, they call

---

2   Under the Trump administration, the number of immigrants locked into detention centers hit an all-time high of over fifty-five thousand people a day.

for "tightening asylum law," "stronger signals of deterrence," and "tighter border security."

"Most familiar to and accepted by people today is the right of states to control *entry*, a prerogative that has come to be understood as one of the quintessential features of sovereignty," writes sociologist John Torpey. But, Torpey explains, the expectation of national immigration controls is a recent phenomenon. Before World War I, "a German analyst of the international passport system was unable to muster any consensus for the view that states had an unequivocal right to bar foreigners from entry into their territory."

How soon we forget. When pundits, liberals, and conservatives decry or dismiss the call for open borders, do they know what they are decrying or dismissing? The other pole of the conversation—closed borders and draconian anti-immigration policing—is easier to imagine. Pro-border-wall jingoists, nationalists, and isolationists have sharply defined and publicized their vision: higher walls, militarized lockdowns, mass deportations, religious-based immigration bans.

But, as world populations are increasingly uprooted and increasingly mobile, the attempt to wall humans off is neither feasible in the long term, nor, in any term, humane.

To move, to be moved upon. To cross a border, to raise a border. Both actions call forth some of our most elemental passions. We move to survive. We defend our position. We migrate. We linger.

Through politics, through careful thought and action, the two positions are reconcilable.

TWENTY-ONE ARGUMENTS FOR OPEN BORDERS

"The right of locomotion; the right of migration; the right which belongs to no particular race, but belongs to all and all alike. It is the right you assert by staying here, and your fathers asserted by coming here. It is this great right that I assert for the Chinese and Japanese, and for all other varieties of men equally with yourselves, now and forever."

—Frederick Douglass, in 1869 speech, "On Composite Nationality"

"Of all the specific liberties which may come into our minds when we hear the word 'freedom,' freedom of movement is historically the oldest and also the most elementary."

—Hannah Arendt

1. Borders have not always been
2. Immigrants Don't Steal Jobs—They Create Them
3. Immigrants Don't Drain Government Coffers
4. Borders Don't Stop Crime and Violence; They Engender Crime and Violence
5. Immigrants Don't Threaten Communities; They Revitalize Them
6. Migrants Rejuvenate
7. Open Borders Doesn't Mean a Rush to Migrate
8. The Nonsense of Nationalism
9. Closed Borders Are Unethical
10. Brain Drain Ain't a Thing

Most arguments for open borders begin by addressing counterarguments, trying to assuage fears of overcrowding, overrun public services, tanking economies, or generalized chaos. It's important work to do, as careful counterarguments easily deflate nativist fearmongering. However, the case for open borders must ultimately be a positive one, explaining why the freedom to move—coupled with the freedom and possibility to remain—is a necessary good, and why a world *not* divided into exclusive nation states with militarized borders would be more egalitarian, would promote and cultivate diversity instead of fear, and would help form a world where sustainability and justice take precedence over extraction and exploitation.

When we open borders, there won't be an overwhelming influx of migrants, wages won't plummet, there won't be a paralyzing run on government services, and crime won't increase. All true—but policies are rarely won by defining what they won't do. In fact, allaying imagined fears can, paradoxically, solidify them. As Harsha Walia notes, "All movements need an anchor in a shared positive vision, not a homogeneous or exact or perfect condition, but one that will nonetheless dismantle hierarchies, disarm concentrations of power, guide just relations, and nurture individual autonomy alongside collective responsibility."

Why is the fundamental right of movement lagging, even back-sliding, throughout the world? Why do states decry and prosecute impingements on the right to free speech, the free press, or the right to freedom from government oppression throughout the world, and yet so enthusiastically impinge on the right to free movement? Is the right to freedom of movement somehow different from the right to free speech, or the right to liberty? Why is the fundamental right to leave your country enshrined in the UN Declaration of Human Rights, but not the right to enter another country? In a world (almost) completely carved into nation states, the right to leave is only a half right without the concomitant right to enter.

Unauthorized migration, whether it is asylum seekers fleeing for their lives or the poor for better opportunity, should be understood as a radical political act. It is an individual act, and often driven by necessity, but it is also an affront and subversion of a violent system of colonial subordination. Colonizers in the United States saw themselves, and were celebrated, as subjects bucking oppressive rule. Today's migrants, exercising their fundamental right of mobility, are migrating in a much more peaceful manner than the settlers and colonizers of yore. Today's migrants are not threats to freedom, but much-needed threats to a global system of oppression. In their mere movement, they are freedom fighters.

Just as courageous activists sat at lunch counters, stood down tanks, refused to pick up weapons, or raised their voices against and toppled oppressive institutions, it is time to call forth such courage and turn the system of closed borders into a relic of backwardness, to shove it into history's dustbin.

Opening borders is possible. We just need to find out how to get there. A necessary step toward guaranteeing and exercising the right to free movement includes understanding its implications and promises. Below is a short and far from exhaustive list of some of the simple arguments about why open borders would be an economic, environmental, and ethical boon.

1. Borders Have Not Always Been

In the nineteenth-century United States, many couldn't imagine beyond the strictures of slavery, with even most abolitionists advocating to let the "peculiar" institution wither into history. The problem with the gradual lapse of slavery, however, was that even as the abolition movement grew, slavery, in what would be its dying years, became both more entrenched and more profitable. Slavery-driven cotton production and cotton exports in the South nearly doubled during the 1850s. The market value of an enslaved person increased from around $1,000 in 1850 to $2,250 by 1860—more than a 100 percent leap in ten years. Then, by the middle of the next decade, slavery was legally abolished.

To get a sense of the moral certainty and presumed durability of slavery—even in its last years—consider a few lines of this 1860 editorial from the *Atlanta Confederacy*: "We regard every man in our midst an enemy to the institutions of the South, who does not boldly declare that he believes African slavery to be a social, moral, and political blessing." If a man didn't declare slavery to be such a blessing, the editorial continued, he "should be requested to leave the country."

The political volte-face came five years later, upending an entrenched status quo and profoundly altering the lives of millions of people. (Of course, slavery was effectively reinstituted in different forms in subsequent years.) Radical change may seem a distant dream, but all political institutions are constructs only kept functioning by concerted human will and bureaucratic inertia. Redirect or nix that will, dismantle the bureaucracy, and the institutions, one day to the next, may come tumbling down. In the open space, in the sunlight, new and more just institutions can be built. "No one in the twelfth century foresaw capitalism," Jacqueline Stevens writes. "Naysayers in the sphere of social change, those who extrapolate the future from the present, are the ones whom history has repeatedly defeated."

Today, perhaps only support for late-stage capitalism stands as more of a mainstream given, practically a shibboleth, than support for border restrictions. Ironically, borders also hark back to capital's predecessor—feudalism—in that they divide and deny based merely on the happenstance of birth.

Some scholars see nations' push to close and hypermilitarize borders over the last decades as a last-gasp effort to restore the slipping grip of nationalism. As political theorist Wendy Brown writes, "Walls do not merely index, but accelerate waning state sovereignty: they blur the policing and military functions of states; they generate new vigilantisms at borders; they expand the transnationalist identifications that in turn spur demands for greater exercises of state sovereignty, more effective walling, and less flexibility in responding to globalization's vicissitudes and volatilities." As global trade and connectivity continue to increase, as climate change pushes people from their homes, walled-off nations are dead-duck efforts to hoard increasingly diffuse geopolitical power.

Historically speaking, closed borders are still in short pants. For the first century of the United States' existence, there were zero federal immigration laws, and there were no substantial fences or walls along the US–Mexico border until the late 1990s. Immigration scholar Reece Jones calculates that as recently as 1990 there were only fifteen international border walls throughout the world. That number today is in the eighties. But change works in both directions, and the number may soon fall back to fifteen, or to zero.

Borders haven't always been. And they certainly haven't always been as they are now—militarized zones where human beings are stripped of their rights merely for crossing an imaginary line. Nor will borders, as they are now, always be.

2. Immigrants Don't Steal Jobs—They Create Them

Economic studies across the political spectrum tell us that immigrants create more jobs than they take, and that the ones they do snag are essential for the basic functioning of much of Western society. A US Department of Labor study conducted under the Bush administration noted that the perception that immigrants take native jobs is "the most persistent fallacy about immigration in popular thought." A comprehensive 2016 report from Cornell University found that migration resulted in "little to no negative effects on overall wages and employment of native-born workers in the longer term."

Much of the confusion comes from the "lump of labor" fallacy, which the Cato Institute defines as the "fundamental misconception that there is a fixed amount of work in a society." As economist Jonathan Portes explains, "It's true that, if an immigrant takes a job, then a British worker can't take that job—but it doesn't mean he or she won't find another one that may have been created, directly or indirectly, as a result of immigration."

British Revenue and Customs figures show that from 2013 to 2014, recent arrivals to the UK paid £2.54 billion more in income tax and national insurance than they received in tax credits or child benefits. The UK's Office of Budget Responsibility has estimated that migrants' labor contribution is helping to grow the economy by an additional 0.6 percent a year. That economic growth equals more jobs all around.

No matter which way you crack it or where you conduct your study, migrants boost labor markets. Even in times of downturn or crisis, migrant workers remain critical in keeping economies revving. Shortly after the 1929 stock market crash, the United States launched the Mexican Repatriation Act, in which as many as two million people were deported from the United States, many of them US citizens. The logic was that jobs were scarce, and getting rid of a big chunk of the labor supply would help. Studies later showed, however, that, especially in rural areas from which a lot of Mexicans and Mexican Americans were deported, wages for natives actually decreased. Production levels also went down, farmers struggled with harvests, and shops had fewer patrons. As one labor economist noted, each migrant farmworker "creates three jobs in the surrounding economy—in equipment and sales and processing and packaging."

During the COVID-19 pandemic, a congressional study concluded that "foreign-born workers are key contributors to the US economy, making up more than 17 percent of the labor force and creating about one-fourth of new businesses." Immigrants, that is, provide the labor power and innovation that fuels economic growth, working in both service sector jobs and in health care and research.[1]

In 2021, the Center for Migration Studies counted that 19.8 million foreign-born workers qualified as essential workers (69 percent of all such immigrant workers), which is a higher percentage than native-born workers. These foreign-born workers are also overrepresented in key occupations in health care and the food supply chain. The same congressional report found that immigrants make up 22 percent of all workers in the US food supply chain, even though they comprise only 17 percent of the labor force. A separate study found that young Hispanic males work more than native born men of the same age.

According to the Migration Policy Institute, foreign-born workers are even more concentrated in specific areas of the supply chain, comprising more than three in ten workers in agriculture, crop production, meat processing, and commercial bakeries. Among agricultural laborers, graders, and sorters, the share of foreign-born workers is over half. In California alone, immigrants make up 69 percent of the state's agricultural workers. In Alaska, immigrants constitute 70 percent of the seafood processing workers, and in

---

1   Notably, it was a Turkish couple who migrated to Germany who invented the Pfizer vaccine for COVID-19.

Nebraska 66 percent of the meat-processing workers are immigrants. Many of them are undocumented, pay into the welfare pot far more than they can take out, and are ostracized and sometimes hunted down and deported as they work jobs essential to the basic functioning of society.[2] In short, the economy, as well as food production and health care systems—in the United States and elsewhere—*existentially* depends on migrants.

And those essential jobs the immigrants are working beget more jobs—which, as long as labor rights are upheld, can be good for everyone.

3. Immigrants Don't Drain Government Coffers

In 2016, immigrants contributed an estimated $2 trillion to the US GDP. Two years later, economists tabulated that immigrants added over $450 billion to state, local, and federal taxes. The same year, immigrants wielded more than $1.2 trillion in spending power in the United States, by which they purchased groceries, clothes, cars, homes, appliances, and all sorts of useful and useless goods from both local and big businesses. Meanwhile, proposed cuts to US legal immigration, economists estimate, could tank the GDP by 2 percent over twenty years, shrink growth by over 12 percent, and flush more than 4.5 million jobs. American Rust Belt states would be hit particularly hard, as they rely on immigration to stabilize populations and revive economies.

For all they pour in, immigrants can't collect on a lot of public services and tend to use the ones to which they do have access much less than natives. For instance, according to a 2015 study, immigrants use emergency room services at half the rate of native residents.

---

2   According to a withering 2023 investigation from *The New York Times*, many of them are also children, too young to legally work but nonetheless toiling away—and sometimes even dying on the job—at major American companies.

In the UK, one study calculated that the average European migrant arriving to the UK will contribute £78,000 more than they take out in public services and benefits. The average non-European migrant will make a positive net contribution of £28,000 while living in the UK. The average UK citizen, meanwhile, takes out about as much as they pay in across their lifetime.

Such studies repeat themselves across the globe. In the United States, authorized migrants have to pay into the welfare system for *at least five years* before they can draw any benefits. Studies have estimated that migrants to the United States pay tens of billions more in payroll taxes than they receive in social security benefits. Unauthorized migrants, meanwhile, almost exclusively pay into the pot—unable to draw much of anything out.

As *Wall Street Journal* editorial board member Jason Riley poses: "What does it mean to cite welfare costs as a reason to restrict immigration? Those who do are suggesting that a person's worth to society is nothing more than the sum of his tax payments. By that standard, however, most natives are 'worthless,' since some 60 percent collect more in government services than they pay in taxes."

Native residents don't have to guard their wallets because of migration. Immigrants don't hurt the economy, though they are often hurt *by* the economy.

4. Borders Don't Stop Crime and Violence; They Engender Crime and Violence

In 1917, as some of the first lengths of wall and fence were being raised along the US–Mexico border, and as emergency measures were put in place to limit migration, a new law increased the head tax at the border to eight dollars (equivalent to $162 today) and, for the first time, expanded the tax to Mexican citizens. As Reece Jones notes, "[T]he result was the emergence of smuggling networks, which would take people across the border for half that amount, saving the laborers money." For over a century, increased immigration enforcement and border militarization have led to expanded and more profitable smuggling networks. Prohibitions against drugs (including alcohol) and anti-immigration crackdowns created the ultraviolent transnational paramilitary networks (or cartels) that have plagued large parts of Mexico, Central and South America, and border regions throughout the hemisphere for decades. State forces and politicians criminalize drugs and migration even as they back and create criminal networks (which traffic drugs and migrants), accept bribes, and contribute to a spiral of violence that has, in Mexico alone in the last twenty years, resulted in the deaths of nearly half a million people and the disappearance of almost one hundred thousand more. The border has not kept the crisis at bay; it has helped create it.

In 1994, just over five thousand noncitizens were held in US federal prisons. By 2011, over 30 percent of all federal prison sentences were for immigration violations alone. Arrests of noncitizens for immigration offenses rose 440 percent from 1998 to 2018—from 19,556 a year to 105,748 people locked behind bars because they moved. This was a policy choice. These migrants don't have to be criminalized and imprisoned. We can eliminate these "crimes" by simply not deeming them crimes. (Recall that immigrants commit violent crimes at far lower rates than natives.)

Legalizing migration and drugs would—overnight—eliminate nearly all the profits on which transnational criminal groups rely and free up the piggish immigration and drug-enforcement budgets to address the root causes of addiction and forced migration.

In 1925, as historian Rachel St. John reports, the head of the Los Angeles Immigration District explained, "each added restrictive measure increased the incentive to illegal entry and to smuggling."

That tight relationship between restriction and illegal profiteering extends throughout history and throughout the world, with criminal networks, human traffickers, and corrupt politicians gaining power and enacting violence as they navigate and make use of borders to plunder, upsell, exploit, and stash the pickings.

The rich, meanwhile, cross borders at their leisure. Just glance at the footloose escapades of the super-wealthy, or the multiplying financial scandals of opulent globetrotters parking their stores of loot practically wherever they please—jurisdiction shopping, as it's known—in order to avoid paying taxes. Journalist Atossa Araxia Abrahamian notes that "ultra-high-net-worth individuals" need nation states with closed borders to dodge taxes and keep their money "encased and concealed." In other words, the border system works both ways: it criminalizes migrants and spurs violence among the poor at the same time as it protects the criminal activity of the rich.

Borders also foment crime among their defenders, as border enforcement agencies around the world are some of the most opaque and abusive agencies operating today. In the United States, hundreds of Border Patrol agents are arrested every year for crimes and corruption. The arrest rate within the ranks of Customs and Border Protection is 0.5 percent of the overall force of about sixty thousand people, which may seem small but is five times higher than the arrest rate for any other federal law enforcement agency. CBP officers also use excessive force, threaten, and sexually abuse those they detain at a higher rate than other law enforcement agencies. And they are rarely held responsible for any of it. Frequently operating in the far reaches of the desert and outside of public view, Border Patrol culture can be summed up, as one whistleblower put it to me, "kick ass and ask questions later." (Those questions are hardly ever asked.)

In the EU, agents of the European Border and Coast Guard Agency, known as Frontex, don dark clothes and beat, render, and disappear migrants. In 2021, *Der Spiegel* reported on Europe's "violent shadow army" that was beating up refugees and pushing their boats back to sea. Journalists captured a pack of over twenty men guarding the border with Croatia who began beating a group of migrants with clubs and yelling at them to "Go! Go to Bosnia!" The thuggish shadow army receives indirect funding—filtered through the national governments—from the European Commission. In

2015, I reported on Mexican border agents basically using Central American migrants riding on a northbound train for target practice—killing one Honduran teenager. It is such heinous acts, not the peaceful crossing of concocted border lines or the "crime" of a family moving toward safety, that constitute the actual threat to society.

5. Immigrants Don't Threaten Communities; They Revitalize Them

When migrants arrive to a community, crime rates drop, property values jump, and neighborhoods get a shot of cultural energy and economic vitality. There are exceptions, of course, and xenophobes have made much hay out of particular cases when, for example, an unauthorized migrant commits a violent crime. After the 9/11 attacks, the United States specifically targeted and criminalized Muslim migrants, reframing immigration as a national security issue. But of the 180 people arrested for plotting terrorist attacks in the United States in the two decades following 9/11, only four were found to have illegally crossed US borders. Three crossed the US–Mexico border, but when they were children younger than five—one wasn't even a year old. Their radicalization (though they did not commit any actual attacks) took place *in* the United States. No one has ever been killed in a terrorist attack on US soil by anyone who illegally crossed the US–Mexico border.

One study calculated the chance of an American being killed in a terrorist attack by a refugee is about 1 in 3.86 billion.[3]

It's not just about national security, but neighborhood security as well: researchers found that first-generation Mexican

---

3   More protection is generally needed within the state, and even from the
    state, than from people crossing state borders. As Rudolph J. Rummel
    calculates in *Death by Government*, in the twentieth century, there were
    35 million direct victims of wars between states, while 165 to 170 million
    people were massacred by their own states.

immigrants are 45 percent less likely to commit a violent offense than third-generation Americans. "For every ethnic group without exception," write Rubén Rumbaut and Walter Ewing in a 2007 study that has been replicated many times since, "incarceration rates among young men are lowest for immigrants, even those who are the least educated." According to the same study, even while the undocumented population in the United States doubled from 1994 to 2007, the violent crime rate declined 34.2 percent—and the property crime rate dropped 26.4 percent. Since 2007, the undocumented population has gone down, and crime has inched back up. A 2021 *Axios* study found that while crime rates shot up in many cities throughout the country, violent crime rates in eleven of the largest communities along the US–Mexico border stayed below the national average. A 2018 study in the journal *Criminology* found that "increases in the undocumented immigrant population within states are associated with significant decreases in the prevalence of violence."

The pattern holds in Europe. One study found that when workers from Eastern European states came to the UK, the impact on crime was minimal. (Some research, however, does indicate that the increase in asylum seekers to the UK in the 1990s—mainly from war-torn Middle Eastern countries—coincided with a slight increase in the total number of property crimes. Causation in this research is not clear, and some speculate that the rise in property crime had to do with lower employment rates for immigrants.)

A study in Germany found no "evidence for a systematic link between the scale of refugee immigration and the risk of Germans becoming victims of a crime in which refugees are suspects." A 2015 report, also from Germany, found that on average, refugees commit just as many crimes as the local population. Despite a relatively large influx of refugees to Germany in 2014 and 2015—and despite high profile stories about refugees committing crimes—by 2018, when the number of refugees in Germany was at a record high, the crime rate in Germany was at its lowest level since 1992.

6. Migrants Rejuvenate

Many US cities—St. Louis, Detroit, Philadelphia, Cleveland, Baltimore, Buffalo, New Orleans, Pittsburgh, Newark, Milwaukee—have been emptying out in recent decades. In his book *One Billion Americans*, journalist Matthew Yglesias calls for *re*populating the "hard-core depopulation belt composing about a third of rural counties that currently have fewer residents than they had in 1950." These cities, suburbs, and rural areas could use new workers, more taxpayers, and the revitalizing spirit immigrants bring everywhere they go.

Not only does the United States need more migrants—the current US fertility rate is below the number of births per woman needed to maintain a steady population—but it has more than enough room to welcome them. With an average of 86 people per square mile, the United States is far less densely populated than many other countries throughout the world. And only about 5 percent of US land is developed. The country could quadruple the population and still be less dense than France. The country also has enough essential resources to provide a growing population.

The United States provides 8,800 cubic meters of freshwater per person. If the US population tripled, the country would still provide 2,900. For comparison, Spain only has 2,400 cubic meters of freshwater per person; the UK has 2,200; Germany has 1,300; and the Netherlands has 650. It's harder to calculate the total amount of water wasted, but in the United States alone, it's easily over 1 trillion gallons a year. Despite worrying droughts and unconscionable waste, there remains—if we are mindful—water enough.

The real problem with resources or services isn't that migrants are consuming them but that much of the world wastes so damn much. The best estimate is that Americans waste between 30 and 40 percent of the food supply, or over one hundred billion pounds of food every single year. Other nations in the global North don't do quite as badly, but they still throw out food by the billions of tons.

None of this is to promise unwavering homogeneity. If more migrants came, your city would change, but that's what cities do. In 1920, New York City's population was 44 percent immigrant. The same year, Cleveland was 41 percent immigrant. (Today those numbers are about 36 and 6 percent, respectively.) Those cities thrived in subsequent decades, and when people today pine for those cities' heydays, they are pining for immigrant cities.

7. Open Borders Doesn't Mean a Rush to Migrate

Across the globe, about 14 percent of the global population—around seven hundred million people—would, according to recent Gallup polls, like to migrate. Financial burdens, family ties, and fear of the unknown, however, keep a lot of them at home. Plus, many of those potential migrants wouldn't migrate in the same direction. Despite the lure of the Hollywood-baked American dream and economic and political pressures in "sending countries," most people want to stay at home.

Puerto Ricans have enjoyed the unimpeded right to migrate to the far wealthier mainland United States since 1904, but they haven't left the island empty. Similarly, Eastern European countries added to the EU free-migration zone did not swarm Western European countries with their citizens. Absent lethal climactic or political threats, most people tend to want to stay where they are.

Despite the United States being the top desired destination country, according to a recent Gallup poll, its total potential population gain—if borders were opened and respondents to the poll actually followed through—would be far below a number of other countries, including Singapore, New Zealand, Saudi Arabia, Canada, and Australia. And while 31 percent of sub-Saharan Africans said they would like to migrate, 21 percent of European Union citizens responded similarly. Twenty-seven percent of Europeans outside the EU also claimed they wanted to migrate. Migration is not a one-way street but a back-and-forth shuffle. (Walls and strict immigration enforcement are partially changing that, turning would-be temporary migrants into permanent and precarious denizens.)

A recent study of Central Americans who participated in a poll asking whether or not they want to migrate to the United States found that only 3 percent of those who responded positively actually made preparations to head north. (It is unclear how many, in the end, ventured from their homes.) This means, if we return to the polls cited above of total potential migrants worldwide, probably only about twenty-one million of those seven hundred million people who want to migrate actually would, which is a much more absorbable quantity, especially when spread throughout receiving countries. And even given that the closed-border regime may have convinced many of those people to stay at home—and some of them may, with open borders, venture forth—migration is still expensive and uprooting, and many people don't want to leave their homes, jobs, families, language, and community.

8. The Nonsense of Nationalism

The modern concept of sovereignty is based on the idea of collective self-rule: that a nation of people has the authority to determine how they will be organized and governed, as well as who can be a member of the sovereign body. According to the International Covenant on Civil and Political Rights, a United Nations resolution signed and ratified by almost every country on earth, "All peoples have the right of self-determination." It's frequently assumed that such self-determination includes the right to exclude. That presumed right, however, especially in regard to forcibly displaced people, bars migrants from their own self-determination. If people are pushed out of one place and denied access to another, their self-determination is reduced to a figment.

And the manner in which most populations have gained the power to exercise such self-determination is by violently wresting it from others, namely the Indigenous or natives. The call for national self-determination thus typically turns out to be a euphemism for something much more pernicious: class- and race-based domination and oppression.

And yet, political thinkers and ethicists have long leaned on this problematic crutch of national self-determination to advocate for closed borders. Much-cited political theorist Michael Walzer claimed that nations must maintain a "community of character," and thus be allowed to deny entry to migrants. Otherwise, he fears, citizens will become "radically deracinated" from their territory and culture. Sarah Song, in her book, *Immigration and Democracy*, similarly claimed that "the right to control immigration derives from the right of the *demos* to rule itself."

But the "character" of those violently forged communities—nation states—is typically formed by oppressive majority rule: those in power dehumanizing and killing the Indigenous and minorities, forcibly assimilating intractable subjects, or establishing an *esprit national* through erasure and selective historical celebration and mythical heroization. There is little more nationalistically binding than a shared antagonist. As Georgy Arbatov, policy advisor and Soviet representative in the United States, put it in 1987: "This time we will deal you a fatal blow by depriving you of an enemy."

So to deny entrance to migrants in order to determine the character of a nation is to forge ethnically exclusive states. And if it's character change you fear, there are more responsible targets than immigrants. As journalist Jeremy Harding points out in *Border Vigils*, it would take decades of immigration to "bring about the degree of 'cultural difference' that such a bad patch of international trading, a brisk downsizing, or a decision by a large corporation to start outsourcing can inject into a social landscape in a year."

Another problem with relying on the concept of national self-determination to drive immigration policies is that it's a slippery slope. If you can determine who is let in, what is to stop a country from determining who must be put out, or banished? Or, as legal scholar

Ilya Somin writes, the right of national self-determination "would imply the power to coerce even currently existing residents to keep them from changing their cultural practices." If the majority or ruling party is permitted to determine that a culture or demographic sector be static, what impositions might they levy against current residents? Could laws be passed to restrict how people talk, act, celebrate, make or engage with art, how many children they have? Such regulations would certainly be nationally deterministic.

The reality is that humans don't group into tidy and geographically distinguishable communities. Rather, we all bear multiple identities and cycle through various overlapping communities. The actual borders of the United States do not trace neatly onto the legal territory of the United States, nor France onto territorial France, nor China on China. Rather, the United States has outsourced its border-enforcement regime to Mexico, Central America, and elsewhere, reaching far beyond its territory with economic and cultural breaches, thus extending its effective borders beyond the standard logo map. As legal scholar E. Tendayi Achiume puts it, such imperial overreach extra-territorializes "the demos beyond nation-state borders such that its boundaries are contiguous with those of neocolonial empire." The national self-determination of the United States, in other words—through martial, cultural, and economic conquest—determined the character of many foreign communities. Even within the United States, sovereignty waxes and wanes, and culture dramatically morphs from location to location.

To submit to the hoky fiction of national self-determination is to open the door to government imposition and control, laying out the mat to the thought or culture police.

9. Closed Borders Are Unethical

In *The Ethics of Immigration*, political theorist Joseph Carens writes that birthright privileges, or *jus solis*—unearned preferential access to wealth, freedom, quality health care, and myriad other benefits—are akin to feudal class privileges, in that they grant "great advantages on the basis of birth but also entrench these advantages by legally restricting mobility, making it extremely difficult for those born into a socially disadvantaged position to overcome that disadvantage, no matter how talented they are or how hard they work."

We are all dependent on others, and that dependency today bleeds across borderlines. We all have developed into who we are, as both individuals and communities, because of this interdependence. As such—so goes the ethical argument—we are morally obligated to show compassion and offer care to each other. Closed borders interrupt this reciprocal nature of care and mutual responsibility. Politicians and nativists (as well as "the border" itself, which takes on its own weight and influence) dissuade people from caring for the other, induce fears of consequence for expressing or extending such care, and create conditions that make it impossible to care.

Besides bestowing or withholding privileges and interrupting reciprocity, closed borders also dehumanize people, make them suffer, and kill them. Closed borders subject some people, based on where they were born and what visas or passports they are granted, to prolonged detention, torture, isolation, removal from family, and deportation—all for an act that is quintessentially human: moving toward safety, freedom, or opportunity. It is hard to see an iota of ethics in such a setup.

As British philosopher Maurice Cranston has it:

> One of the things that is meant by saying that men have a natural right to freedom of movement is to assert that the desire to move is a natural, universal, and reasonable one; and hence that it is not so much a man's desire to move that needs to be justified as any attempt to frustrate the satisfaction of that desire.

The justifications, however, fall short.

Consider how 9-1-1 calls are handled in the wilderness of the US Southwestern borderlands. The humanitarian aid organization

No More Deaths has extensively documented how emergency response to presumed citizens who call 9-1-1 when they are lost or in distress in the desert is rapid, robust, and usually results in rescue. When the emergency call comes from a suspected noncitizen or recent border crosser, however, there is typically no response. If any agency reacts to an emergency distress call from a noncitizen, it is the Border Patrol, the same people charged with hunting down border crossers and whose response often amounts to little or no medical treatment—even when desperately needed—and a swift deportation.[4]

The same applies in the Mediterranean, where despite the ancient and revered practice of rescue at sea, as well as long-established maritime law that obligates nearby ships to respond to distress calls, SOS calls from migrant rafts or boats are routinely ignored. And when some people do respond and try to rescue migrants adrift at sea, they are sometimes prosecuted as human smugglers. As these examples show, when it comes to the tradition of the Good Samaritan, migrants are officially exempt.

How is it that we can so readily turn our backs on fellow humans in desperate need? No More Deaths, for whom I have been

---

4   In northern Mexico, I interviewed and spent a long afternoon with a man who, after living for almost four decades in Los Angeles, where his whole family still resided, tried crossing the desert to reunite with them after being caught up in an immigration raid. He was caught by the Border Patrol, pushed into the back of a truck ("dog-catchers," they sometimes call them), where, after the truck slipped off the road and flipped, the man broke his back—luckily avoiding serious spinal damage. Border Patrol agents gave him a back brace and a bottle of pain pills, and then swiftly deported him. I remember him shaking his pill bottle like a maraca, somehow finding the strength to joke about the pain waiting for him after he'd swallow the last of the pills. Less than a week later, still planning his next move, he died. The cause of death was deemed a heart attack, though it's hard to imagine the stress and the recent severe injury weren't a factor. I spoke with his daughter in LA a few days later: she wanted to hear about her father's last days. I didn't have much to report, but explained that despite his intense pain and confusion, he was exceedingly polite with me, and that he lamented the fact that he had no money treat me to a Coke.

a volunteer, has also extensively documented Border Patrol agents and anti-immigrant zealots dumping out, shooting, stabbing, or poisoning water bottles left for migrants, many of whom die of dehydration in this same crossing corridor. The *nonresponse* may come from "motives of policy, rather than from a hardened nature, or from innate brutality," as Frederick Douglass explained the cruel acts committed by a slaveholder. It is the policy (in this case closed borders) that drives the malice.

Much of the world, since Douglass's time, has learned that racism is an unmitigated evil, and yet many still openly embrace or excuse dehumanizing and deadly discrimination based on birth location. Further examples of the incalculable harms of that discrimination abound, but here's one stat that drives it home with particular force: in 2012, under the Obama administration, the parents of around 150,000 US-citizen children were deported. Many of those parents were handcuffed and removed in front of their children. Whatever the reason they were unauthorized to be in the country (which is a civil, not a criminal offense) the cruelty and lasting generational trauma inflicted by such arrests and deportations is undeniable. Such are the miseries the border drives into people, the pain it draws—loss, deprivation, imprisonment—as punishment for seeking life, security, dignity.

Historian Roxanne Dunbar-Ortiz asks a pointed question about the asymmetry of ethics between the state and migrants: given that "the United States has not acted lawfully with other nations, including the Native American nations on its soil, through most of the nineteenth and twentieth centuries. . . how can it now expect the human victims of that enormous illegality to obey the laws of the United States and stay home or wait thirty years for a visa to rejoin their families?" Her answer is "reparations or migration: choose."

(Both is also an option.)

10. Brain Drain Ain't a Thing

"Brain Drain" is the false assumption that there is a fixed and limited amount of "skilled" labor, and therefore that professionals from poorer countries should not be allowed to migrate.

Those who assume that the emigration of doctors and nurses harms countries with underdeveloped health systems fail to consider the impact of other factors unrelated to migration—such as the lack of medical resources, low wages for public health workers, paltry education, or little promise of career advancement—all of which both hold back access to adequate care and push workers to seek opportunity elsewhere. Many studies have shown that skilled emigration does not slow down economic growth (or higher-quality care in terms of public health) but, on the contrary, speeds it up.

A 2015 study on physicians who migrated from Romania found that more than half of the participants "collaborated with the country of origin during their stay abroad." As researcher Linda Semu summarized, "We need to view migration not in terms of brain drain or brain gain, but in terms of brain circulation that allows for exchange of knowledge and experience between places of origin and places of residence."

Meanwhile, "brain drain" certainly exists *within* countries, including the United States, as rural medical workers can't find jobs in their home counties and flock to the cities. For the same reasons, Nairobi, the largest city of Kenya, is home to just 8 percent of Kenya's population but 66 percent of its physicians. As serious as the issue is, such rural-to-urban skilled migration goes largely uncriticized.

Many skilled migrants who were "drained" away from their countries of origin return with newly acquired education and experience, as well as money. One study shows that "a 10 percent increase in the proportion of a nation's population that emigrates leads to a 2 percent decline in the proportion of people living on less than $1 per day." The same study found that a "10 percent increase in remittances is sufficient to reduce a country's poverty rate by 3.5 percent." Remittances currently make up 29 percent of Haiti's GDP and 17 percent of El Salvador's—to name two countries that heavily rely on their compatriots abroad. Halting "brain drain" would devastate both of these economies.

Remittances, of course, aren't the only means by which a skilled or "unskilled" immigrant can help their country of origin. Professional migrants of all skill levels form networks abroad that create opportunities for those remaining at home, as well as help foster the trade of technology, ideas, goods, and services.

And if we were to forbid migration for the good of the home or sending community, what would stop us from forbidding native professionals from merely changing careers? Could we forbid nurses, for example, from leaving their profession and taking up novel writing or landscaping for fear of a shortage of health care workers?

"The brains in question," as Ilya Somin puts it, "do not belong to the government."

11. The Libertarian Case

Libertarians have their idiomatic vision of open borders—based on letting people engage in free and mutually consensual activity, wherever that may be. Theirs is an appealing case (though it may come packaged along with other less palatable policies) for anyone interested in protecting basic individual freedoms.

The line of thinking also questions the distinction between migration within national borders and migration across them: Why is internal migration readily allowed and international migration subject to apoplectic crackdown?

As capital is allowed to freely flow, libertarians argue, people should be allowed the same.

Libertarian philosopher Robert Nozick argues for a minimal state whose only legitimate function is the protection of people's natural rights. Barring migration, thus, is not within the state's bailiwick. "Individuals have the right to enter into voluntary exchanges with other individuals," Joseph Carens writes. "They possess this right as individuals, not as citizens." If an American farmer wants to contract a Mexican laborer, the thinking goes, the government shouldn't intervene in this voluntary and mutually beneficial agreement.

Border checkpoints, whether at the borderline or in the interior of the country, which slow down, stop, and regularly inspect both citizens and noncitizens are a point of particular ire for libertarians.

Eminent domain is also a clear violation of libertarian principles: the government taking people's property by force to impose a major infrastructure project, a move that has been used to construct border walls from Texas to Poland. Border enforcement and immigration restrictions are major and invasive impediments to individual liberties, no matter what side of the line you are on.

Libertarians, however, also claim that our obligation to strangers is minimal, amounting to little more than leaving them alone (a dubious presumption, in my view). Denying strangers the freedom to migrate violates that *laissez faire et laissez passer* (let be and let pass) obligation. As Jason Riley summarizes: "No self-respecting free-market adherent would ever dream of supporting laws that interrupt the free movement of goods and services across borders." Nor should they, then, dream of interrupting the free movement of people.

12. Dehumanizing Border Machinery Targets Native Residents Too

The technology of borders is not exclusive to the borderlands. The US Border Patrol has been deployed against uprisings from Los Angeles to Portland to Miami, with agents roaming Amtrak trains and inspecting Greyhound buses, flying helicopters over the Super Bowl, and buzzing drones over protests in the Dakotas.

Between 2017 and 2019, Border Patrol's secretive Tactical Terrorism Response Teams detained and interrogated more than six hundred thousand travelers—about a third of them US citizens. Besides invasive tech surveillance, the increasing use of interior checkpoints in the United States has also shifted the target from noncitizens to just about everybody, though particularly to people of color.

Arivaca, a small town in southern Arizona, suffered the installation of two Border Patrol checkpoints blocking the only exits from town. A local watchdog organization, People Helping People, noted that the agency engaged in a pattern of racial profiling of Latino motorists at the Arivaca Road checkpoint. Their study found white drivers passed through the checkpoint almost ten times more than nonwhite drivers, though white drivers were rarely asked to show identification or stopped for further inspection. Overall, approximately 16 percent of Latino drivers had to show identification—for merely driving down the road—while only 0.6 percent of white-occupied vehicles had to, meaning that Latinos were scrutinized twenty-six times more frequently than whites. There are nearly two hundred such checkpoints throughout the US Southwest, and similar tales of discrimination, harassment, and abuse prevail.

Such internal policing is not limited to the United States. In 2019, Mexican immigration authorities faced severe criticism when agents attacked four Indigenous Mexican citizens, accusing them of being migrants, beating, and even tasing one young Tzeltal Maya man (a Mexican citizen) and forcing him to sign a deportation document that falsely stated that he was Guatemalan. In 2022, Mexico's Supreme Court ruled immigration checks on buses racist and discriminatory, and therefore unconstitutional, though the practice continues.

In Kenya, citizens have been placed under biometric surveillance and sent to refugee camps in their own country. And in North Korea, border guards have shot residents crossing into the Chinese–North Korean border's "buffer zones"—spaces over a kilometer from the border lockdown line, where guards are ordered to open fire on anyone who enters. In one incident border guards shot and killed a resident who had trailed after his escaped goat.

Border guards the world over are looking to obtain and maintain "full operational control" of the ever-expanding borderlands. The danger, for all of us, is that the border is inching ever closer and ever deeper into our daily lives (and "inch" is not an adequate verb to capture the pace of the threat). Ankle bracelets and apps increasingly restrict and monitor mobility. When US Border Patrol agents apprehend someone, they now typically collect DNA samples as well as take fingerprints, photographs, and, increasingly, an iris image and sometimes voice prints—all to be stored in a massive Department of Homeland Security biometric database. At this point, the repository holds biometric data on a quarter billion people.

As political philosopher Thomas Nail points out, the US Border Patrol's mobile surveillance towers (previously named "Cerberus," after the three-headed hound of Greek mythology that prevented people from escaping the underworld) are attached to trucks and can be positioned at any point along the border. In 2016, DHS worked with a data-mining project that is also called Cerberus. Yet a third company of the same name, Cerberus, operated a surveillance flight that, together with the Arizona National Guard, flew reconnaissance missions over a Phoenix protest in 2020. Guarding people from escaping the underworld seems to be a fitting analogue for border security technologies. The reach of bordering has gone so deep that in one town in Maryland, after a series of fights at the local high school, administrators reached out to Homeland Security officials to monitor students' social media accounts.

Following the law of the hammer, these globally proliferating tools of border enforcement are looking for nails, which could be any of us. As Jacqueline Stevens estimates, the federal government detained or deported around twenty thousand US citizens between 2003 and 2010, and between 1 and 2 percent of all people detained for deportation are estimated to be US citizens.

Closed borders mean less freedom for everyone, not just those on the "other" side of them. As Tohono O'odham activist and scholar Nellie Jo David put it, about her experience living in the southern Arizona borderlands, "We live in war, we live with these planes and if we're stopped out there on the reservation or in and around Ajo"—the nearby former mining town on traditional Indigenous land—"how many Border Patrol will show up? They treat it like it's a war scenario." Open the door to a data-collection or surveillance-tech corporation (or government agency), and they'll take your whole home.

13. Opening Borders Is Economically Smart

"When it comes to policies that restrict emigration, there appear to be trillion-dollar bills on the sidewalk," economist Michael Clemens famously wrote in 2011. "For eliminating labor mobility barriers, the estimated gains range from 50 to 150 percent of global GDP." As of late 2021, the global GDP is over $80 trillion, which means open borders would, according to his reckoning, add $40–100 trillion in total global wealth.

Clemens's estimated potential windfall is almost certainly overblown, mostly because it assumes a much higher rate of migration that would likely occur, and it also likely undercounts downstream changes to productivity rates, as well as the basic costs of massive migration. But his point still stands: opening borders would both increase wealth and distribute wealth more equally. With open borders, hunger, homelessness, and other forms of poverty, privation, and precarity would decrease.

In 2017, the nonprofit ProPublica found that for every 1 percent increase in US immigrant population, GDP rises 1.15 percent. The immigrant-sparked increase doesn't just take place at the national level: a Winthrop Rockefeller Foundation report from 2007 about Latino immigrants' impact on Arkansas's economy found they "have a small but positive net fiscal impact on the Arkansas state budget." Overall, immigrants "cost" the state of Arkansas $237 million in 2004 but made direct and indirect tax contributions of $257 million. More convincing is the fact that immigrant Arkansans generated around $3 billion in business revenues. The report also estimated that without immigrants, "the output of the state's manufacturing industry would likely be lowered by about $1.4 billion—or about 8 percent of the industry's $16.2 billion total contribution to the gross state product in 2004."

That's migrants' clear positive effect on state and national economies. We also need to consider the effect (of both bordering and crossing borders) on the migrants themselves.

Economists have observed up to 1,000 percent wage gaps for workers doing nearly identical jobs between the United States and Haiti, Nigeria, or Guatemala. It's hard to argue against the decision to go from earning less than five dollars a day to fifteen dollars an hour for doing the same labor, and yet the Haitian, Nigerian, or Guatemalan worker is forced to risk their life to do so. Such wage gaps are not an unfortunate and inevitable part of the economic order. Rather, they are intentionally enforced and exploited.

Analyzing the effect of imposed austerity measures and the North American Free Trade Agreement (NAFTA, which reinforced a growing trend to shift jobs from the American Midwest and southern, rural Mexico to the northern Mexican border) on manual labor jobs in northern Mexico, Justin Akers Chacón, in his book *The Border Crossed Us*, calculates that in 1992 the bottom 29 percent of workers in the *maquila* industry earned 64 percent less in wages than they made in 1976. By 2002, wages for those same workers fell 14 percent below what they were in 1983. Over the same period, productivity rates doubled.

In the first decade of the implementation of NAFTA, the wage gap between the United States and Mexico grew by more than 10 percent. This same period saw the first substantial wall infrastructure go up, dovetailing with the exploitative economic policies just mentioned. As writer Suketu Mehta summarizes: "Between 1970 and 2010, Mexico lost $872 billion in illicit financial outflows, and most of the money ended up in American banks. Roughly over the same period, 16 million Mexicans immigrated to the United States. "They weren't doing anything wrong," Mehta concludes, "they were just following the money."

Simultaneously, 50,000 midwestern auto workers, mostly in the midwest, lost their jobs. Many of those jobs went to Mexico, where, Akers Chacón reports, productivity rates increased over 66 percent between 1990 and 1999. During the same period, however, real wages fell by about 20 percent. Unionization rates also dropped over the same period. In other words, the *open-borders-for-capital* and *closed-borders-for-people* schema is a lose-lose for both American and Mexican workers. Closed borders is a win only for the corporations, which use the border as a wedge to lower wages, undercut worker protections, and keep the assembly line zipping.

Opening borders would immediately strip corporations of a key tool of exploitation, offering workers easier access to decent wages and facilitating collaboration and collective organization.

Akers Chacón notes that in Nicaragua, more than 120,000 garment workers produce clothing for major US companies, while an estimated 600,000 people make auto parts in Mexico, a huge share of which end up in GM, Chrysler, and Ford factories in the United States. Those foreign workers are employed by the same corporations as workers in the US, but, Akers Chacón writes, are "divided by borders and subject to more intensive (and US-abetted) degrees of labor repression in their home countries."

Of the hundreds of free-trade agreements recorded by the World Trade Organization (depending on how you count, there are between 360 and 800 of them), only 40 contain provisions that allow for some migration of workers, typically reserved for highly specialized professions.

14. Open Borders Are an Urgent Response to the Climate Crisis

According to prevailing estimates, as many as half a billion people will be forced from their homes by climate crises in the coming decades. Consigning them to refugee camps or slums will not only be dangerous for them—and a disgraceful mark of ignominy on the world—but a grave and politically volatile abdication of basic human decency. Tens of millions of people amassed behind border walls will push us closer to political despair and explosive violence. Borders are as much a solution to the radical changes to come as an umbrella is to a hurricane. As we work toward sustainability, as we work toward survivability, opening borders is an essential step not only toward keeping people safer from the accumulating disasters, but to finding a collective solution.

People currently enjoying relative luxury in the global North will also be forced to move because of climate change. In 2020 alone, according to the Internal Displacement Monitoring Center, thirty million people were displaced by climate disasters—more than three times as many as were displaced by conflict. In the United States alone, Hurricanes Katrina, Harvey, Maria, and Irma have pushed millions to leave their homes, in some cases forever. In 2021, more than 40 percent of Americans lived in counties hit by climate disasters.

The United States, Germany, Japan, the UK, Canada, France, and Australia collectively spent more than twice as much on border and immigration enforcement (over $33.1 billion) as on climate finance ($14.4 billion) between 2013 and 2018. Despite the major world powers spending significantly more on border enforcement than decarbonization or mitigation efforts, any hope for a solution continues to recede. Closed doors don't cool or calm an increasingly hot and erratic climate. Nor do they lock in place an upheaved global population.

As we tilt toward and beyond eight billion people on this warming planet, nobody will be able to stave off or hunker away from the effects of climate change.

Rising populations throughout the world, and especially in the global South, will burn more oil and coal to power their cities, use massive amounts of nitrogen-based fertilizers to grow their food, and continue to desire the luxuries and comforts some have already attained. It is almost certainly impossible that we will slow that massive energy need enough to achieve current targets for mitigating climate change. But, working with developing countries and breaking out of zero-sum power competitions that sacrifice responsible reform and blow past treaty obligations as nations strive for world hegemony[5]—as well as embracing denser living, planet-healthier diets, and different forms of mobility—is the only path toward sustainable human existence. Borders are an impediment to that goal.

15. Open Borders As Reparations and Decolonization

The United States has what could be termed "an imperial debt" to a number of countries throughout the world. "US responsibility for helping to create the conditions that drive much of the out-migration from Honduras," Joseph Nevins writes, "should negate any justification by the US government to deport and deny rights of

---

5   The US Department of Defense is, by far, the world's largest institutional emitter of greenhouse gasses, according to a study from Brown University. In 2017, the Pentagon's total greenhouse gas emissions were not only higher than emissions from all US iron and steel production, but were larger than many industrialized countries, including Sweden, Denmark, and Portugal. A lot of those emissions are, like the self-devouring snake, gassed into the atmosphere to protect oil reserves. Russia, China, Israel, Saudi Arabia, and other countries don't do much better. Militaries throughout the world are estimated to account for up to 5 percent of all global emissions: more than civilian aviation and shipping combined.

residence to people of Honduran origin." Given that Honduras is less exception to and more exemplar of the destabilizing effects of US imperialistic intervention, the same argument could be made for dozens of other countries, including but not remotely limited to Iraq, Iran, Afghanistan, Pakistan, Yemen, Somalia, the Congo, El Salvador, Guatemala, Nicaragua, Mexico, Haiti, the Dominican Republic, Cuba, Indonesia, the Philippines, Laos, and Cambodia.

Sri Lankan novelist and activist A. Sivanandan's famous and succinct line explains why migrants move to countries that had colonized their homes: "We are here because you were there."

And it's not just the United States that has such an imperial debt: many European countries—Britain, France, Germany, Belgium, Portugal, Italy, Spain—played lead roles in genocidal invasions and ignored borders in the Americas and Africa to snatch up land and smuggle away riches. To go back to Nevins's analysis on the US role in Honduras, the same calculus can easily be applied to Belgium and the Democratic Republic of the Congo, Germany and Cameroon, as well as France and huge swaths of Africa.

Western countries have also run up what could be termed a "climate debt"—as they are responsible for the overwhelming majority of carbon dioxide emissions, while poorer countries overwhelmingly suffer the destabilizing effects.

Given the failures of independence movements in Africa and the Americas to undo ongoing effects of colonial violence, migration remains a needed mitigating process that, as E. Tendayi Achiume writes, "enhances individual self-determination within neocolonial empire." For a citizen of a Global South country to assert political equality with a Global North citizen, and to cross the border to change or improve their economic situation, Achiume claims, "is migration as decolonization." A formal recognition of that right would be open borders.

Researchers Sara Amighetti and Alasia Nuti argue that "postcolonial migrants," or people from former colonies, are "essential contributors" to the colonizing nation's identity (in fact, the economic prosperity and freedom that citizens of the colonizing nation enjoy are, in many regards, predicated on the colonial relationship between the countries) and thus they should be able to migrate to the colonizing state they are effectively already a part of.

According to international law (as stipulated by the United Nations–appointed International Law Commission), countries are required "to make full reparation" for internationally wrongful acts. Such full reparation includes "restitution, compensation, and satisfaction," which means reestablishing the conditions before the act was committed, paying money, as well as acknowledging and apologizing for the committed harms. Given the impossibility of the first form of remediation, the unlikelihood of the second, and the important but not completely satisfying nature of the third facet of reparation, opening the doors and offering citizenship to colonialism's victims (both direct and generational) is a worthy form of both reparative justice and recompense.

How can a country that has so disrupted and dispossessed a population presume to deny that population the right to seek security and dignity? One ready and simple form of expiation for colonial and neocolonial disruptive meddling would be, rather than the torture and imprisonment of those fleeing political or climactic conflagrations, to offer them welcome.

16. World Religions Agree: Open the Borders

"And if a stranger dwells with you in your land, you shall not mistreat him," Yahweh tells Moses in the Book of Leviticus. "The stranger who dwells among you shall be to you as one born among you, and you shall love him as yourself; for you were strangers in the land of Egypt."

Many of the world's religions proclaim and promote—at least rhetorically—principles of welcoming the stranger, offering succor, aid, water, and honor to those in need. Many of the world's religions also venerate the wanderer, pilgrim, or migrant—all those driven from their homes. It is a wonder, then, that so many practitioners of the major religions rebuke the figure of the migrant, calling for walls to block them out or immigration agents to send them home.

"Hospitality begins at the gate, in the doorway, on the bridges between public and private space," writes social-ethics scholar Christine D. Pohl in *Making Room: Recovering Hospitality as a Christian Tradition*. Hospitality, that is, begins at the border.

Sanctuary, the practice of offering protective welcome to the migrant, is part of America's prophetic tradition, harking back to the slavery abolitionists, whose spirit was rooted in their own legacy of religious, political, and economic persecution. In Europe, too, some Christians have long leaned on their faith to welcome and protect the persecuted. But such tradition and spirit are today, more than ever, running up against a wall of anti-immigrant policies.

In the Gospel of Matthew, Jesus articulates one of the religion's foundational maxims that speaks, or should speak, to how we treat migrants today: "Thou shalt love thy neighbour as thyself." Love, even tough love, does not abide a deportation.

Jewish history and tradition is, in many ways, a history of migration. According to one count, the Torah commands hospitable and just treatment to the migrant thirty-six times. In just the last century, Jews have been stripped of rights, persecuted, deported, and slaughtered, suffering some of the most heinous crimes in human history. Their plight, and countries' hard-hearted refusal to offer them welcome, gave rise to the basic standards of international human rights, including international accords on refugee and asylum law. With a long history of near-constant displacement, Judaic tradition, in its ideal, is devoted to honoring and welcoming the stranger. This tradition is reflected in the Talmud, where, for instance, Rabbi Yosie says, "Let your home be open always to those who suffer and seek relief."

One of Buddhism's first and central precepts is respecting life, with a committed focus on compassion and nonviolence. *Karuna* (compassion) and *mudita* (empathetic joy) call one to care for and to delight in the security and happiness of others, whatever form they take and wherever they may be from.

With Islam, welcome and hospitality form the cornerstone of both the religion and, more broadly, Islamic culture. Scholar Tahir Zaman writes that "matters pertaining to protection and assistance are referred to 396 times in the Qur'an . . . 20 make specific reference to *hijra* (flight) and *aman* (asylum)." In Surah 4:36 of the Quran, the prophet Muhammad writes, "Do good unto your parents, and near of kin, and unto orphans, and the needy, and the neighbor from among your own people, and the neighbor who is a stranger, and the friend by your side, the wayfarer, and your servants."

The Hindu Tradition, in the Taitiriya Upanishad 1.11.2, similarly importunes: "Let a person never turn away a stranger from his house, that is the rule. Therefore a man should, by all means, acquire much food, for good people say to the stranger: 'There is enough food for you.'"

Living to the standard of any of the world's major religions requires an openness, a welcome, and a hospitality that closed borders do not permit. As Rabbi Y'hudah said in the Talmud, "Hospitality to wayfarers is greater than welcoming the presence of the Divine."

17. Closed Borders Are Racist

The nationality granted to you at birth determines whether you are free to move across international borders or are blocked by them. Not only border walls, but a web of multilateral visa agreements privilege certain passport holders and allow their free movement, while denying and immobilizing others. Such discrimination, while based in nationality, overlaps with both class and race. Citizens of Global North nations, made up of predominantly white citizens, are generally able to cross borders with ease. Citizens of the Global South, predominantly Black or Brown, are denied that same freedom.

The logic of apartheid and Jim Crow lives on when applied to migrants. "Looking at the data, it becomes apparent," writes sociologist Steffen Mau, that "most countries with either black or Islamic majorities are exempted from visa-free travel on a large scale." Even within Third World countries, whiter citizens have the wealth and connections to obtain passports and authorization for international travel. The pattern holds for nonauthorized migration as well: Black and Brown people are more readily denied, suspected, detained, and deported.

In an investigation I cowrote for *Business Insider*, journalist José Olivares and I teased out commonly overlooked statistics and patterns, finding that in the United States the specific mistreatment of Black migrants in the immigration detention system rears its head in myriad ways. Detention center officials and guards offer Black migrants less food, frequently enact retaliatory violence against Black migrants, submit them to longer periods of detention than white migrants, demand of Black migrants significantly higher bond rates, send Black detainees to solitary confinement for longer periods, and disproportionately shackle Black migrants with electronic ankle monitors.

In the two-year period from 2018 to 2020, the average bond paid by the Refugee and Immigrant Center for Education and Legal Services (RAICES) to get immigrants out of detention was $10,500. During that same period, bonds for Haitian immigrants averaged $16,700—54 percent higher than for other immigrants. While asylum statistics are not categorized by race, patterns show that bond prices are higher for migrants coming from majority Black nations.

According to other statistics—also compiled by RAICES— among the ten nationalities with the most asylum decisions from 2012 to 2017, Haitians had the second-highest denial rate at 87 percent, despite coming from an extremely politically unstable country beset by persistent violence (often enabled or provoked by US policy). Previously, Jamaicans and then Somalians had the highest asylum denial rates, as well the highest rates of deportation over the same time period.

While only 7 percent of noncitizens in the United States are Black, Black immigrants make up 20 percent of those facing deportation on criminal grounds. And while African and Caribbean immigrants made up only 4 percent of people in immigration detention centers between 2013 and 2017, they represented 24 percent of all people subjected to solitary confinement.

"The modern day immigration system is a modern day Jim Crow," Allen Morris, a researcher with RAICES, told me. "The whole system is rooted in white supremacy. It's not built to let Black immigrants come here."

18. Walls Don't Work

Whether or not walls "work" in fact depends on how you define the latter: because walls do work to endanger, strip rights, marginalize, and kill migrants. Walls may also work politically, even as they fail practically. Border walls successfully function as nationalist symbols, spur the border industrial complex, and line the pockets of international security companies. What they don't do very well is keep people on one side or the other.

Scores of reports pepper local news channels about migrants quickly shimmying up and over wall segments along the US–Mexico border, even the latest and tallest barrier designs. I've personally witnessed border crossers scale a segment of an eighteen-foot wall between Nogales and Nogales, slip down the other side, and vanish into the city, all in about fifteen seconds.

As early as 1951, a Border Patrol report noted that just four days after holes in the Calexico fence were repaired, eleven of the newly patched panels had been torn out, fourteen new holes had been cut in the wall, and at least seven new breaches were counted in barbed wire portions of the fence.

Newly raised walls are quickly crossed by cut-out doors, rope-ladders, grappling hooks, drones, tunnels, or even makeshift wall-bridges. Barring moats of fire or minefields, or the permanent, hyper-militarized infrastructure of the Demilitarized Zone between North and South Korea,[6] walls—no matter how "smart" or brutally medieval—don't keep people out. As fast as a wall can be built, it can be breached. Hence the simplicity of former DHS Secretary Janet Napolitano's quip: "Show me a 50-foot wall, I'll show you a 51-foot ladder."

Draconian immigration enforcement measures don't do much better than walls. In one of the most drastically anti-human immigration policies in recent years, the Trump administration ripped thousands of children away from their parents in an attempt to punish them and dissuade more families from trying to cross the border. And yet, in the immediately following months of implementing that heinously cruel policy, *more families crossed the border* than in the preceding months. That's because they were fleeing crushing poverty, deadly violence, and utter hopelessness in their home countries. They were doing what anybody would do—seek dignity and safety—and neither the wall nor Trump's anti-immigrant barking kept them at home.

As poet Warsan Shire writes in "Home":

> no one leaves home unless
> home is the mouth of a shark . . .
>
> you have to understand,
> that no one puts their children in a boat
> unless the water is safer than the land

---

6 Although it's rare for people to cross the DMZ itself, it does happen, and about a thousand North Koreans defect every year by other means.

19. "Smart" Walls Are Stupid

Steel walls aren't the only kind that kill. Geographer Samuel Norton Chambers found a "significant correlation between the location of border surveillance technology, the routes taken by migrants, and the locations of recovered human remains in the southern Arizona desert." In other words, "smart walls" drive migrants into the dangers of the remote desert just as much as dumb walls do.

The surveillance technology Chambers was studying is proliferating throughout the world's borderlands. Along the US–Mexico border alone, there are nearly four hundred permanent surveillance towers with high-powered multispectrum cameras tracking movement along huge swaths of land. Beyond these permanent towers, there are hundreds more mobile surveillance units mounted on or dragged behind trucks, as well as unmanned drones, surveillance blimps, automated license plate readers, facial recognition and phone-hacking technology, vehicle forensic kits (used to obtain information from vehicles' "infotainment" systems, which can include geographical data, cell phone metadata, text messages, and even when and which doors have been opened), as well as sprawlingly massive and constantly bloating databases to collect and filter the petabytes of information.

Decades of anti-migrant policies have weaponized the landscape, both physically and digitally. And while these tech-walls cost billions and successfully function to push migrants into the more forbidding and dangerous reaches of the desert (or into the sea if heading to Europe), they don't do so well at stopping migration. In 2006, tech giant Boeing was awarded a multi-billion-dollar contract by DHS to install surveillance towers (the initial plan was to build 1,800 100-plus-foot towers), radar equipment, and ground sensors, and to integrate lots of data on border crossers. After five years of reining in expectations, the government concluded that the terrain was too varied, the technology insufficient, and the project an absolute failure.

In the UK, a faulty algorithm in an immigration database incorrectly flagged seven thousand students for deportation—and then the government deported them. A report from Migration and Technology Monitor called such efforts at automating immigration enforcement "a human laboratory of high risk experiments." At a refugee camp in Jordan, people aren't allowed to access food until they are identified using an optic scanner. Refugees consigned to the camp are not only worried about the management of their personal biometric data, but they also complain that their family members are restricted by mistakes in the system. As typically only a single member is allowed to purchase food with their eye scan, if they're sick, poked in the eye, or, more frequently, the technology doesn't work, people go hungry.

European countries are experimenting with voice prints and, increasingly, using electronic ankle shackles for monitoring, a process referred to as "tagging" migrants. Laws in Austria, Germany, Denmark, Norway, the United Kingdom, and Belgium allow governments to seize asylum seekers' mobile phones, from which data is extracted and used as part of asylum procedures. Privacy concerns abound.

Meanwhile, the European Commission is exploring a complex new border militarization plan that includes the ROBORDER Project, which sounds as scary as it is—combining militaristic unmanned aircraft, boats, and sensors to guard Europe's borders. There was also the proposed "wall of drones" that the Trump administration explored: "smart" drones meant to monitor the US–Mexico border and interrogate people referred to as "intruders" in a promotional video. The trial drones had the capacity to tase border crossers.

And, in both the United States and Europe, border bots are being installed at border crossing kiosks in order to read people's faces and determine if they are lying. Such technology has, unsurprisingly, misidentified and wrongfully criminalized people.

The invasive and dystopian use of tech to surveil migrants and restrict their mobility is also increasingly being outsourced by governments to the private sector, which presents a host of ethical and human rights issues.

"Smart walls" function in much the same way standard walls do: they don't stop migrants but, rather, slow or divert them into more dangerous routes. At the same time, these high-tech efforts fail in novel ways by misreading, misidentifying, invasively collecting, perpetually hoarding, and over-sharing personal data—malfunctioning in new, consequential, discriminatory, and potentially deadly ways.

20. The Right to Migrate / The Right to Remain

You are where you are right now because either you, your parents, or your ancestors migrated there.

A 2018 genetic analysis of human specimens from the Neolithic period, Copper Age, and Bronze Age revealed that nearly every population on earth has moved in the last ten thousand years. "The orthodoxy, the assumption that present-day people are directly descended from the people who always lived in that same area," one of the study's authors wrote, "is wrong almost everywhere."

While Indigenous populations rightly claim long and rich histories in the territories they inhabit, many of them, too, have long been on the move. Humans are a mobile species. We are also a nostalgic species, forging ties and identities based on place. The two truths can conflict, but they don't have to. Showing respect, addressing injustices, and offering welcome can help guide us toward a more just and less violent future.

Decolonization is a key step, but it's not just about giving the land back. Who the land "belongs" to is, always has been, and always will be a source of contention. Indigenous people deserve apology and compensation for the massive and murderous robbery of the past centuries, but that doesn't necessarily mean drawing and enforcing new borders. Rather, we need to wholly reconsider our relationship to land, embracing the spirit of a shared commons—commons, that is, in the sense proffered by scholar-activist Silvia Federici: "not as a gated reality, a grouping of people joined by exclusive interests separating them from others, as with communities formed on the basis of religion or ethnicity, but rather as a quality of relations, a principle of cooperation and of responsibility to each other and to the earth, the forests, the seas, the animals." Workers and anyone who cares for rather than exploits or destroys the land should be permitted to enjoy and live on and in the land.

Humans have always been roaming, curious, and on the run. It is only modern nation states and the machinery of borders that have turned our innate and natural mobility into *migration*, into something visa-stamped and permitted, or deemed illegal and punished. As migration scholar Nicholas de Genova has put it, "If there were no borders, there would be no migrants—only mobility." A surprisingly easy way to eliminate illegal migration would be to—simply—eliminate closed borders

But the appeal for open borders rings empty without the attending fight to improve conditions in the countries migrants flee. Nobody should be forced to migrate—whether it be due to state violence or oppression, climate change or the inability to find employment. One of the essential aspects of the push for open borders is the push for a more just and safer world, a world in which nobody is driven out of their homes because of fear or want.

The best policies are those that force nobody to migrate, affording people the right and the means to live in, cultivate, and enjoy their home and community. An open-borders vision is one where such a life is not constrained by where that community lies, or where one is able to seek or find such a community. An open-borders world is a world in which "this" and "that" side of the border are not distinguished by violence on this side and safety on that side, by prosperity and opportunity spatially juxtaposed by poverty and choicelessness.

It is a world of greater freedoms and less oppression, where opportunity and safety are, when needed, available. At the same time, it is a world in which we fight to help basic needs be met before anyone is uprooted. To this end, Reece Jones has recommended the creation of a Department of Human Rights and Free Movement as a replacement to the Department of Homeland Security. In comparison to the zones of death and rightlessness that militarized borders foster, such a department would offer more security—both personal and national.

21. The Simple Argument

Barring small island nations, all countries' borders have been drawn in blood. Genocidal slaughter and ruthless imperialism helped form the United States and bottom-lined the wealth of France, the UK, Spain, Germany, Israel, and other countries in the global North. To claim the right to stop a migrant from crossing a line that was previously and flagrantly trespassed by the controlling elite (or their ancestors) is absurd and, in the most basic sense, unfair.

The 1884 Berlin Conference, in which imperial European powers slashed lines across a map of Africa and divvied up territorial claims, is only the most blatant example of how borders are violently imposed onto people and landscapes. The source of some of history's most destructive episodes is the claim that only certain people belong on certain tracts of land, and that others are interlopers who must be denied or deported. Doing away with such brattish selfishness and blinkered xenophobia would ease, not exacerbate, geopolitical tension.

A country is not a house. Locking your doors at night is not the same as barring a migrant from a country's territory. When we deny the migrant welcome, we are exposing and dishonoring our own home—forgetting the history of the land and conquest, or the traditions of freedom and hospitality practiced there. Paradoxically, we deracinate ourselves by claiming exclusive attachment to space. We lose our own home by denying it to others.

The Spanish word *querencia*, with a taproot in the verb *querer*—to desire or to love—refers to the place one feels at home, from where we draw our strength and spirit. *Querer* itself has origins in Proto-Indo-European: to seek, to ask. To establish or reestablish querencia, our home anchor and spirit, is to drop a root. But the lurking question in that root, that seeking—the desirous nature of both roots and humans—also reveals our inherent transience, the itch to seek, to ask, and the constant motion of being itself.

Roots are on the move. In our increasingly mobile world, for those who are uprooted and unroofed, as well as for those who feel firmly planted, we are all always still seeking and asking, *queriendo*, always building and finding home, whether we have one now or not.

The way to go home, the way to stay home, is to welcome the migrant.

ACKNOWLEDGMENTS

Deep and first thanks to Andy Hsiao, friend and consummate editor. Thanks also to Róisín Davis, friend, comrade, and agent. To Ben Mabie, for pushing and believing in the book. And to Katy O'Donnell at Haymarket, as well as to the whole team there, for taking a chance and championing the project. Special thanks to Sam Smith, a committed and fantastic copy editor, as well as Jameka Williams.

José Olivares, my compa and collaborator, it's been such a pleasure and honor to work with you—I'm glad to further lean on our reporting here. I've been thrilled to get to work with a number of great interns, including Brianna Flinkingshelt, Leonel Ignacio Martín, Sophia Diez-Zhang, Anna Pastore, and America Bañuelos. Thanks to Earlham College's Border Studies Program, especially Kate Morgan. I want to thank Cecile Pilot, Isabella Alexander-Nathani, Vivian Yee, Anan AbuShanab for consultations, and Valerie Forman for her expertise and friendship.

I workshopped some very early versions of a couple chapters with two writers' groups, whose whip-smart members include Joel, Alison, Patri, Liz, Kristen, Daniela, Sarah, Allie, and then Rux, Charlie, Gabe, Kimi.

Thanks to Nellie Jo David, Amber Ortega, Lorraine Eiler, Ieva Jesionyte for inspiration, chats, and openness. Rachel Dolnick for help with Jewish stances towards migration. Russ McSpadden for the friendship, wisdom, and some great trips out in the borderlands. And to raconteur and all-around expert, Myles Traphagen. Thanks to Gus, Bria, Niko, and Lev for lifelong friendship and spiritual ballast. And to Amy Joseph for being around and wonderful.

El equipo de El Faro—los mejores y más comprometidos investigadores y periodistas que hay, especialmente José Luis Sanz, Roman Gressier, Óscar Martinez, Julia Gavarrete, y Nelson Rauda.

My team at Arizona Luminaria, especially my editor Dianna Nañez. I have so much all-abiding respect and appreciation to the founding trio: Dianna, Irene McKisson, and Becky Pallack. Thank you for building something that matters, and matters beautifully, and for giving me the chance to be a part of it.

Thanks to the many editors who have poured their expertise and sharp eyes into the many articles that, intentionally or not, were base research for this book. Frank Reynolds, who I dearly miss collaborating with at *The Nation* and who edited my first article on open borders. Ali Gharib at *The Intercept*, who has sharpened many a nut graf, as well as Cora Currier, Maryam Saleh, and Eve Bowen at *New York Review of Books*. Thanks to Ratik Asokan for his daunting erudition, the occasional editing, and the friendship.

Thanks to Sean Rys for an early read of opening chapters. And to Sophie Smith for her wisdom and cutting intelligence on the border and on all things.

The whole crew at the Open Borders Conference, especially Jamila Hammami and all the organizers and participants.

Thanks to my brilliant friend and mentor John Granger, to whom I am indebted, in no small part, for all of my sentences.

Thanks to my family, of course, especially my loving sister, Tiffany, to Marko for the productive conversations, and to Julian and Livia. Gracias a mis suegros, migrantes los dos, quienes adoro como la familia que son. And to my wonderfully supportive parents. And to my mother, again, as well as uncle and grandparents, who crossed borders to find freedom and build the home I see the world from.

Thanks in advance to everyone who has read or glanced at this work, and to all of those unnamed here who have helped and inspired the project: my gratitude.

And last: to Elías, that dazzling rocket of soul, and to Daniela, for her daily presence—what could be more?—for her love and for our life.

A NOTE ON SOURCES

What most informs my work, thinking, and writing on borders and immigration are the thousands of conversations I've had with migrants, including my mother, uncle, grandparents, in-laws, cousins, second and third cousins, as well as countless friends, acquaintances, sources, and contacts from Romania, Mexico, Peru, Scotland, Venezuela, Colombia, Ecuador, Haiti, Cuba, Nicaragua, El Salvador, Honduras, Guatemala, Ukraine, Russia, Belarus, Syria, Palestine, Iran, Iraq, Tunisia, Nigeria, the Democratic Republic of the Congo, India, Pakistan, China, Vietnam, the Philippines, and elsewhere.

Their knowledge, experience, wisdom, openness, and courage are not secondary to the excellent books, articles, talks, expert opinions, and presentations that are published, paid for, and lauded in traditional and social media or in the award circuits, but are the roots and foundation of all scholarship and understanding on the subject. And yet, these lived experiences and testimonies are harder to cite, are often overlooked, and are not given enough credit in publishing, journalism, and academia.

Aid workers, activists, good neighbors and Good Samaritans who defend the rights of migrants have also been integral in my understanding and approach to borders and immigration. So has my formative experience being threatened by anti-immigrant militia in the Arizona deserts, conversations with immigration restrictionists, and politicians nonplussed about policy.

The excellent scholars and writers on whom this book and my understanding of borders heavily lean are Harsha Walia, Todd Miller, Aaron Reichlin-Melnick, Austin Kocher, Dara Lind, Lee

Gelernt, Adam Wola, Yael Schacher, Matthew Longo, Ari Saw-
yer, Molly Molloy, Suketu Mehta, Nick Estes, Alex Sager, Nandita
Sharma, Itamar Mann, Joseph Carens, Alex Nowrasteh, and Bryan
Caplan.

Journalists José Olivares, Óscar Martinez, Ryan Devereaux,
Melissa Del Bosque, Adolfo Flores, Jennifer Ávila, Alfredo Corcha-
do, Aura Bogado, Hamed Aleaziz, Molly O'Toole, Jonathan Blitzer,
Tanvi Misra, Sarah Stillman, Felipe De La Hoz, Gaby Del Valle,
Alexis Okeowo, Michelle García, Camilo Montoya-Galvez, Jack
Herrera, Caitlin Dickerson, Matt Katz, Kate Morrissey, Alisa Zai-
ra Reznick, Emily Green, Lomi Kriel, Mazin Sidahmed, Kendal
Blust, and Valerie Gonzalez do the sort of on-the-ground, breaking,
and investigative work that is essential to my basic understanding
of how borders work and how migrants cross them or are crossed
by them. And despite my stark disagreement with them, John Judis,
Jason DeParle, Michael Walzer, and George Borjas provide insight
and important backdrop.

The listed authors and titles above and below are partial, and I
stick mostly to works that drove thinking more than simply made
an appearance (the latter of which are mostly cited in the text itself).
Facts, figures, and fine points that aren't easily googleable I reference directly in the text.

Chapter 1

James C. Scott's *Seeing Like a State* and *Against the Grain* call into
question both the formation of states and our current relation to
them. Poet Wendy Trevino's *Cruel Fiction* beautifully and mov-
ingly takes on the very premise of bordering. Jacqueline Stevens's
States without Nations is one of the smartest books detailing the
difference between the nation and the state, convincingly detailing that the laws of nation states foster and perpetuate inequality
rather than freedoms. Simon Winchester's *Land* is a bright historical and international survey of human's legal relationship to land.
Michael Walzer's *Spheres of Justice* is one of the most important

political-philosophical texts analyzing, and often defending, the rights of citizens. Thomas Nail's *Theory of the Border* is one of the few true philosophical takes that focuses exclusively on bordering. Wendy Brown's *Walled States, Waning Sovereignty* highlights, among other trends, the rising anxiety of the United States and other countries as they face increased globalization and mobility and react with militarized borders. Suketu Mehta's *This Land Is Our Land* is an impassioned memoir-cum-overview of the of heart-hardening of US immigration policy. Andreas Malm's *How to Blow up a Pipeline*, recently adapted for film, is an aptly titled panegyric to mass mobilization and direct action. Nick Estes's *Our History Is the Future* is a brilliant conversation-reset on how we understand and discuss Indigeneity and our relationship to land claimed by the United States. Rachel St. John's *Line in the Sand: A History of the Western US-Mexico Border* is an illuminating and granular telling of how that border was drawn. *John Brown*, by David S. Reynold, is a gripping and eerily relevant biography.

Chapter 2
Author and scholar Larissa Behrendt is essential reading for understanding the history of Australia. *The Journals of Captain Cook* are a window into the murderous presumption of white supremacy. Nandita Sharma's *Home Rule* is a whip-crackingly smart rethink about the rise of nation states and their exclusionary stance toward migrants. Behrouz Boochani, a Kurdish-Iranian refugee, wrote one of the more remarkable books I've read: *No Friend But the Mountains*, "penned" on WhatsApp messages from Australia's prison camp/penal colony on Manus Island. Claudio Saunt's *Unworthy Republic* is a terrifying and important retelling of the early decades of the United States and its campaign to dispossess, banish, and slaughter the Indigenous. In a similar spirit, Kevin Kenny's *Peaceable Kingdom Lost* tracks colonizers' rapacious conquest of land in North America. Roxanne Dunbar Ortiz's *Not "a Nation of Immigrants"* breaks through the mythos of America as an inclusive

and welcoming nation state. One of the most moving and brilliant works I read in my research was Mahmood Mamdani's *Neither Settler nor Native*, which, among other revelations, dates the rise of nation states not to European empires' treaties of the mid-seventeenth century but to the genocidal campaigns waged by those empires in the Americas beginning in the late fifteenth century. Eli Kedourie's *Nationalism* is a treasure of historical fact and political conceptualizing about the rise of nationalism. Matthew Longo has written one of the more crystalline and troubling takes on the many implications of border enforcement in *The Politics of Borders*. David Bacon's *Illegal People* is a seminal text in connecting economic/trade policy to the rise of the current border-enforcement regime in the United States. Fewer books better take on the juridical-philosophical questions of bordering, through both historical and contemporary examples, than Itamar Mann's *Humanity at Sea*. Chief Clinton Rickard's autobiography, *Fighting Tuscarora*, recaps much of the ongoing fallout from the genocidal anti-Indian campaigns waged in North America. John Torpey's *The Invention of the Passport: Surveillance, Citizenship, and the State* is full of relevance about the rise of biometric surveillance and the border regimes. Doreen Manuel's (with Peter McFarlane) *Brotherhood to Nationhood: George Manuel and the Making of the Modern Indian Movement* chronicles the rise of Canada's Indigenous movement. And Mae Ngai's *Impossible Subjects: Illegal Aliens and the Making of Modern America* details the many and profound contradictions in immigration policy in the US from the late nineteenth through the twentieth century.

Chapter 3

Shafa's story, as presented in this chapter, is based entirely on a few BBC articles, one of which was an oral history. I reached out repeatedly to BBC to try to track down the author and see if I could get an update or get in touch with Shafa, to no avail. Other details, besides those cited in text, come from conversations with Giuseppe

Loprete, of the UN's Office of International Migration, and with other former officials and activists who have worked in the Sahel, including volunteers with Alarme Phone Sahara.

Chapter 4

Mirta Ojito's *Finding Mañana* informed my understanding of the personal experience of the boatlift. I also spoke with two other Marielitos on background. George Borjas, another Cuban immigrant to the United States, wrote *We Wanted Workers*, which seeks to take a dispassionate view on the economics of immigration—a useful read, as much as I disagree with many of Borjas's conclusions. Some great political background about Cuban emigration is found in William M. LeoGrande and Peter Kornbluh's *Back Channel to Cuba*. "While anti-Asian racism is critical in the nation's immigration history," historian Hidetaka Hirota writes in *Expelling the Poor*, "the origins of immigration control lay in economic and cultural nativism against the Irish in Atlantic seaboard states." Hirota emphasizes that anti-Irish state laws and deportation practices specifically targeted Irish women, especially those with children. Few have done better than Daniel Denvir, with his *All-American Nativism*, to trace the story of US anti-immigrant ideology. Thomas Piketty's dense *Capital and Ideology* is a useful resource to both to consider the big picture of the global inequality regime and understand its details in both Europe and the US. Harsha Walia, probably the clearest thinker advocating for a world beyond borders, is essential reading. Her latest, *Border and Rule: Global Migration, Capitalism, and the Rise of Racist Nationalism*, as well as *Undoing Border Imperialism*, have been trailblazers.

Chapter 5

Just taking this opportunity to mention *Terminator* again . . . I also watched a lot of YouTube videos about the Attari–Wagah border gate for this chapter. See also Frances Stonor Saunders's brilliant three-part series in the *London Review of Books*, "The Suitcase," adapted from a book of the same name. I leaned on Reece Jones, once again, who has done important work on the Indian-Bangladeshi enclaves. Suchitra Vijayan's *Midnight's Borders* is a comprehensive history of India's borders, highlighting their artificial and consequential origins. I learned an immense amount from Ratik Asokan's "The Long Struggle of India's Sanitation Workers," an article published in the *New York Review of Books*. Joshua Keating's *Invisible Countries: Journeys to the Edge of Nationhood* provides a portrait of a number of quasi-states, including Somaliland, Kurdistan, and a Mohawk territory straddling the United States and Canada.

Chapter 6
David Wallace-Wells's *The Uninhabitable Earth* is a terrifying and very readable compendium of the current and coming catastrophes wrought by climate change. Sonia Shah's *The Next Great Migration* takes on the history of our understanding of migration—human and animal. Ken Burns does his evocative usual with material about the forced displacement of "okies" in *The Dust Bowl*. Abrahm Lustgarten's "The Great Climate Migration" is a book's worth of material packed into a single article about mostly Central Americans pushed out of their homes by climate change. In *Storming the Wall*, Todd Miller chronicles climate migration from the Philippines to Central America, making a convincing plea to offer welcome.

Chapter 7
I'm very glad to be able to give even passing mention to Joseph Andras's *Tomorrow They Won't Dare to Murder Us*, a fabulous novel about a French revolutionary in Algeria. Kelly Lytle Hernández's *Migra!* is a scathing history of the US Border Patrol. See also Francisco Cantú's beautiful and revealing memoir, *The Line Becomes a River*. Anna Funder's *Stasiland* is some of the best essaying about totalitarian surveillance, of which bordering is a gateway drug.

Imagined Communities, by Benedict Anderson, chronicles the rise and contradictions in modern nation states, with Indonesia as a compelling case study. In *Border Vigils*, Jeremy Harding beautifully reports tensions along the line in Italy, Africa, and the southern United States.

Chapter 8

Books in this chapter that I haven't previously cited include Jason Riley's *Let Them In: The Case for Open Borders*, an early take on open borders from a conservative perspective. Atossa Araxia Abrahamian's *The Cosmopolites* explores the globetrotting elite, and how they use borders to their financial and legal advantage. Rudolph J. Rummel's *Death by Government* is a study of democide and a poignant argument that people often have much more to fear by looking up, at their own government, than by looking beyond their border. See also the work of Salvadoran journalist Óscar Martínez, whose first book, *The Beast*, changed the way I and many others understood migration. *The Security Principle*, by Frédéric Gros, reads modern conceptions of security through a philosophical lens.

FURTHER READING

Abrahamian, Atossa Araxia. *The Cosmopolites: The Coming of the Global Citizen.* Columbia Global Reports, 2015.

Akers Chacón, Justin. *The Border Crossed Us: The Case for Opening the US-Mexico Border.* Haymarket Books, 2021.

Anderson, Benedict. *Imagined Communities.* Verso Books, 2016.

Bacon, David. *Illegal People: How Globalization Creates Migration and Criminalizes Immigrants.* Beacon Press, 2009.

Boochani, Behrouz. *No Friend But the Mountains: Writing from Manus Prison.* Anansi International, 2019.

Brown, Wendy. *Walled States, Waning Sovereignty.* Zone Books, 2010.

Cantú, Francisco. *The Line Becomes a River: Dispatches from the Border.* Riverhead Books, 2018.

Chomsky, Aviva *They Take Our Jobs! And 20 Other Myths About Immigration.* Beacon Press, 2018.

Del Valle, Gaby and Felipe De La Hoz. *Border/Lines* Newsletter. https://borderlines.substack.com

Denvir, Daniel. *All American Nativism.* Verso Books, 2020.

Dozal, Gabriel. *The Border Simulator.* One World, 2023.

Dunbar Ortiz, Roxanne. *Not "A Nation of Immigrants": Settler Colonialism, White Supremacy, and a History of Erasure and Exclusion.* Beacon Press, 2021.

Estes, Nick. *Our History Is the Future.* Verso Books, 2023.

Estes, Nick; Yazzie, Melanie K.; Nez Denetdale, Jennifer; Correia, David. *Red Nation Rising: From Bordertown Violence to Native Liberation.* PM Press, 2021.

Funder, Anna. *Stasiland.* Harper Perennial, 2011.

García Hernández, César Cuauhtémoc. *Welcome to the Wretched: In Defense of the "Criminal Alien."* The New Press, 2024.

Goodman, Adam. *The Deportation Machine: America's Long History of Expelling Immigrants.* Princeton University Press, 2020.

Gros, Frédéric. *The Security Principle.* Verso Books, 2019.

Harding, Jeremy. *Border Vigils: Keeping Migrants Out of the Rich World.* Verso Books, 2012.

Hernández, Kelly Lytle. *Migra!: A History of the U.S. Border Patrol.* University of California Press, 2010.

Hirota, Hidetaka. *Expelling the Poor: Atlantic Seaboard States and the Nineteenth-Century Origins of American Immigration Policy.* Oxford University Press, 2017.

Jones, Reece. *Violent Borders*. Verso Books, 2016.

Keating, Joshua. *Invisible Countries: Journeys to the Edge of Nationhood*. Yale University Press, 2018.

Kenny, Kevin. *Peaceable Kingdom Lost: The Paxton Boys and the Destruction of William Penn's Holy Experiment*. Oxford University Press, 2011.

Kocher, Austin. *Austin Kocher*. Newsletter. https://austinkocher.substack.com

Longo, Matthew. *The Politics of Borders: Sovereignty, Security, and the Citizen after 9/11*. Cambridge University Press, 2017.

Lustgarten, Abrahm. "The Great Climate Migration." *New York Times* and *ProPublica*, 2020.

Malm, Andreas. *How to Blow Up a Pipeline*. Verso Books, 2021.

Mamdani, Mahmood. *Neither Settler nor Native*. Belknap Press: An Imprint of Harvard University Press, 2020.

Mann, Itamar. *Humanity at Sea: Maritime Migration and the Foundations of International Law*. Cambridge University Press, 2017.

Martínez, Óscar. *The Beast: Riding the Rails and Dodging Narcos on the Migrant Trail*. Verso Books, 2014.

Mehta, Suketu. *This Land Is Our Land: An Immigrant's Manifesto*. Macmillan Publishers, 2019.

Miller, Todd and Melissa del Bosque. *The Border Chronicle*. Newsletter. https://www.theborderchronicle.com.

Miller, Todd. *Storming the Wall: Climate Change, Migration, and Homeland Security*. City Lights Publishers, 2017.

Nail, Thomas. *Theory of the Border*. Oxford University Press, 2016.

Ngai, Mae. *Impossible Subjects: Illegal Aliens and the Making of Modern America*. Princeton University Press, 2014.

Ojito, Mirta. *Finding Mañana: A Memoir of a Cuban Exodus*. Penguin Books, 2006.

Reynold, David S. *John Brown, Abolitionist: The Man Who Killed Slavery, Sparked the Civil War, and Seeded Civil Rights*. Vintage Books, 2006.

Saunt, Claudio. *Unworthy Republic: The Dispossession of Native Americans and the Road to Indian Territory*. W. W. Norton & Company, 2020.

Scott, James C. *Against the Grain: A Deep History of the Earliest States*. Yale University Press, 2017.

Scott, James C. *Seeing Like a State: How Certain Schemes to Improve the Human Condition Have Failed*. Yale University Press, 1999.

Shah, Sonia. *The Next Great Migration: The Beauty and Terror of Life on the Move*. Bloomsbury Publishing, 2020.

Shull, Kristina. *Detention Empire: Reagan's War on Immigrants and the Seeds of Resistance*. University of North Carolina Press, 2022.

St. John, Rachel. *Line in the Sand: A History of the Western US-Mexico Border*. Princeton University Press, 2012.

Stevens, Jacqueline. *States Without Nations: Citizenship for Mortals*. Columbia University Press, 2011.

Stonor Saunders, Frances. "The Suitcase." *London Review of Books* 42, no. 15 (July 2020):https://www.lrb.co.uk/the-paper/v42/n15/frances-stonor-saunders/the-suitcase.

Torpey, John. *The Invention of the Passport: Surveillance, Citizenship, and the State.* Cambridge University Press, 1999.

Trevino, Wendy. *Cruel Fiction.* Commune Editions, 2018.

Vijayan, Suchitra. *Midnight's Borders: A People's History of Modern India.* Melville House, 2021.

Walia, Harsha. *Border and Rule: Global Migration, Capitalism, and the Rise of Racist Nationalism.* Haymarket Books, 2021.

Walia, Harsha. *Undoing Border Imperialism.* AK Press, 2013.

Wallace-Wells, David. *The Uninhabitable Earth: Life After Warming.* Tim Duggan Books, 2019.

Walzer, Michael. *Spheres of Justice: A Defense of Pluralism and Equality.* Cambridge University Press, 2014.

INDEX

9/11, 191
9-1-1 calls, 199

abolition of Border Patrol, 153
abolition of ICE, 149–50
abolition of prisons, 148, 170
Aboriginal people, 26–27, 29–33, 88n4
see also Indigenous peoples; Indigenous peoples, genocide of
Abrahamian, Atossa Araxia, 190
Achiume, E. Tedayi, 197, 211
Act to Encourage Immigration, 1864, 49
Adelanto Detention Center, 148
Administrative Procedure Act, 143
affectedness, 161
Afghanistan borders, 111
Africa and the climate crisis, 122–23
African borders, 61
African Continental Free Trade Area, 159
African free transit zones, 159
African migrants, 59–60, 63–65, 74
African nation states, 62
African states, fluxation of, 113
Afrin occupation, 21
Agamben, Giorgio, 148
Agarwal, Ruchir, 136n8
Age of Discovery, 29
agricultural workers, 86, 186, 203
Akers Chacón, Justin, 158n10, 207–8
Alarme Phone Sahara, 64–65
Alaska seafood processing workers, 186
Albrecht, Glenn, 127
Alexander VI (pope), 43

Algéria and France free transit zone, 159
Algeria to France migration, 99
Ambonese people, 117
American Rust Belt states, 187
America's Voice, 6
Amighetti, Sara, 211
Anderson, Benedict, 104n2, 116, 117, 176
Andorra, 2
Anglo-Saxon Superiority (Demolin), 91
Angola, 113
animal migration, 127–35, 138–39
Anti-Fascist Protection Rampart, 106
anti-immigration rhetoric, 5–6, 8–9
Apache people, 53
apartheid, 8, 13, 164
"A Proposal to End the COVID-19 Pandemic" (International Monetary Fund), 136n8
Arbatov, Georgy, 196
Arendt, Hannah, 177, 178, 180
Arivaca Road checkpoint, 204
Arizona border, 4, 8, 206
Arkansas and Latino immigrants, 206–7
artificial states, 113–14
Assam, Muslims in, 112–13
asylum seekers
Cuban, 92–100
denial of, 215–16
detention of, 33–34
European Union and, 19
policies on, 139, 139n9
taxes and, 79
see also immigrants; migrants
Atlanta Confederacy, 183

ABOUT HAYMARKET BOOKS

Haymarket Books is a radical, independent, nonprofit book publisher based in Chicago. Our mission is to publish books that contribute to struggles for social and economic justice. We strive to make our books a vibrant and organic part of social movements and the education and development of a critical, engaged, and internationalist Left.

We take inspiration and courage from our namesakes, the Haymarket Martyrs, who gave their lives fighting for a better world. Their 1886 struggle for the eight-hour day—which gave us May Day, the international workers' holiday—reminds workers around the world that ordinary people can organize and struggle for their own liberation. These struggles—against oppression, exploitation, environmental devastation, and war—continue today across the globe.

Since our founding in 2001, Haymarket has published more than nine hundred titles. Radically independent, we seek to drive a wedge into the risk-averse world of corporate book publishing. Our authors include Angela Y. Davis, Arundhati Roy, Keeanga-Yamahtta Taylor, Eve Ewing, Aja Monet, Mariame Kaba, Naomi Klein, Rebecca Solnit, Olúfẹ́mi O. Táíwò, Mohammed El-Kurd, José Olivarez, Noam Chomsky, Winona LaDuke, Robyn Maynard, Leanne Betasamosake Simpson, Howard Zinn, Mike Davis, Marc Lamont Hill, Dave Zirin, Astra Taylor, and Amy Goodman, among many other leading writers of our time. We are also the trade publishers of the acclaimed Historical Materialism Book Series.

Haymarket also manages a vibrant community organizing and event space in Chicago, Haymarket House, the popular Haymarket Books Live event series and podcast, and the annual Socialism Conference.

ALSO AVAILABLE FROM HAYMARKET BOOKS

Angela Davis: An Autobiography
Angela Y. Davis

Border and Rule
Global Migration, Capitalism, and the Rise of Racist Nationalism
Harsha Walia, afterword by Nick Estes, foreword by Robin D. G. Kelley

The Border Crossed Us
The Case for Opening the US-Mexico Border
Justin Akers Chacón

From #BlackLivesMatter to Black Liberation (Expanded Second Edition)
Keeanga-Yamahtta Taylor, foreword by Angela Y. Davis

Our History Has Always Been Contraband
In Defense of Black Studies
Edited by Colin Kaepernick, Robin D. G. Kelley,
and Keeanga-Yamahtta Taylor

Resisting Borders and Technologies of Violence
Edited by Mizue Aizeki, Matt Mahmoudi, and Coline Schupfer
Foreword by Ruha Benjamin

Solito, Solita
Crossing Borders with Youth Refugees from Central America
Edited by Jonathan Freedman and Steven Mayers

Unbuild Walls
Why Immigrant Justice Needs Abolition
Silky Shah, foreword by Amna A. Akbar